MW00974753

The Essential College Experience

with Readings

JOHN N. GARDNER

Distinguished Professor Emeritus, Library and
   Information Science
Senior Fellow, National Resource Center for the
   First-Year Experience and Students in Transition
University of South Carolina, Columbia

Executive Director, Policy Center on The First Year of
   College, Brevard, North Carolina

A. JEROME JEWLER

Distinguished Professor Emeritus, College of Journalism
   and Mass Communications
University of South Carolina, Columbia

Bedford/St. Martin's
Boston • New York

**The Essential College Experience with Readings,
Sixth Edition**
John N. Gardner, A. Jerome Jewler

Executive Editor: *Carrie Brandon*
Development Editor: *Julie Kelly*
Editorial Assistant: *Nicholas Murphy*
Marketing Manager: *Casey Carroll*
Senior Project Manager, Editorial Production: *Lianne Ames*
Senior Print Buyer: *Mary Beth Hennebury*
Permissions Editor: *Stephanie Lee*
Production Service: *Lachina Publishing Services*
Text Designer: *Diane Beasley*
Cover Designer: *Diana Coe*
Cover Printer: *Malloy Lithographing*
Compositor: *Lachina Publishing Services*
Printer: *Malloy Lithographing*
Cover Illustration: © *Comstock Images/ Getty Images/RF*

ted in the United States of America
6 7 09

formation, write: Bedford/St. Martin's, 75 Arlington Street
, MA 02116   (617-399-4000)

f Congress Control Number: 2005924649

312-68349-9
8-0-312-68349-8

Brief Contents
and Readings

Contents

3   Learning Styles and Personality   39

4   Active Learning   53

5   Critical Thinking   71

6   Listening, Note Taking, and Participating   89

7   Reading to Remember   111

8   Taking Tests   127

11   Careers and Service Learning   187

12   Relationships   203

Preface

It's hard to believe that we've been writing about college success for new college students for so many years. In fact, we've spent most of our academic lives helping new students avoid both the pitfalls and the pratfalls of getting accustomed to a new way of life.

To prepare this text, *The Essential College Experience with Readings, Sixth Edition* we drew not only on our years of research in this field but also on talks with actual students, actual classroom experiences, and what we learned from our colleagues at two- and four-year campuses around the country.

We have based all of our books on this belief: that anyone of any age who is admitted to college will have a much greater chance of success, as long as he or she knows how to deal with the detours and potholes that come with the first year of college. We will provide in this book a road map to navigate these challenges and opportunities.

So we say to you: "Read each chapter, practice what it says, and save yourself a lot of potential trouble!"

One of the most important things you'll learn in college is to resist the notion that the information you read, see, or hear provides the complete story. If you were studying Thomas Jefferson, for example, you might read a fascinating article on his self-designed home, Monticello, without learning about his political beliefs, his attitude toward slavery, or why he is considered one of our greatest presidents. If you really wanted to capture the essence of this great man, you'd have to gather information from more than one source.

This book is different from our previous texts in that it includes readings following each chapter. These readings were carefully chosen to provide further insights into the chapter topic, insights that will be useful for class discussion or individual assignments. And working with readings as well as textbook content is good practice for all of your other courses, in which more than likely you will be reading from multiple sources.

Drawing on our experience in the field, we have included 15 chapters in *The Essential College Experience with Readings,* covering what we believe are the "musts" for success in college:

- A list of strategies to be used as the need arises.
- The basics of time management to keep you on deadline with time remaining for fun or important responsibilities.
- An understanding of how you learn best so you can master assignments in the most productive way.
- Coverage of the importance of participating in class—asking questions, offering answers, and so forth—to help immerse you in "active learning," which is how most of us learn best.
- Practice in the critical-thinking process, the basis for this text and the hallmark of sound analysis.
- Suggestions for reading a textbook for maximum understanding and retention of material.
- Strategies for taking tests and exams, from the true/false variety to the full-blown essay exam.
- Ways to sharpen your writing and speaking skills for greater impact in the classroom.
- A guide to research and college libraries, because you will have many occasions to "find the answers."
- An explanation of the career-planning process, which it's never too early to learn, as well as the opportunity to learn about careers through service learning.
- Coverage of the importance of good, honest relationships.
- The benefits of appreciating diversity of people, ideas, and experiences, one of which is learning to look at a situation from a different point of view.
- Concrete information on alcohol, other drugs, and sex. No judgment, just the facts.
- Tips on staying healthy (food, exercise, sleep, etc.) and keeping safe on campus.

Remember, the authors of this book believe that:

- Every student who persists and follows the advice in this text possesses the ability to achieve.
- We, as educators, are responsible for providing dedicated support to help students succeed through graduation.
- You must always seek the truth. For only through truth do real learning and growth take place.

Acknowledgments

Although this text speaks through the voices of its two editors, it represents contributions from many others. We gratefully acknowledge those contributions and thank these individuals whose special expertise has made it possible to introduce new college students to "their college experience" through the holistic approach we deeply believe in:

> *Chapter 2:* Jeanne L. Higbee, University of Minnesota, Twin Cities
> *Chapter 3:* Tom Carskadon, Mississippi State University
> *Chapters 6-8:* Jeanne L. Higbee, University of Minnesota, Twin Cities
> *Chapter 9:* Constance Staley, University of Colorado, Colorado Springs, and R. Stephens Staley, Colorado Technical University
> *Chapter 10:* Charles Curran and Rose Parkman Marshall, University of South Carolina, Columbia
> *Chapter 11:* Philip Gardner, Michigan State University, Linda Salane, Columbia College, and Edward Zlotkowski, Bentley College
> *Chapter 12*: Tom Carskadon, Mississippi State University
> *Chapter 13:* J. Herman Blake, Iowa State University, and Joan Rasool, Westfield State College
> *Chapter 14:* Sara J. Corwin, Bradley H. Smith, Rick L. Gant, and Georgeann Stamper, University of South Carolina, Columbia
> *Chapter 15:* JoAnne Herman and Danny Baker, University of South Carolina, Columbia

Special thanks are also owing to these reviewers whose wisdom and suggestions guided the creation of this text:

Ollie Baylis-Payne, *Contra Costa College*
Marilyn R. Bowers, *Walters State Community College*
Anne Hawthorne, *Cuyahoga Community College*
Bill Horstman, *Mesa State College*
Elizabeth S. Kennedy, *Florida Atlantic University*
Karen M. Kus, *East Carolina University*
Judith M. Lang, *Whitworth College*
Polly McMahon, *Spokane Falls Community College*
Anna Katherine Roope, *Virginia Technical Institute*
Diane Savoca, *St. Louis Community College*
Mary Scott, *North Carolina Central University*
Vicki Stieha, *Northern Kentucky University*
Mary Walz-Chojnacki, *University of Wisconsin-Milwaukee*
Phyllis N. Weatherly, *Floyd College*

Finally all this could not have happened without the support of the Wadsworth team, without whom this book would never be. Special thanks to Cathy Murphy of Editrix for her superb guidance and judgment and to Carolyn Merrill, Executive Manager of College Success, whose visionary leadership made this project possible.

Our special thanks also go to Susan Badger, CEO of Thomson Higher Education; Sean Wakely, President of Wadsworth Thomson; Eden Kram, Assistant Editor for College Success; Lianne Ames, Senior Production Project Manager; and Katie O'Keeffe-Swank, Project Manager, Lachina Publishing Services.

We could have done it without you, but it wouldn't have been nearly as good.

John N. Gardner
A. Jerome Jewler

College Makes the Difference

N o matter your age, no matter your background, the fact that you were admitted to college means something. It means that you have been afforded a great opportunity that could be, and we hope will be, life-transforming. We believe that if you follow the advice and inspiration offered in this book, your chances of succeeding in college will be greatly increased—even if it takes you five or six years or more to finish, as it does for many students today. We are especially concerned about the sad fact that many entering students drop out or flunk out, with the highest rates of those occurrences during the first year. We especially want to prevent or reduce this from happening to more students.

What can go wrong so quickly? Well, take the student who left campus before the first day of classes because she was so intimidated by the social activities the school had arranged for new students. Or the fellow who wanted to meet other students so much that he went out every night and never cracked a book. Or the guy who maxed out his credit card the first week of the term and had no money for food. Or the one who lacked clear goals for college and couldn't manage her time. Or the student who never learned how to use the library, the Internet's research capabilities, and other sources to flesh out a topic. Or the student of color who felt out of place on a predominantly white campus. Or the returning student who found it was nearly impossible to balance the responsibilities of work, family, commuting, and studies.

This book, as you will see, is for all of these students and more. It is a game plan for succeeding in college, a carefully chosen list of strategies that, if followed, can help you achieve more than you ever dreamed possible. Many of them may strike you as common sense, and many of them are. Nonetheless, you will benefit from carefully reading them and thinking about what they mean to you.

Strategies for Success

Get Ready: The Basics

1. **Show up for class.** When you miss even one class, you're missing something. You're also sending your instructor a message that you don't care. If you know you are going to miss class because of an appointment, sickness, or an emergency, contact your instructor as soon as possible and certainly before the next class meeting. The most dangerous classes to miss are those at the start of the term.

2. **Complete work on time.** Not only may you face a grade penalty if you don't, you will most certainly irritate some of your teachers if you are perpetually late with assignments. Some instructors may have a policy of not accepting late work or of penalizing you for it. Ask to make sure. If your work is late because of illness or an emergency, let your instructor know. It may help.

3. **Set up a weekly schedule.** And stick to it. Learning how to manage your time can make the difference between success and frustration. Get an appointment calendar you can write in or a personal digital assistant (PDA) and always keep it handy. Consider using a computer calendar program as a backup to your written one.

4. **Give yourself a realistic workload.** If you are a full-time student, limit your workweek to 15 hours. Many students begin a downhill slide after that. Need more money? Consult a financial aid officer. Try to find a job on campus. Students who do and who work fewer than 15 hours have a higher graduation rate than those who work off campus and/or more than 15 hours. If you're stressed, enroll part-time. Stress is the enemy of learning.

5. **Discover how you learn best.** Explore learning style theory, which suggests that we are all individuals with differing approaches to the world around us, the information we receive, the decisions we make, and the way we choose to live and to learn. Perhaps you'll understand why you hate being alone and love to plan things in detail, while your best friend— or more important, your instructor—is just the opposite.

6. **Have realistic expectations.** At first you may be disappointed in the grades you make, but remember that college is a new experience and things can, and probably will, improve. Remember, you are not alone. Millions of other students have faced the same uncertainties you may be facing. Hang on to that positive attitude.

Get Set: Study, Study, Study

7. **Improve your study habits.** Master the most effective methods for reading textbooks, listening, taking notes in class, studying for exams, and using information sources on campus. Visit your academic skills center whenever you need help with your studies.

8. **Develop critical thinking skills.** Challenge. Ask why. Seek dependable information to prove your point. Look for unusual solutions to ordinary problems. Never accept something as fact simply because you found it on the Internet or someone tells you it's true. And don't be swayed by your emotions.

9. **Participate in class.** Research indicates that students who involve themselves in class discussions usually remember more about the discussion than students who do not. As a result, they usually enjoy the class more and earn higher grades.

10. **Learn how to remember more from every class.** Effective listening not only results in better notes but also helps you improve memory techniques—an important skill as exams approach.

11. **Learn from criticism.** Criticism can be healthy. And helpful. It's how we all learn. If you get a low grade, ask to meet with your instructor to discuss what you should do to improve your work.

12. **Study with a group.** Research shows that students who collaborate in study groups often earn the highest grades and survive college with fewer academic problems. If you have family responsibilities, consider inviting several other students to your home for a study group session.

Go: The Extra Mile

13. **Get to know at least one person on campus who cares about you.** It might be the teacher of this course, some other instructor, your academic advisor, someone at the counseling or career center, an advisor to a student organization, or an older student. You may have to take the initiative, but it will be worth it.

14. **Get involved in campus activities.** Visit the student activities office. Work for the campus newspaper or radio station. Join a club or support group. Play intramural sports. Most campus organizations crave newcomers—you're their lifeblood.

15. **Become engaged in campus life and work.** You can do this by engaging in a practicum, an internship, or a field experience. Or you can perform community service as a volunteer. Or work with a faculty member on his or her research. Or enroll in a study abroad program. Students who are more engaged with their studies report they had a more beneficial college experience.

16. **Find and use campus helping resources.** Academic, personal, and career services are usually free and confidential. Successful students use them. If you're a minority student, a student with a disability, or a returning student, locate the campus office that is designed to meet your specific needs.

17. **Meet with your instructors and advisors.** Meet with an instructor, whether or not you have something specific to discuss. Students who do tend to stay in college longer. Your instructors are required to have office hours posted on their office doors; they expect you to visit. Also, find yourself a terrific academic advisor or counselor, someone you can talk to for support and guidance.

18. **Enlist the support of your spouse, partner, or family.** As a returning student, you may need to adjust household routines and duties. Let others know when you need extra time to study. A supportive partner is a great ally, but a nonsupportive partner can threaten your success in college. If your partner feels threatened and tries to undermine what you are doing, sit down and talk it over, or seek counseling.

19. **Take your health seriously.** How much sleep you get, what you eat, whether you exercise, and what decisions you make about drugs, alcohol, and sex all will affect your well-being and how well you will do in classes. Find healthy ways to deal with stress. Your counseling center can help.

20. **Learn how to be assertive, yet tactful.** If you don't, others may walk all over you. If it's difficult for you to stand up for yourself, take assertiveness training. Be proud of your heritage. Stand tall and refuse to tolerate disrespect. Your counseling center probably offers workshops that can teach you to stand up for your rights in a way that respects the rights of others.

First-Year Commitment: Hangin' In

Why do so many students drop out of college during or at the end of the first year? This comment from Columbia University professor Andrew Delbanco in *The New York Times* may provide a clue:

> *Every year I read that our incoming students have better grades and better SAT scores than in the past. But in the classroom, I do not find a commensurate increase in the number of students who are intellectually curious. . . . Many students are chronically stressed, grade-obsessed and, for fear of jeopardizing their ambitions, reluctant to explore subjects in which they doubt their proficiency.*[1]

---

[1]Andrew Delbanco, "Academia's Overheated Competition," *The New York Times,* March 16, 2001.

Taking a cue from this quote, when you "doubt your proficiency" in a certain subject, are you creating a negative "self-fulfilling prophecy," an attitude that could help your worst nightmare come true?

What other circumstances make the first-year dropout rate so high?

For those fresh out of high school, a major problem involves newfound freedom. Your college teachers are not going to tell you what, how, or when to study. If you don't live at home, your parents can't wake you in the morning, see that you eat properly and get enough sleep, monitor whether or how well you do your homework, or remind you to allow enough time to get to class. In almost every aspect of your life, getting it done suddenly depends on you.

For returning students, the opposite is true: a daunting lack of freedom. Working, caring for a family, commuting, and meeting other adult commitments and responsibilities compete for the time and attention it takes to do your best or even simply to persist in college. And the easiest thing to do is quit.

Whichever problem you are facing, what will motivate you to hang in? And what about the enormous investment of time and money that getting a college degree requires? Are you convinced that the investment will pay off? Or are you having thoughts such as these:

- This is the first time someone has not been there to tell me I had to do something. Will I be able to handle all this freedom? Or will I just waste time?
- I've never been away from home before, and I don't know anybody. How am I going to make friends?
- I have responsibilities at home. Can I get through college and still manage to take care of my family? What will my family think about all the time I'll have to spend in classes and studying?
- As a minority student, will I be in for some unpleasant surprises?
- In high school, I got by without working too hard. Now I'll really have to study. Will I be tempted to cut corners, maybe even cheat?
- Will I like my roommate? What if he or she is from a different culture?
- Can I afford this? Can my parents afford this? I wouldn't want them to spend this much and then have me fail.
- Looking around class makes me feel so old! Will I be able to keep up at my age?
- Will some teachers be biased toward students of my age or culture?

High School vs. College

Besides what we've already said, the mere differences between high school and college can threaten your survival—if you let them.

- College classes are larger and longer.
- College classes do not meet every day.

- College tests are given less frequently.
- You will do more writing in college.
- Your teacher will rarely monitor your progress. You're on your own.
- You will have to choose from many more types of courses.
- While peer pressure keeps many high school students from interacting with faculty, in college it's the norm to ask a teacher for counsel.
- You and your teachers will have more academic freedom—freedom to express different views, for example.
- College teachers usually have private offices and keep regular office hours.
- High school is more "textbook focused," while college is more "lecture focused."
- In high school, you learn facts; there's little or no room for discussion or disagreement. In college you will be encouraged to do original research and to investigate differing points of view on a topic.
- College faculty are more likely to create and transmit original knowledge and research.
- High school students have much less freedom in school, even though they enjoy freedom out of school. In college, you'll have more freedom.
- College students have more work, both in class and out of class.
- College students often live far from home.

Returning Students

Even returning students must deal with major life changes when they choose to begin college. Once their children have "flown the nest," returning students may find college a new beginning, a stimulating challenge, a path to a career, or all of these things. Yet working full-time and attending college at night, on weekends, or both can put added stress on your life, especially if you have a family.

Returning students tend to work harder than younger students because they realize how important an education can be. Consequently, they also tend to earn higher grades although many fear they won't be able to keep up with their younger counterparts.

Those Who Start, Those Who Finish

In 1900, fewer than 2 percent of Americans of traditional college age attended college. Today, new technologies and the information explosion are changing the workplace so drastically that few people can support themselves and their families adequately without some education beyond high school.

Today, more than 60 percent of high school graduates go on to college, with over 4,000 colleges serving more than 15 million students. Nearly half of those enrolling in college begin in two-year institutions. Adult students are also enrolling in record numbers. In the new millennium, more than one-third of college students are over age 25.

In addition to higher earnings, according to the Carnegie Commission on Higher Education, as a college graduate you will have a less erratic job history, will earn more promotions, and will likely be happier with your work. You will be less likely than a nongraduate to become unemployed. As the saying goes, "If you think education is expensive, try ignorance."

As the statistics in Table 1.1 indicate, it pays to go to college in more ways than one. Not only does income go up, as a rule, with each degree earned, but the unemployment rate goes down. You not only stand to earn more with a college degree, you also stand to find it easier to get a job and hold on to it.

College Education and Quality of Life

Of course, college will affect you in other ways. A well-rounded college education will expand life's possibilities for you by steeping you in the richness of how our world, our nation, our society, and its people came to be.

As a result of your college education, you will understand how to accumulate knowledge. You will encounter and learn more about how to appreciate the cultural, artistic, and spiritual dimensions of life. You will be more likely to seek appropriate information before making a decision. Such information also will help you realize how our lives are shaped by global as well as local political, social, psychological, economic, environmental, and physical forces. You

Table 1.1   Unemployment and Earnings by Educational Attainment for Year-Round, Full-Time Workers Age 25+

2001 UNEMPLOYMENT RATE (%)	EDUCATION ATTAINED	2000 MEDIAN EARNINGS ($)*
1.2	Professional degree	80,230
1.1	Doctorate	70,476
2.1	Master's degree	55,302
2.5	Bachelor's degree	46,276
2.9	Associate degree	35,389
3.5	Some college, no degree	32,400
4.2	High school graduate	28,807
7.3	Less than high school diploma	21,391

* These are median earnings, meaning half the group earned less and half the group earned more.
SOURCE: Bureau of the Census, Bureau of Labor Statistics, 2002.

will grow intellectually and personally through interaction with cultures, languages, ethnic groups, religions, nationalities, and social classes other than your own.

You will also:

- Know more, have more intellectual interests, be more tolerant of others, and continue to learn throughout life.
- Have greater self-esteem and self-confidence, which help you realize how you might make a difference in the world.
- Be more flexible in your views, more future oriented, more willing to appreciate differences of opinion and more interested in political and public affairs.
- Have children with greater learning potential who will achieve more in life.
- Be an efficient consumer, save more money, make better investments, and spend more on home, intellectual, and cultural interests as well as on your children.
- Be able to deal with bureaucracies, the legal system, tax laws, and advertising claims.
- Spend more time and money on education, hobbies, and civic and community affairs.
- Be more concerned with wellness and preventive health care, and consequently—through diet, exercise, stress management, a positive attitude, and other factors—live longer and suffer fewer disabilities.

Where to Go for Help

To find the college support services you need, ask one of your instructors or your academic advisor/counselor; consult your college catalog, phone book, and home page on the Internet. Or call or visit student services (or student affairs). Most of these services are free.

Academic Advisement Center: Help in choosing courses, information on degree requirements.

Academic Skills Center: Tutoring, help in study and memory skills, help in studying for exams.

Adult Reentry Center: Programs for returning students, supportive contacts with other adult students, information about services such as child care.

Career Center: Career library, interest assessments, counseling, help in finding a major, job and internship listings, co-op listings, interviews with prospective employers, help with résumés and interview skills.

Chaplains: Worship services, fellowship, personal counseling.

Commuter Services: Information on off-campus housing, roommate lists, orientation to community. Maps, information on public transportation, child care, and so forth.

Computer Center: Minicourses, handouts describing computer resources on or near campus.

Counseling Center: Confidential counseling on personal concerns. Stress management programs.

Disabled Student Services: Assistance in overcoming physical barriers or learning disabilities.

Financial Aid and Scholarship Office: Information on financial aid programs, scholarships, and grants.

Health Center: Medical treatment as well as strategies for preventing certain conditions. Help in personal nutrition, weight control, exercise, and sexuality. Information on substance abuse programs and other health issues. May include pharmacy.

Housing Office: Help in locating on- or off-campus housing.

Legal Services: Legal aid for students. If your campus has a law school, it may offer assistance by law students.

Math Center: Help with math skills and courses.

Physical Education Center: Facilities and equipment for exercise and recreational sports.

Writing Center: Help with writing assignments.

Setting Goals for Success

Now that you've read the strategies for success, what should you be doing to accomplish them? One method is to set specific goals for yourself, beginning now, that will help you maximize your potential in college.

We know from years of working with new college students that many hold a number of negative self-fulfilling prophecies. A self-fulfilling prophecy is something you predict is going to happen ("I can't write," "I'm going to fail math," "I'm going to ace this course," "I'm going to make the honor roll," and so on). By thinking that's how things will turn out, you greatly increase the chances that they will. In fact, many people actually act out their prophecies, whether positive or negative, to make them come true. Instead of taking a pessimistic attitude, learn to change negative goals into positive ones by stating your goals loud and clear.

College is an ideal time to begin setting and fulfilling short- and long-term goals. A short-term goal might be to set aside three hours this week to study chemistry; a long-term goal might be to devise a strategy for passing chemistry with an A. It's okay if you don't yet know what you want to do with the rest of your life or what your major should be. In fact, you should use this time to explore any number of fields and expose yourself to new learning experiences. More than 60 percent of college students change majors at least once. Using the strategies for success as a starting point, practice the following process by setting some short-term goals now:

1. **Select a goal.** State it in measurable terms. Be specific about what you want to achieve and when (for example, not "improve my study skills" but "master and use the recall column system of note taking by the end of October").
2. **Be sure that the goal is achievable.** Have you allowed enough time to pursue it? Do you have the necessary skills, strengths, and resources? If not, modify the goal to make it achievable.
3. **Be certain you genuinely want to achieve the goal.** Don't set out to work toward something only because you feel you should or because others tell you it's the thing to do. Be sure your goal will not have a negative impact on yourself or others and that it is consistent with your most important values.
4. **Know why the goal matters.** Be sure it has the potential to give you a sense of accomplishment.
5. **Identify and plan for difficulties you might encounter.** Find ways to overcome them.
6. **Devise strategies for achieving the goal.** How will you begin? What comes next? What should you avoid? Create steps for achieving your goal and set a timeline for the steps.[2]

In this first chapter we have laid the foundations for college success. Subsequent chapters will take closer looks at specific strategies, beginning with the critical skill of time management in Chapter 2.

As for the strategies for success we described at the beginning of this chapter, review them periodically as you work through this book. As you revisit them, ask yourself if you feel you've developed skills in some of these areas. Which strategies have you mastered? Which do you still need to work on?

YOUR PERSONAL JOURNAL

Each chapter of this book will ask you to write reflectively about the material you've just read. What did I learn? What's the most valuable thing I learned? What doesn't work for me? Why doesn't it work and how can I make it work?

---

[2]Adapted from *Human Potential Seminars* by James D. McHolland and Roy W. Trueblood, Evanston, Illinois, 1972. Used by permission of the authors.

This is another way to remember the content of the chapter, so you might try it with your other classes as well. Choose one or more of the following questions. Or choose another topic related to this chapter and write about it.

1. Go back to the list of concerns on page 5. Which of them are you feeling right now? How do you think you can begin overcoming them?
2. Of the 20 strategies, which one will give you the greatest challenge? Which will be easiest? Why?
3. What behaviors are you thinking about changing after reading this chapter? How will you go about changing them?
4. Which will be the hardest behaviors for you to change? Why?
5. What else is on your mind this week? If you wish to share it with your instructor, add it to this journal entry.

READINGS

How to Avoid First-Year Pitfalls*

You can sidestep some of the most common problems new college students face.

By Mark Rowh

Freshman year at college can be traumatic. But many of the classic pitfalls can be avoided. Here is a look at 10 common problems to anticipate and how to prevent them.

1. A SLOW START

Cynthia Hernandez, coordinator of new student programs at Texas A&M University, says it's important to avoid a slow start with your course work. "Don't make the mistake of assuming that this is a trial year academically," she says. "A low GPA your first two semesters can impact your entire academic career."

As simple as it may sound, a key factor is having the right kind of study skills. "Many students feel they didn't have to study in high school in order to get good grades," says Lori Bolden, assistant dean of students for first-year student programs at Lehigh University in Pennsylvania. "That's not often the case at the college level. If you are one of those students, it would be a good idea to start fine-tuning your study skills in preparation for the academic year."

To get off to a solid start, make studying the most important part of your day. Do all assigned work. Read course material carefully, and reread if necessary. Get a syllabus (or course outline) for each course, and follow it faithfully.

2. SKIPPING CLASS

Since colleges allow students much more flexibility than they had in high school, it's all too easy to fall into the trap of cutting class when you want to do something else, or are simply not in the mood to attend. But that can be a real mistake.

"Avoid taking cuts from class," says Carol Williamson, vice president of student affairs at Salisbury University in Maryland. "Some faculty never take attendance, but you should not consider this the OK to skip class. Attending class is a must, as much for what you learn there as for your demonstrating your interest to the professor."

3. NEGLECTING PAPERWORK

Filling out forms is a big part of college life. Be sure to take the necessary time to complete any required forms, whether in person or online. If not, you can face any number of problems, from not getting the classes you want to finding you've missed financial aid deadlines.

A special tip: If you decide to drop a class, be sure to fill out the appropriate form. "A common mistake for new students is to stop going to class believing the professor will know you intended that to translate into dropping the class from your schedule," Williamson says. "You must formally withdraw from a class or else you will receive an F because it has remained on your schedule."

4. OVERLOOKING KEY RESOURCES

What happens if your initial grades are not what you expected, or you find yourself struggling to master difficult material? Even if you get discouraged, don't give up, and don't be shy about seeking help. Bolden notes that it can be a serious mistake to overlook the resources available to every student.

"Many students feel like they have to get through college without any help, but college is a challenge for everyone in one way or another," she says. "Resources are available on campus because we know that students may need to use them. You're not a loser if you have a tutor, talk to your professors after class, go to the counseling center, or use any other helping resource on campus."

5. OVERCOMMITTING

Bonnie Gorman, associate dean for first-year students and director of first-year programs at Michigan Technological University, cautions against getting involved in too many activities. "There is a lot to do at college besides studying that will enhance your future career," she says, "but don't overcommit yourself. In the first semester, select just one or two things you'd like to do, and then get involved."

6. WASTING TIME

"Time management is key to being a successful student," says Jodi Koslow Martin, dean of first-year students at Aurora University in Illinois. "Don't wait until the last minute to write a paper or study for a test. You will produce your best work if you plan for your assignments in advance."

Keep in mind that unlike high school teachers, who often remind students when work is due, college professors expect students to be responsible for assignments on their own. "Review your syllabi and write down when your assignments are due," Gorman says. "It's unlikely that your professors will remind you. They expect you to keep track of these things. Whatever you do, get your homework and studying done first, then have fun."

7. HANGING ON TO THE PAST

Unless you're commuting to school, a major part of college life is getting used to living in a new environment. "Avoid the temptation to visit home every weekend," says Martin. "If you go home every weekend, you will not get a feel for what life is like on campus, and it will be harder for you to feel at home in your new community."

At the same time, be open to new relationships rather than dwelling on the past. "Don't stay overly involved with high school relationships," says Mary Anne Pugh, associate dean of students at Randolph-Macon College. "Constantly going home, either physically or mentally, interferes with adjusting to college and making new friends."

8. THE DEBT FACTOR

For many students, personal finances can quickly develop into a problem. Too often, this means overusing credit cards that are increasingly available to virtually anyone. "Credit card debt is a huge pitfall to avoid," Williamson says. "You may have your own credit card, or be bombarded by offers to obtain your own card. Be careful!"

She says that a common temptation is to treat friends when socializing. "But the bills pile up fast," she says, "and you do not want to be mired down in debt. You will owe enough upon graduation for student loans—don't add to the debt by running up to the limit on credit cards."

To avoid such problems, limit the number of credit cards you have, and use them only after careful thought. Pay off your balances each month. If you find yourself building up a significant balance on any account, quit adding new charges until you have paid it off.

9. PARTYING HEARTY

Everyone wants to have a good time, but don't overdo it. Too much partying, especially when you're first adjusting to the academic demands of college, can be disastrous. And avoid parties with alcohol.

"People assume that everybody at college drinks, but this is not true," Gorman says. "Go to events where alcohol is not the main focus, and you will likely meet other people who want to do more than just drink."

10. ISOLATION

One of the biggest mistakes you can make is to isolate yourself from the mainstream of college life. Even though academics should be your first priority, get involved in other activities.

"Find one or two healthy social outlets other than partying or studying," says Pugh. "These may include athletics, intramurals, volunteering, or joining a club or organization. You will have time for these, and they will help you connect with your new community and help keep you grounded."

Of course no matter how well you plan ahead, not everything will be perfect. But hang in there. Most students are able to adjust well to the challenges of college life. Along the way, avoiding unnecessary problems can make the experience a much less stressful one.

EIGHT TIPS FOR SUCCESS

Amy Hitlin, director of the Office of Academic Advising at Meredith College in North Carolina, offers these tips to help first-year college students achieve academic success:

1. Be sure to sit near the front of the class.
2. Read the chapters assigned before you get to class.
3. Make a schedule and keep it.
4. Study ahead for tests; do not cram.
5. Get plenty of sleep, and make time to eat.
6. Review, recite, and rewrite your notes.
7. Make sure your study conditions work for you. For example, find a quiet place to read without interruptions.
8. Make a practice test for yourself as part of your studying routine.

CHECKING OUT CAREER SERVICES

Even for those just starting college, it may be a good idea to check out services related to planning for employment. That way, you can lay the groundwork for important steps later.

Stephen Cantine, director of the Career Services/ Internship Program at Cazenovia College in New York, advises: "Connect with all offices on campus, even ones you don't think are essential for meeting your immediate needs. The career services office, for example, usually handles all part-time and summer jobs. Also, most career services offices have at least a hand in internships; and at many small colleges, they house the whole program."

He says that visiting the career services office during your freshman year will not only ensure that you are positioning yourself to succeed later, but it will also help the career services staff get to know you.

Finding Your Niche*

Learn how to feel comfortable in your new home away
from home—college.
By Joan Axelrod-Contrada

Finding your niche in college is like putting on the right pair of gloves. College life will feel just right: not too snug and confining, not too loose and unstructured. You know you fit in—somewhere, somehow—even if you're a little different from most students. Whether your idea of fun is a serious discussion about international economics, or jamming at a jazz club, you're able to find like-minded students who share your interests and passions. Humans are social creatures, after all. No one wants to feel like a stranger in a strange land for too long.

"I think finding your niche means finding a place where you belong—a place that feels like home, with folks who have interests and lifestyles similar to your own," says Jeanne Horrigan, director of the New Students Program at the University of Massachusetts in Amherst.

So how do you go about finding your niche? First and foremost, get involved in student activities. "It's the main way to help you find your niche," says Horrigan. Participation in student activities can help you develop new interests, get ready for a career, and learn important leadership skills.

GET INVOLVED

Student activities offices (check college Web sites for online links) list offerings ranging from theater groups to volunteering to skydiving.

Perhaps, though, you're worried that such activities will interfere with your schoolwork. It's possible. However, some college advisors say that getting involved can actually enhance your learning and boost your time-management skills. "Too much unstructured time is no good for anyone," says Leslie Goldberg, an educational consultant in Hingham, Massachusetts. The trick is

---

to choose activities with relatively modest time commitments so you don't get overwhelmed.

Many college students start with activities they enjoyed in high school, then branch out to something new. Goldberg recommends signing up for three groups, then dropping one, since finding the right outside activities is often a matter of trial and error.

Still not sure what you want to do? Goldberg suggests getting involved in residence-hall planning and community service.

MEET YOUR PROFESSORS

College advisors also recommend that you get to know your professors. Professors can become mentors who will help you find internships or write letters of recommendation. And don't worry if you have no idea what your major will be. Your college's academic advising office can help you with course selection. As long as you keep track of what you like and don't like about your classes, you're on the right track.

"One of the most popular majors is 'undecided,' " says Sidonia Dalby, coauthor of *The Panicked Parents' Guide to College Admissions.* "Everyone grows and changes."

College is a time of adjustment, so expect some rough times. "If I could strike one phrase from the English language it would be, 'These are the best years of your life,' " says Paul Cody, Ph.D., a staff psychologist at the Counseling Center at the University of New Hampshire. "College life for most people includes some difficult times."

BE PATIENT

The important thing is to persevere. According to Goldberg, "When students isolate themselves or run home, finding a niche in that particular college will never happen."

Colleges offer plenty of services and programs to help you adjust. Freshman orientations give you the lowdown on choosing residence halls and classes, and resident assistants (RAs) can help you adjust to having a new roommate and missing your old pals. And if after a while you're still seriously unhappy, you can always transfer. It takes some students more than one try to find their niche.

BIG FISH, LITTLE FISH

Ria Jodrie, a sophomore at Skidmore College in Saratoga Springs, New York, spent much of her first semester in college missing her boyfriend and tight-knit circle of friends back home. A popular, well-rounded student in high school, she auditioned for a couple of singing groups but failed to make the cut. She was so lonely she considered transferring.

"In high school, I had been a bigger fish," says Ria. "It took me a while to realize that I wasn't as big a fish as I thought I was. It was hard not being as popular right away."

Ria went to see a counselor and found that just having someone to talk to made her feel better. In her second semester, Ria joined the softball team, which gave her a new circle of friends. And her perseverance finally paid off—she also got into a singing goup. Now Ria loves Skidmore.

FOLLOWING A DREAM

Other students find their niche through a career goal. Keith Gormley, a junior at Emerson College in Boston, played football in high school but dreamed of a career in radio. He turned down a football scholarship to major in radio broadcasting at Emerson. The crowd at Emerson was much different—more arty—than what he was used to, but Keith adjusted quickly because he found others who shared his interest in music.

Now an RA and deejay at two radio stations, he encourages students to get involved even if they miss their friends from back home. "I tell them they'll never make any friends at all if they don't try," says Keith.

FROM SMALL TOWN TO BIG SCHOOL

While Ria and Keith chose relatively small colleges, Kim McLaughlin faced the challenge of adjusting to a big state school that was not her first choice. Kim was accepted at Ithaca College, which was her first choice, but for financial reasons she agreed to give the University of Massachusetts at Amherst a try. The size of UMass, with its 18,000 students, was daunting at first—bigger than her entire hometown of Spencer, Massachusetts.

At first, Kim stuck close to her residence hall and, like Ria, spent much of her time emailing her friends back home. But before long, Kim heeded her mother's advice and got involved in student activities.

"Going to the first meeting or practice is always the hardest," Kim recalls. "No one is begging you to join. You don't know anyone, and other people do. It's so much easier to hang out in your room with your roommates."

But Kim knew she wanted to be busier than she was, and so she joined the marching band, went out for rugby, and eventually became an RA. She now fits into a number of different niches. She has academic friends for her studious side and teammates from the rough-and-tumble sport of rugby for her "wild and crazy" side. Residence hall activities provide her with an outlet for her creative side.

Kim plans to eventually pursue a career in travel and believes that her extracurricular experience will help in her career. "Every time you join a group, you're developing your personal skills," she says. "Not every group is the same. You have to adapt to the group."

No matter what your circumstances, you too will find your niche. It just takes a little openness, flexibility, creativity, and time.

DISCUSSION

Some of the most important student learning in college takes place in discussions with other students. You learn from them, they learn from you, and you all get to practice critical thinking and other college-level skills. Below are a few questions that lend themselves to discussion. Your course instructor will provide specific directions as to which ones you will use, how the discussions and groups are to be structured, where and when discussions are to take place, etc. Your investment in these will determine what you derive from the discussions and what you give others.

1. What is the purpose of college? Every student will answer this question differently, based on goals, objectives, and needs. What have you learned in this chapter that helps you define the reasons you are in college now and at your particular institution? Discuss with other students in your class.
2. This chapter is about *college success*—what it is and how to achieve it. Think about some of the successful college students you know. What characteristics of these students have helped them adjust to college? Which of these characteristics could you adopt?
3. Reread the list of strategies for success in this chapter. Choose one that you have already mastered and one that you know you need to do some work on. Share these with a group of your fellow students and take note of some similarities and differences.
4. Using the list of 10 common pitfalls/problems presented in this chapter's first reading, "How to Avoid First-Year Pitfalls," brainstorm with a group of students additions to (or deletions from) this list. Discuss which of these pitfalls are most important to address, and which are least important.
5. In the second reading, "Finding Your Niche," the author gives a number of examples of how real college students discovered how to get the most out of college. Which example made the biggest impression with you? Why? Discuss what you and others in your group need to do in order to "connect" to college as soon as possible, and why it's important to find your niche.

CHAPTER 2

Time Management

Jeanne L. Higbee of the University of Minnesota, Twin Cities, contributed her valuable and considerable expertise to the writing of this chapter.

IN THIS CHAPTER, YOU WILL LEARN

- How to take control of your time and your life
- How to use goals and objectives to guide your planning
- How to combat procrastination
- How to use a daily planner and other tools
- How to organize your day, your week, your school term
- The value of a "to do" list
- How to avoid distractions

How do you approach time? Because people have different personalities and come from different cultures, they may also view time in different ways. Some of these differences may have to do with your preferred style of learning. Time management involves

- Deciding where your priorities lie
- Understanding when, how, and why you procrastinate
- Anticipating future needs and possible changes
- Placing yourself in control of your time
- Making a commitment to being punctual
- Carrying out your plans

The first step to effective time management is recognizing that *you* can be in control.

How often do you find yourself saying, "I don't have time"? Once a week? Once a day? Several times a day? The next time you find yourself saying this, stop and think about that statement. Do you not have time, or have you made a choice, whether consciously or unconsciously, not to make time for that particular task or activity? When we say that we don't have time, we imply that we do not have a choice. But we *do* have a choice. We *do* have control over how we use our time. We *do* have control over many of the commitments we choose to make. Being in control means that you make your own decisions. Two of the most often cited differences between high school and college are increased autonomy, or independence, and greater responsibility. If you are not a recent high school graduate, you have most likely already experienced a higher level of independence. But returning to school creates additional responsibilities above and beyond those you already have, whether those include employment, family, community service, or other activities. Whether you are beginning college immediately after high school, or are continuing your education after a hiatus, now is the time to establish new priorities for how you spend your time. To take control of your life and your time, and to guide your decisions, it is wise to begin by setting some goals for the future.

Setting Goals and Objectives

What are some of your goals for the coming decade? One goal may be to earn a two-year or four-year degree or technical certificate. Perhaps you plan to go on to graduate or professional school. You already may have decided on the career that you want to pursue. As you look to the future, you may see yourself buying a new car, owning a home, or starting a family. Maybe you want to own your own business someday, want time off to travel every year, or want to be able to retire early. Time management is one of the most effective tools to assist you in meeting these goals.

Your goals can be lofty, but they should also be attainable. You do not want to establish such high goals that you are setting yourself up for failure. Some goals may also be measurable, such as completing a degree program or earning a 3.0 or higher grade point average (GPA). But other goals, like "to be happy" or "to be successful," may mean different things to different people. No matter how you define success, you should be able to identify some specific steps you can take to achieve this goal. Perhaps one of the goals you will set is to find a good job—or a better one than the one you now have—upon completion of your degree Now, at the beginning of your college experience, is an important time to think about what that means. A few of your objectives may be to determine what is a "better" job and to make yourself more competitive in the job market.

A college degree and good grades may not be enough. When setting goals and objectives and thinking about how you will allocate your time, you may want to consider the importance of:

- Having a well-rounded resume when you graduate
- Setting aside time to participate in extracurricular activities
- Gaining leadership experience
- Engaging in community service
- Taking advantage of internship or co-op opportunities
- Developing job-related skills
- Participating in a study abroad program
- Pursuing relevant part- or full-time employment while you are also attending classes.

When it is time to look for a permanent job, you want to be able to demonstrate that you have used your college years wisely. That requires planning and effective time management, which in themselves are skills that employers value.

Beating Procrastination

You've just begun to study for tomorrow's history test and a friend pops in and asks you to go to a concert. You drop the books, change clothes, and you're out the door.

That's procrastination. It can be an enemy for some and a friend for others. While it is sometimes sensible to delay taking action, most people procrastinate too long and risk the possibility of never getting down to business. Generally, the more you procrastinate, the greater the danger of having tough times in college and throughout life.

Some of the smartest, most committed, and most creative people procrastinate. Being a procrastinator doesn't mean you are lazy or unmotivated. You shouldn't beat yourself up about it. Instead, use that energy to understand what is motivating you to procrastinate, even when you know you're sabotaging your success.

If the risks of procrastination are so high and the results so grim, why do we do it in the first place? Often, because as we anticipate meeting a particular obligation, we are struck by fear and its corollaries:

- **Performance anxiety.** Fear of doing a poor job. A lack of self-esteem may result in your believing that you cannot master a task no matter what you do, so you don't even try.
- **Dreading the outcome.** Fear of what will follow. If you do a poor job, you may be scolded by the teacher, or worse, fail the course.
- **Disliking the task.** Fear of specific steps. You may dread the early part of the project but may feel comfortable about what follows.
- **Boredom.** Fear of monotony. You've read the first two assigned articles and almost fell asleep. What's the point of continuing?[1]

Overcoming procrastination takes self-discipline, self-control, and self-awareness. Here are some ways to achieve this state of mind:

- Always anticipate the good that will come from finishing the task on time. Don't slip back into fear or doubt. Focus on your goal and its positive effects. Remind yourself that you can learn skills or gain the knowledge that you need to accomplish a task.

---

[1]Schwartz, Andrew E. and Dallett, Estelina L. "Procrastinate." *The CPA Journal,* April 1993, v63, n4, p. 83(3). Reprinted with permission.

- Do the awkward or difficult task early in the day. You will then feel the exhilaration that comes with accomplishing a dreaded task. It will carry you through the day and even set you up right for the next one.
- Focus on good results as they occur. Give yourself credit for all that you do. Seek quality overall rather than perfection in everything. Rather than pressuring yourself too much, face your requirements and your talents realistically.[2]

Here are other ways to beat procrastination:

- Say to yourself, "I need to do this now, and I am going to do this now. I will pay a price if I do not do this now." Remind yourself of the possible consequences if you do not get down to work. Then get started.
- Although it's tough for procrastinators to do, use a "to do" list to focus on the things that aren't getting done. Working from a list will give you a feeling of accomplishment and lead you to do more.
- Break down big jobs into smaller steps. Tackle short, easy-to-accomplish tasks first.
- Promise yourself a reward for finishing the task. For more substantial tasks, give yourself bigger and better rewards.
- Eliminate distractions. Say no to friends and family who want your attention. Agree to meet them at a specific time later. Let them be your reward for studying.
- Don't make or take phone calls or instant messages during planned study sessions. Close your door.

A very different management view describes procrastinators as those who

- Eagerly volunteer for impossible workloads.
- Want to take on more important tasks but seem to lack the ability to succeed.
- Agree to or suggest impossible deadlines.
- Often fail to deliver. His or her procrastination may be due to perfectionism, a fear of failure, or even a fear of success.
- Follow through only when constantly monitored.
- Spend more time on giving the appearance of progress than on actual progress.
- Blame bad luck or others when confronted with failure to deliver, or says, "I knew you'd want it done right."[3]

Recent research indicates that college students who procrastinate in their studies also avoid confronting other tasks and problems and are more likely to

---

[2]Ibid.
[3]Deep, Sam, and Sussman, Lyle. "When an employee says 'can do'—but doesn't" [excerpt from *What to Say to Get What You Want*], *Executive Female*, May–June 1992, v15, n3, p16(1).

develop unhealthy lifestyles that include higher alcohol consumption, smoking, insomnia, poor diet, and lack of exercise. If you cannot get your procrastination under control, it is in your best interest to seek help at your campus counseling service before you begin to feel you are losing control over other aspects of your life as well.

Setting Priorities

This book is full of suggestions for enhancing academic success. However, the bottom line is keeping your eyes on the prize and being intentional in taking control of your time and your life. Keeping your goals in mind, establish priorities in order to use your time effectively.

First, determine what your priorities are: attending classes, studying, working, or spending time with the people who are important to you. Then think about the necessities of life: sleeping, eating, bathing, exercising, and relaxing. Leave time for fun things like talking with friends, watching TV, going out for the evening, and so forth; you deserve them. But finish what *needs* to be done before you move from work to pleasure. And don't forget about personal time. Depending on your personality and cultural background, you may require more or less time to be alone.

If you live in a residence hall or share an apartment with other college students, communicate with your roommate(s) about how you can coordinate your class schedules so that you each have some privacy. If you live at home with your family, particularly if you are a parent, work with your family to create special times as well as quiet study times.

Setting priorities is an important step. You are the only one who can decide what comes first, and you are the one who has to accept the ramifications of your decisions.

In setting priorities, you may have to prioritize the assignment that is due tomorrow over reading the chapters that will be covered in a test next week. Understandably, you do not want to procrastinate on all the reading until the night before the exam. Planning is critical or you will always find yourself struggling to meet each deadline.

Use a Daily Planner

In college, as in life, you will quickly learn that managing time is an important key not only to success, but to survival. A good way to start is to look at the big picture. Use the *term assignment preview* (Figure 2.1) on pages 24–25 to give yourself an idea of what's in store for you. Complete your term assignment preview by the beginning of the second week of classes so that you can continue to use your time effectively. Then purchase a "week at a glance"

Figure 2.1   **Term Assignment Preview**

Using the course syllabi provided by your instructors, enter all due dates on this term calendar. For longer assignments, such as term papers, divide the task into smaller parts and establish your own deadline for each part of the assignment. Give yourself deadlines for choosing a topic, completing your library research, developing an outline of the paper, writing a first draft, and so on.

	Monday	Tuesday	Wednesday	Thursday	Friday
Week 1					
Week 2					
Week 3					
Week 4					

	Monday	Tuesday	Wednesday	Thursday	Friday
Week 5					
Week 6					
Week 7					
Week 8					

	Monday	Tuesday	Wednesday	Thursday	Friday
Week 9					
Week 10					
Week 11					
Week 12					

	Monday	Tuesday	Wednesday	Thursday	Friday
Week 13					
Week 14					
Week 15					
Week 16					

organizer for the current year or personal digital assistant. Your campus bookstore may sell one designed just for your school, with important dates and deadlines already provided. If you prefer to use an electronic planner, go to the calendar link on your college's Web site and enter the key dates you need to know in your planner. Regardless of the format you prefer (electronic or hard copy), enter the notes from your preview sheets into your planner, and continue to enter all due dates as soon as you know them. Write in meeting times and locations, scheduled social events (jot down phone numbers, too, in case something comes up and you need to cancel), study time for each class you're taking, and so forth. Carry your planner with you in a convenient place. *Now* is the time to get into the habit of using a planner to help you keep track of commitments and maintain control of your schedule.

This practice will become invaluable to you in the world of work. Check your notes daily for the current week and the coming week. Choose a specific time of day to do this, perhaps just before you begin studying, before you go to bed, or at a set time on weekends. But check it daily, and at the same time of day. It takes just a moment to be certain that you aren't forgetting something important, and it helps relieve stress!

Maintain a "To Do" List

Keeping a "to do" list can also help you avoid feeling stressed or out of control. Some people start a new list every day or once a week. Others keep a running list, and only throw a page away when everything on the list is done. Use your "to do" list to keep track of all the tasks you need to remember, not just academics. You might include errands you need to run, appointments you need to make, email messages you need to send, and so on. Develop a system for prioritizing the items on your list—highlight; use colored ink; or mark with one, two, or three stars, or A, B, C. You can use your "to do" list in conjunction with your planner. As you complete each task, cross it off your list. You will be amazed at how much you have accomplished, and how good you feel about it.

Guidelines for Scheduling Week by Week

- Begin by entering all of your commitments for the week—classes, work hours, family commitments, and so on—on your schedule.
- Examine your toughest weeks on your term assignment preview sheet (see Figure 2.1). If paper deadlines and test dates fall during the same week, find time to finish some assignments early to free up study time for tests. Note this in your planner.

- Try to reserve two hours of study time for each hour spent in class. This "two-for-one" rule is widely accepted and reflects faculty members' expectations for how much work you should be doing to earn a good grade in their classes.
- Break large assignments such as term papers into smaller steps such as choosing a topic, doing research, creating a mind map or an outline, writing a first draft, and so on. Add deadlines in your schedule for each of the smaller portions of the project.
- All assignments are not equal. Estimate how much time you will need for each one, and begin your work early. A good time manager frequently finishes assignments before actual due dates to allow for emergencies.
- Keep track of how much time it takes you to complete different kinds of tasks. For example, depending upon your skills and interests, it may take longer to read a chapter in a biology text than in a literature text.
- Set aside time for research and other preparatory tasks. Most campuses have learning centers or computer centers that offer tutoring, walk-in assistance, or workshops to assist you with computer programs, databases, or the Internet. Your campus librarian can be of great help also.
- Schedule at least three aerobic workouts per week. (Walking to and from classes doesn't count!)

Use Figure 2.2 to tentatively plan how you will spend your hours in a typical week.

Organizing Your Day

Being a good student does not necessarily mean grinding away at studies and doing little else. Keep the following points in mind as you organize your day:

- Set realistic goals for your study time. Assess how long it takes to read a chapter in different types of texts and how long it takes you to review your notes from different instructors, and schedule your time accordingly. Give yourself adequate time to review and then test your knowledge when preparing for exams.
- Use waiting time (on the bus, before class, waiting for appointments) to review.
- Prevent forgetting by allowing time to review as soon as reasonable after class.
- Know your best time of day to study.
- Don't study on an empty or full stomach.
- Pay attention to where you study most effectively, and keep going back to that place. Keep all the supplies you need there and make sure you have

Figure 2.2   Weekly Timetable

A chart like this can help you organize your weekly schedule and keep track of how you're spending your time. Checking it at the end of each week is a good way to make yourself aware of ways that you may have misjudged how you use and manage your time.

	Sunday	Monday	Tuesday	Wednesday	Thursday	Friday	Saturday
6:00							
7:00							
8:00							
9:00							
10:00							
11:00							
12:00							
1:00							
2:00							
3:00							
4:00							
5:00							
6:00							
7:00							
8:00							
9:00							
10:00							
11:00							
12:00							

adequate lighting, a chair with sufficient back support, and enough desk space to spread out everything you need.

- Study difficult or boring subjects first, when you are fresh. (Exception: If you are having trouble getting started, it might be easier to get started with your favorite subject.)
- Avoid studying similar subjects back to back if you might confuse the material presented in each.
- Divide study time into 50-minute blocks. Study for 50 minutes, then take a 10- or 15-minute break, and then study for another 50-minute block. Try not to study for more than three 50-minute blocks in a row, or you will find that you are not accomplishing 50 minutes' worth of work. (In economics, this is known as the law of diminishing returns.)
- Break extended study sessions into a variety of activities, each with a specific objective. For example, begin by reading, then develop "flash cards" by writing key terms and their definitions or formulas on note cards, and finally test yourself on what you have read. You cannot expect to be able to concentrate on reading in the same text for three consecutive hours.
- Restrict repetitive, distracting, and time-consuming tasks like checking your email to a certain time, not every hour.
- Be flexible! You cannot anticipate every disruption to your plans. Build extra time into your schedule so that unexpected interruptions do not necessarily prevent you from meeting your goals.
- Reward yourself! Develop a system of short- and long-term study goals and rewards for meeting those goals.

Making Your Time Management Plan Work

With the best intentions, some students using a time management plan allow themselves to become overextended. If there is not enough time to carry your course load and meet your commitments, drop any courses before the drop date so you won't have a low grade on your permanent record. If you are on financial aid, keep in mind that you must be registered for a certain number of credit hours to be considered a full-time student and thereby maintain your current level of financial aid.

Don't Overextend Yourself

Learn to say no. Do not take on more than you can handle. Do not feel obligated to provide a reason; you have the right to decline requests that will prevent you from getting your own work done. If you're a commuter student, or if you must carry a heavy workload in order to afford going to school, you may prefer scheduling your classes together in blocks without breaks.

Although block scheduling allows you to cut travel time by attending school one or two days a week, and may provide more flexibility for scheduling employment or family commitments, it can also have significant drawbacks. There is little time to process information or to study between classes. If you become ill on a class day, you could fall behind in all of your classes. You may become fatigued sitting in class after class. Finally, you might become stressed when exams in several classes are held on the same day.

Block scheduling may work better if you can attend lectures at an alternative time in case you are absent, if you alternate classes with free periods, and if you seek out instructors who allow you flexibility in completing assignments.

Reduce Distractions

Where should you study? Avoid places associated with leisure—the kitchen table, the living room, or in front of the TV. They lend themselves to interruptions by others. It's not usually a good idea to study in bed. Either you will drift off when you need to study, or you will learn to associate your bed with studying and not be able to go to sleep when you need to. Instead, find quiet places to do your work.

Try to stick to a routine as you study. The more firmly you have established a specific time and a quiet place to study, the more effective you will be in keeping up with your schedule. If you have larger blocks of time available on the weekend, for example, take advantage of that time to review or catch up on major projects, such as term papers, that can't be completed effectively in 50-minute blocks. Break down large tasks and take one thing at a time; then you will make more progress toward your ultimate academic goals.

Here are some more tips to help you deal with distractions:

- Don't snack while you study. (Ever wonder where that whole bag of chips went?) However, it's fine to take your textbook with you to lunch or dinner, if you're dining alone. With a healthy meal in front of you, you can multitask, feeding your mind while you're feeding your body.
- Leave the cell phone, TV, CD player, tape deck, and radio off, unless the background noise or music really helps you concentrate on your studies or drowns out more distracting noises (people laughing or talking in other rooms or hallways, for instance).
- Don't let personal concerns interfere with studying. If necessary, call a friend or write in a journal before you start to study, and then put your

worries away. You might actually put your journal in a drawer and consider that synonymous with putting your problems away.

• Develop an agreement with the people you live with about "quiet" hours.

Time and Critical Thinking

Few questions in higher education have a right or wrong answer. Good critical thinkers have a high tolerance for ambiguity. Confronted by a difficult question, they suspend judgment until they can gather information and weigh the merits of different arguments. Thus, effective time management does not always mean making decisions or finishing projects hastily. Effective critical thinkers resist finalizing their thoughts on important questions until they believe they have developed the best answers possible.

This is not an argument in favor of ignoring deadlines, but it does suggest the value of beginning your research, reading, and even the writing phases of a project early, so that you will have time to change direction if necessary as you gather new insights. Give your thoughts time to incubate. Allow time to visit the library more than once. Talking about your ideas with other students or your teacher can also be helpful. Sometimes insights come unexpectedly, when you are not consciously thinking about a problem. If you are open-minded and prepared to let your mind search for new insights, you may experience an epiphany—a sudden intuitive leap of understanding, especially through an ordinary but striking occurrence. If you begin a project as early as you can, you will have time to give it the level of thought it deserves.

YOUR PERSONAL JOURNAL

Following are several topics you can write about. Choose one or more. Or choose another topic related to time management.

1. Before you completed this chapter, how successful were you at managing your time?
2. What have you learned from this chapter that will help you apply good time management skills to your college courses?
3. How can you modify the ideas in this chapter to fit your own habits and biological clock?
4. What behaviors are you thinking about changing after reading this chapter? How will you go about changing them?
5. Is there anything else on your mind this week that you'd like to share with your instructor? If so, add it to your journal entry.

READINGS

How to Manage Your Time*
By Andrea Matetic

When Dennis Hensley tells people they can better manage their time, he's speaking from experience. He has a Ph.D. He teaches English and writing at Taylor University–Fort Wayne and has managed to write one book every year he has been there. He has been a full-time freelance writer and has published 44 books, 3,000 newspaper and magazine articles, several songs, short stories, and scripts.

He has been married to Rose for 32 years and has two grown children, Nathan, 29, and Jeanette, 26.

He served in Vietnam for almost two years and managed to read more than 125 books, see 85 movies, travel to Thailand and Taiwan, keep a daily journal, study the Vietnamese language, earn a brown belt in tae kwon do, and write devotions, articles, and comedy pieces while he was there.

Who is this guy? Superman?

No, but he did write a book called "How to Manage Your Time." In that book, published in 1989, Hensley says you don't have to be Superman to get things done. "So, get it straight in your mind right from the start," he challenges. "There are enough hours in the day to do whatever you want to do, but you've got to have discipline."

Hensley illustrates his point by breaking up a typical day into time segments. If you work eight hours, sleep eight hours, and do whatever you want for six hours, you would still have two hours to work on a special goal or project, like writing a book or fixing up an old car.

If you do follow this plan for five days a week, four weeks a month, after one year you will have logged 480 hours—a total of three work months—of progress toward your goal or project. However, he warns, you may have to sacrifice "time-wasting activities," such as channel surfing or Internet browsing, to stay on track.

When his children were young, Hensley would write from 10 p.m. until 3 a.m., sleep until 10 a.m., and write again until 3 p.m. when his children got home from school. Although it was a strange schedule, Hensley was able to write full time and spend evenings with his family.

Now, as a professor, Hensley posts his available hours on his office door and does not carry a cell phone. "I do not own a cell phone because I simply do

---

*Knight Ridder/Tribune News Service, August 3, 2004, p. K1495. Copyright 2004 Knight Ridder/Tribune. Reprinted with permission.

not want to be accessible 24/7. Sometimes I just want total privacy, so I go into my office, lock the door, turn off the phone, and I read and write. . . . I keep my weekends for myself and my wife," he said. In this way, he avoids distractions.

He also advises people to avoid wasting time by getting rid of all "clutter" in the office and home. "Throw out outdated files. Give away books you've already read. Rip outdated materials off bulletin boards. Empty wastebaskets. Donate clothes that no longer fit. Gut the in-files. Pitch old manuals and out-dated reference materials, including disks and floppies and tapes," Hensley says. By doing this, he says, "You'll be able to locate vital materials much faster" and save time.

SETTING PRIORITIES

Hensley offered these additional tips on how to manage time wisely:

1. Set goals regarding family, career, and health and prioritize those goals. Each day, do at least one thing to get closer to accomplishing your goal. "Tasks are not goals," he said. "Stay focused on goals, not busy work. Your goals are what will advance you in life, whereas your tasks are what will eat up your life."

2. Delegate minor activities to others. "Save your prime time for your prime tasks. Hire someone to mow your lawn, deliver your dry cleaning, wash your windows, tune your engine and anything else whenever possible," he said. This will allow you to focus on your more important goals and responsibilities.

3. "Follow yourself around for two days," he advises. Keep a journal of every-thing you do to see what activities need to be eliminated. Some questions to ask are: "How often do you get interrupted by people or cell phones? What jobs are you doing that really are not your responsibility? How are your top-priority goals taking a back seat to daily busy work? What bad habits do you have regarding eating, wasting time, daydreaming, or visit-ing with other people? Once you see your problems, take positive steps to solve them," he said.

4. Find out when your peak hours of productivity are and do your most important work then. Do you work best in the early morning, in the after-noon, or late at night?

5. When sitting in waiting rooms, at the airport, standing in lines, or driving to work, have something to do on hand at all times. Some ideas to con-sider are bringing a tape recorder in the car and dictating speeches, let-ters, or reports on your way to work; taping key words on paper to your dashboard and brainstorming when you stop at traffic lights; having books or reports with you to read or review; and writing business letters longhand.

6. Use your relaxation time wisely as well. Hensley says there's nothing wrong with relaxation, but he does believe some activities, like channel

surfing or coffee breaks, just waste time. More purposeful activities to do during free time, he recommends, are reading, exercising, spending time with friends or family, and even taking brief naps to re-energize yourself.

Getting Started

Sometimes one of the biggest challenges a person faces when starting a project is taking that first step, Hensley writes. "Like everyone, I have certain jobs I must do that I dread. I don't look at the overall task, but at a lot of little 'projects,' " he said. "For example, in writing a book, I won't tell myself that I have to produce 300 pages of finished manuscript. Instead, I'll say that it is going to consist of 24 chapters and that each chapter is actually no more than one good-sized article. So, by doing one article every two weeks—an easy schedule—I wind up with a book completed at the end of each year.

"I do everyday life the same way. If I need to get my yard in shape, I won't look at the whole yard as two days of arduous work. I'll just say that one morning I will trim all the bushes, hedges, and trees. That's enough. The next morning it will be time to weed the garden. Another morning it will be time to edge the lawn. Thus, over a week or so, it all gets done, but I still have a lot of time left each afternoon and evening for other things. "Divide and conquer is the answer to big hateful jobs," he explained.

Taking breaks also can add to wasting time, said Hensley. "When I am really 'in the zone' of writing, I sometimes don't come up for air for two hours at a time. Usually, however, I will take pauses. Instead of a half-hour coffee break that stops all momentum . . . I just pause for five minutes to stretch a bit, refill my coffee mug, grab a granola bar or cheese stick, and then I go back to work," he said.

"The key is to not lose that forward momentum, which is what happens when someone else interrupts you, or you allow yourself to get on a totally different mind-set, as when you turn on the TV or stop by the water cooler to chat with someone for 20 minutes. Not good! Stay on task."

How did Hensley learn to be so focused?

While he was working on his doctorate at Ball State University, he was a reporter at the *Muncie Star.* "I was paid according to how many articles, interviews, and features I wrote and turned in," he said. "That taught me two things: Only what you finish in life really counts; and deadline is a literal, not a figurative term, in that it means, 'Go past this line and you're dead.' "

This is something he emphasizes with his students at Taylor. "It's good that I teach at a private college, because I would never be able to get away with my style of teaching at a public school," he said. "My students are never allowed to come to class late. If a class starts at 9 a.m., I close and lock the door at 9 a.m. Anyone on the wrong side of that door misses that day's lecture and gets an 'F' in the grade book for that day. Similarly, papers may not be turned in late for any reason except death (one's own). In the real world, that's the way it works, so students need to learn that right away.

"Students discover that I am not bluffing about this, so they rise to the challenge. Later, when they go out on internships, their supervisors call me and praise the students for coming every day and coming early. It always makes a good impression and often leads to career job offerings after college."

For those who think they aren't capable of being that focused, determined, and organized, or who make other excuses, Hensley says time management is a choice. "You can always make productive use of your time if you choose to do so. Milton wrote in *Paradise Lost,* 'You can make a heaven of hell or a hell of heaven. It's all in your mind.' He was right about that."

When Mom Goes Back to School*
Middle-aged students are going to college in record numbers, and inspiring younger classmates, including their own kids, to hit the books harder than ever.
By Jennifer Wagner

Vicki Smith stands in line with the other students at the University of Northern Iowa's bookstore, waiting to purchase class materials for her Humanities I and Personal Wellness classes. The petite blond is a sophomore majoring in art education who dreams of one day teaching at the college level. But this undergraduate is a little different from the other coeds: she's 44 years old and the single mother of five children. Her oldest son, Jared, is actually enrolled at the same university.

Returning students like Vicki were for years referred to as "nontraditional," but according to recent studies that phrase may no longer apply. Adult students are in fact the fastest-growing educational demographic in the United States. Between 1970 and 1993, the number of students 40 and older increased a whopping 235 percent, according to statistics gathered by the Education Resource Institute. Attendance is on the rise among students with dependents, as well as among single parents, according to the National Center for Educational Statistics.

Being a student can be difficult enough in terms of balancing hectic class schedules, homework, tests, employment, and social life. Add being a mother and homemaker to the mix, and the thought of going back to school may seem overwhelming at best. And yet each year thousands of these women strap on their backpacks and head off to class.

Jared admits he doesn't know how his mother handles it all. "I take a lot more classes than her, but I don't have as many responsibilities like raising a family and all the things a single mom has to do," he says. "And she spends so much time studying! I like good grades too, but I would never push myself that hard." But Vicki, who says she runs "a pretty tight ship" at home, feels studying is a great example she can set for her children. "Seeing Mom studying is a positive thing for kids."

That certainly was the case with Denise Alexander. The 43-year-old single mother went to college for the first time at the encouragement of a supervisor at her full-time job in New Carrollton, Maryland, where she works as a product analyst. At the same time her daughter, Sheina, had decided to take time off from school and wasn't sure when or if she'd go back.

"I really felt she needed me. I thought that if I could go to college, Sheina might be inspired to go too, get some incentive to go back," says Denise. She was right. Not only was she able to encourage her daughter to go back to school, but Sheina enrolled at her mom's school, Prince George's Community College. What's more, the two even took a couple of classes together. Denise graduated in May 2004. Sheina, who currently has a 4.0 grade point average, will graduate next year.

BACK TO SCHOOL

There's no one reason why women return to school. But divorce, widowhood, and wanting to improve career options number among the most typical motivators. According to the Institute for Higher Education Policy, going back to school provides private and public benefits. College graduates generally enjoy higher salaries and benefits, are employed more consistently, and work in nicer conditions. College-educated people vote more, give more to charity, rely less on government support, and have lower incarceration rates.

Making the switch from being supported to supporting oneself can be a challenge, but often a necessary one. Financial independence for women is key, says Nancy Schlossberg, professor emerita at University of Maryland and author of *Overwhelmed: Coping with Life's Ups and Downs.* "I think it's important for women to do some direct achievement, because chances are women will live alone in later life, either divorced, widowed, or never married."

To Schlossberg, who developed a framework of questions that may assist women in deciding if the time is right to go back to school, education is critical in the long run. "There are times when you have to work, when you will work," she says. "You are going to do much better if you have an education, and you're going to be happier if you have the education that enables you to do what you have to do in life. The question is if you are ready at this time to go for it."

Answering that question may bring into play a whole host of worries, like how to balance the homework with the work at home, how to pay the bills, and how to muster the confidence needed to succeed alongside often-years-younger peers. Yet time after time women around the country rise to meet these challenges head on. Here are a few of the tips that help women go back to school and to keep their personal lives balanced as they do it.

Set Up a Daily Study Time

Time management is an essential issue for all students, and returning women in particular are usually balancing a heavy load of other commitments. Having an assigned time to study in your daily schedule, and making sure everyone in your family knows when that time is, is crucial to keeping up with class expectations.

Redistribute Housework and Chores Whenever Possible

Any extra assistance a spouse, partner, or child can contribute is an added benefit. If the family recognizes that mom is adding on some responsibilities and challenges to her life, they can help by pitching in.

Everything won't happen the same way it did before you went to school. The bathroom might not get cleaned as often, and the meals might not be as elaborate. Family support is key, but each woman needs to recognize her own limits in her daily duties. DON'T OVERCOMMIT. Being overcommitted is a big trap for women returning to school. Something will have to give, whether it's cutting back on work hours or volunteering at a child's school. Don't feel you have to sign up for the same number of courses as a full-time student. It may take you a couple of years longer to get through a traditional four-year program, but you'll be more likely to succeed and you'll be able to work at a pace that won't grind you down. Cutting back on other responsibilities will help a woman succeed in the path to getting a degree.

Consider Doing Homework Together with Children

Clean off the dining room table and sit down together with your books. Children need to see that their parents are in school and are also responsible for doing well at their studies. Share with the children what it's like to be in school. Show them your campus too.

"My daughter and I have study habits that are too different for us to be able to study together," says Denise Alexander. "But we can still talk about our classes and our experiences. Sharing that has been really important, for both of us."

Plan Ahead

Schedule your week ahead of time. Hang the family calendar on the refrigerator so everyone can be aware of each other's schedules, including study times, exams, work hours, and extracurricular activities. Use weekends to plan meals and do grocery shopping for the next week.

Get Technical

Cell phones and email will help keep you connected. Don't worry if you don't have a computer, but be prepared to spend more time away from home in labs or libraries using their equipment for assignments. Schools should be able to help the less technically savvy get up to speed.

Ask for Help

Coping with the transition back to school can be quite daunting, and many schools have systems or personnel in place to help returning women face the new challenges. Norma Kent, a vice president at the American Association of Community Colleges, suggests women ask schools about special programs tailored for either single or returning adult mothers, pointing out that some programs may assist with child care and transportation needs. "For some of them, this is a very courageous thing to go back to college," she says. "In community colleges, women find a real team spirit to help each other succeed. This will make a difference."

DISCUSSION

1. Discuss some of your challenges in dealing with procrastination. How do you attempt to manage it, if you do—or at times, how does it seem to manage you?
2. How are your time management challenges different now that you are in college? How are your coping mechanisms different from or similar to your previous strategies? Share your self-evaluation with some class members and compare notes.
3. Discuss whether on balance you feel that your time demands control you as opposed to your controlling them. After talking about this with other students and noting common themes, check out the concept of "locus of control" for additional insights on how you are doing in this area of self-management.
4. Discuss some of the suggestions in the chapter for time management. How do you think you can or should improve on them or adapt them to your circumstances? Swap some good ideas with other students.
5. Discuss the recommendations from the articles "How to Manage Your Time" and "When Mom Goes Back to School" and develop a list with fellow students of which ones you buy and which ones you don't. Prioritize them if you can.

CHAPTER **3**

Learning Styles and Personality

Tom Carskadon of Mississippi State University contributed his valuable and considerable expertise to the writing of this chapter.

IN THIS CHAPTER, YOU WILL LEARN

- Preferences, psychological types, and learning styles
- What your own psychological type may be
- How to use all learning styles for success
- Study tips for your own psychological type/learning style
- What majors and careers suit your psychological type

Perhaps you find history easier than mathematics or biology easier than English. Part of the explanation has to do with what is called your learning preferences—the way you prefer to acquire knowledge, which is a part of your overall personality.

Learning preferences affect not only how you absorb material as you study but also how you draw conclusions from it. Some students learn more effectively through visual means, others by listening to lectures, and still others through class discussion, hands-on experience, memorization, or a combination of these.

Visual learners have to "see it to believe it." They may have artistic abilities, may find some sounds irritating, and may have trouble following lectures. They may do better using graphics as a learning aid. They tend to remember notes by visualizing precisely where on their notebook page they wrote the information they seek.

Auditory learners remember best what they hear. They may have difficulty following written directions and may find reading and writing exhausting. They may do better by supplementing written notes with a tape of the lecture (with the instructor's permission), summarizing on tape what they read, and participating actively in discussions.

Tactile learners tend to remember what they touch. They like hands-on learning, may have difficulty sitting still, and learn better through physical activity. They may do better in active settings such as lab work and role playing, or using a computer and taking frequent study breaks.

Some people learn better by studying alone, and others prefer study groups. Although no one learning style is inherently better than another, you will need to adapt to the style required in a course.

Learning about Your Personality and Psychological Type

"Personality" is a general term referring to your characteristic ways of thinking, feeling, and behaving. "Psychological type" refers specifically to the personality theory of Carl Gustav Jung, the great 20th-century psychoanalyst. Because different psychological types approach their studies in different ways, we often say that they have different "learning styles." Knowing your psychological type and corresponding learning style helps you identify strategies you are good at, and makes sure you don't neglect necessary elements of learning that come less naturally to you. There are many different theories and tests of personality that describe different psychological types, but in this chapter we will be using the work of Jung, Myers, and Briggs.

The Myers Briggs Type Indicator, or MBTI®, is the most widely used personality test designed for normal individuals, and it is given to several million people worldwide each year. Thousands of research studies have been carried out to support the validity of this test.

Note that all the psychological types we will describe are normal and healthy; there is no good or bad or right or wrong—people are simply different. Various strengths and weaknesses are commonly associated with each preference that makes up a psychological type.

Psychological Preferences

Your psychological type is the combination of your preferences on four different scales. These scales measure how you take in information and how you then make decisions or come to conclusions about that information. They also measure your orientation toward the outer and inner worlds. Like being left-handed or right-handed, these preferences are of an "either-or" nature. But like your hands, you actually use both possible preferences—it's just that one is your natural favorite.

Each preference has a one-letter abbreviation. The four letters together make up your "type." Now here are all the preferences and what they mean.

Extraversion (E) vs. Introversion (I): The Outer or Inner World

The E–I preference indicates whether you direct your energy and attention primarily toward the outer world of people, events, and things or the inner world of thoughts, feelings, and reflections.

Extraverts tend to be outgoing, gregarious, and talkative. They often "think with the volume on," saying out loud what is going on in their minds. They are energized by people and activity, and they seek this in both work and play. They are people of action, preferring to spend more time doing things than thinking about them. At their best, they are good communicators who are quick to act and lead. At their worst, they talk too much and too loudly, they put their feet in their mouths, and they act before they think.

Introverts prefer to reflect carefully on things and think them through before taking action. They think a lot, but they tend to "think with the volume off"; if you want to know what's on their minds, you may have to ask them. They are refreshed by quiet and privacy. At their best, introverts are good, careful listeners whose thoughts are deep and whose actions are well considered. At their worst, they may be too shy and not aware enough of the people and situations around them, and they may think about things so long that they neglect to actually start doing them.

Sensing (S) vs. Intuition (N): Facts or Ideas

The S–N preference indicates how you perceive the world and take in information: directly, through your five senses; or indirectly, using your intuition.

Sensing types are interested above all in the facts, what is known and what they can be sure of. Typically they are practical, factual, realistic, and down-to-earth. They can be very accurate, steady, precise, and patient and effective with routine and details. They are often relatively traditional and conventional. They dislike unnecessary complication, and they prefer to practice skills they already know. At their best, sensing types can be counted on to do things right and keep doing things right, with every detail well taken care of. At their worst, they can plod along while missing the point of why they are doing what they do, not seeing the forest (the whole picture) for the trees (the details).

Intuitive types are fascinated by possibilities: not so much the facts themselves, but what those facts mean, what concepts might describe those facts, how those might relate to other concepts, what the implications of the facts would be, and so on. Intuitive types are less tied to the here-and-now and tend to look further into the future and the past. They need inspiration and meaning for what they do, and they tend to work in bursts of energy and enthusiasm. Often they are original, creative, and nontraditional. They may have trouble with routine and details, however, and they would rather learn a new skill than keep practicing the one they have already mastered. They can be bad at facts and may exaggerate without realizing it. At their best, intuitive types are bright, innovative people who thrive in academic settings and the world of invention and ideas. At their worst, they can be impractical dreamers whose visions fall short because of inattention to practical detail.

Thinking (T) vs. Feeling (F): Logic or Values

The T–F preference indicates how you prefer to make your decisions: through logical, rational analysis or through your subjective values, likes, and dislikes.

Thinking types are usually logical, rational, analytical, and critical. They pride themselves on reasoning their way to the best possible decisions. They tend to decide things relatively impersonally and objectively, and they are less swayed by feelings and emotions—both their own and other people's. Other people's feelings sometimes puzzle or surprise them. They can deal with interpersonal disharmony and can be firm and assertive when they need to be. In all their dealings, they need and value fairness. At their best, thinking types are firm, fair, logical, and just. At their worst, they may be cold, insensitive to other people's feelings, and overly blunt and hurtful in their criticisms.

Feeling types are typically warm, empathic, sympathetic, and interested in the happiness of others as well as themselves. They need and value harmony, and they may be distressed and distracted by argument and conflict. They sometimes have trouble being assertive when it would be appropriate to do so. Above all, they need and value kindness. At their best, feeling types are warm and affirming—they facilitate cooperation and goodwill among those around them while pursuing the best human values. At their worst, feeling types can be illogical, emotionally demanding, reluctant to tackle unpleasant tasks, and unswayed by objective reason and evidence.

Judging (J) vs. Perceiving (P): Organization or Adaptability

The J–P preference indicates how you characteristically approach the outside world: making decisions and judgments, or observing and perceiving instead.

Judging types approach the world in a planned, orderly, organized way; as much as possible, they try to order and control their part of it. They make their decisions relatively quickly and easily. They like to make and follow plans. They begin at the beginning, end at the end, and try to finish one thing before starting the next. They are usually punctual and tidy, and they appreciate those traits in others. At their best, judging types are natural organizers who get things done and done on time. At their worst, judging types may jump to conclusions prematurely and be too judgmental of people.

Perceiving types don't try to control the world as much as adapt to it. Theirs is a flexible, wait-and-see approach. They deal comfortably and well with changes, unexpected developments, and emergencies, adjusting their plans and behaviors as needed. They tend to delay decisions so that they can keep their options open and gather more information. They may procrastinate to a serious degree, however, and they may try to carry on too many things at once, without finishing any of them. At their best, perceiving types are spontaneous, flexible individuals who roll with the punches and find ways to take the proverbial lemons in life and turn them into lemonade. At their worst, perceiving types may become messy, disorganized procrastinators who cannot be relied on.

Because there are two possible choices for each of four different preferences, there are sixteen possible psychological types. The four preferences that make up one of the sixteen types may interact in a unique way. You can read more about this in some of the references listed at the end of this chapter, but for simplicity we will deal mainly with the four main preference choices rather than the sixteen individual types.

Using Your Personality for Better Learning

The key to using psychological type to succeed in college is to use all the attitudes and functions (E, I, S, N, T, F, J, and P) effectively in a logical sequence. As you go about your studies, here is the system we recommend:

1. **Sensing.** Get the facts. Use Sensing to find and learn the facts. What are the facts? How do we know them? What is the factual evidence for what is being said?

2. **Intuition.** Get the ideas. Now use Intuition to consider what those facts mean. Why are those facts being presented? What concepts and ideas are being supported by those facts? What are the implications? What is the "big picture"?

3. **Thinking.** Critically analyze. Use Thinking to analyze the pros and cons of what is being presented. Are there gaps in the evidence? What more do we need to know? Do the facts really support the conclusions? Are there alternative explanations? How well does what is presented hang together logically? How could our knowledge of it be improved?

4. **Feeling.** Make informed value judgments. Why is this material important? What does it contribute to people's good? Why might it be important to you personally? What is your personal opinion about it?

5. **Introversion.** Think it through. Before you take any action, carefully go over in your mind everything you have encountered so far.

6. **Judging.** Organize and plan. Don't just dive in! Now is the time to organize and plan your studying so you will learn and remember everything you need to. Don't just plan in your head, either; write your plan down, in detail.

7. **Extraversion.** Take action. Now that you have a plan, act on it. Do whatever it takes. Create note cards, study outlines, study groups, and so on. If you are working on a paper instead of a test, now is the time to start writing.

8. Perceiving. Change your plan as needed. Be flexible enough to change your plan if it isn't working. Expect the unexpected and deal with the unforeseen. Don't give up the whole effort the minute your original plan stops working; figure out what's wrong. Then come up with another, better plan and start following that.

If you do all of these things in the proper order, you should be able to study successfully for any test from any teacher, and produce a solid and complete piece of work for any paper or assignment.

Your Instructors' Teaching Styles

Once you learn about psychological types, it may be fairly easy to make guesses about what your instructors' types are, and therefore what kind of questions and evaluation criteria they will use. This is risky, however, and not recommended, for two reasons: (1) you may guess wrong, and fail; and (2) many instructors make a conscious effort to "cover all the bases," and therefore test and evaluate in a variety of ways.

To illustrate the perils of studying in just one manner, consider this actual example. Two classes were assigned Henry David Thoreau's famous book *Walden.* All the students read the same book. One instructor gave a very Sensing test, asking only for facts such as the exact location of Walden Pond, the year the book was written, and so on. Students who studied with Sensing only did fine, but Intuitive-only students thought those questions were trivial, didn't study them, and never got a chance to discuss the ideas they had studied.

The other instructor gave a very Intuitive test. The entire test read: " 'I was determined to know beans.' Discuss." The Sensing-only students were stricken—they didn't even know what they were being asked! The Intuitive-only students did fine, happily giving long, abstract discussions of the implications of that quote from Thoreau's book.

Only the students who studied with both their Sensing and Intuition could have passed whichever test they happened to get. Moral of the story: Always cover all the psychological bases when you study.

Helpful Hints for Each Type

Much of the following advice might help any personality type, but because each type tends to have characteristic strengths and weaknesses, some suggestions are particularly apt for certain types.

Tips for Extraverts

1. Studying is your most important activity, so don't let your other activities take up all your study time. Also, don't try to multitask: you can't study effectively while you are simultaneously instant-messaging your buddies, visiting with your friends, eating a meal, watching TV, and so on.
2. Study in groups, put the material into words, and talk about it out loud; but prepare for group study sessions by working carefully with the material beforehand.
3. Participate in class by asking questions or making comments—but think these through before you say them out loud.
4. Get involved in as many class demonstrations, projects, lab exercises, field trips, interest groups, and other course-related activities as you can.

Tips for Introverts

1. Find a quiet, comfortable place where you can study on your own without being disturbed. Don't try to study in your room, unless yours is uncommonly quiet and free of interruptions.
2. Put what you are studying and want to remember into written words.
3. Don't be afraid to ask questions in class; if you have a question, others are probably wondering the same thing, and they will silently bless you for asking. Also feel free to go to your instructor's office hours and ask questions or make comments one-on-one.
4. Don't get "lost in space" with your own thoughts. Be sure to pay attention at all times to what is going on in class, and stay "on task" as you study.

Tips for Sensing Types

1. Some students give broad, sweeping generalizations without supporting facts—but you are more likely to give lots of facts without tying them together. When studying the facts, take time to consider why you are studying them, what concepts they illustrate, and why they are important.
2. Don't accept everything just as it is given to you; think about it, work with it, and make it your own.
3. Ask for more time to do your best on tests—it never hurts to ask. (The worst your instructor can do is say, "No, I'm sorry, I can't.") If you don't have enough time, do everything that is relatively quick and easy for you first, even if that means taking things out of order; then do as much as you can with as many things as possible that are left. Move fast and skip around.

4. Go beyond the obvious on test questions, and watch out for subtle traps. On papers and other assignments, go beyond the minimum; top grades usually go to students who do more than was required, but still stick to the point.

Tips for Intuitive Types

1. Always be able to cite facts, evidence, and examples. Don't skip over the details, whether in studying, writing papers, or taking tests. In math and science courses, show all your work.
2. Don't exaggerate or overstate your case; make sure what you're saying is accurate and well justified.
3. Follow instructions. Often, you may want to do things your own way, but get your instructor's approval to do so first. The safest bet is to do everything as instructed. Then, if you'd like to add something more creative afterwards, fine. Just explain to your instructor what you added and why.
4. Try to work on things steadily, not in fits and starts; find less important parts you can work on when you are not especially inspired. Realize that you may greatly underestimate how much time you will need to study or write papers, so as a rule of thumb, plan for at least twice as much time as you think you will need.

Tips for Thinking Types

1. College isn't always fair. Be prepared for that, and after a certain point, accept it.
2. Don't over-argue your points, just because you feel certain you are right. After a certain point, you can't simply "logic" people into submission. If it's not a major point, simply express yourself and then let it go.
3. Don't neglect the human side of things. People's likes and values do matter and must be taken into consideration.
4. Remember to praise as well as criticize.

Tips for Feeling Types

1. Don't expect special favors because you are a nice person. Your teachers fail lots of nice people every year. They don't enjoy doing it, but if you don't meet the same expectations as everyone else, you aren't going to pass the course.
2. Work as hard on things that you find disagreeable as you work on things you like. It's best to start with what you don't want to do, and then reward yourself by doing work that you like.

3. Stand up for yourself and your point of view, but learn to use and accept logical arguments.
4. Remember to constructively criticize as well as praise.

Tips for Judging Types

1. Avoid absolute statements, those with drastic and extreme opposites.
2. Keep an open mind. Get all the facts and considerations before you make up your mind, and don't jump to conclusions—about ideas or people—too quickly.
3. Don't be afraid to change your mind—that's a big part of what college is about.
4. Don't panic if your plans don't work; just change them and try again. It's not good to miss a deadline, but no student has ever been executed for it. Explain your situation to your instructor, and do the best you can.

Tips for Perceiving Types

1. Procrastination is your worst enemy! Beware of it and learn to defeat it. If you don't know where to start, start anywhere—just start.
2. Don't present all sides of something and then leave it hanging; come to conclusions, even if tentative.
3. Don't abandon all of your plans just because you fail to live up to some of them. You will get better at it. Just modify your plan, then continue to follow it.
4. Don't assume your teachers will cut you a break and accept things late. Poor planning on your part may not constitute an emergency on theirs; if they let everyone turn things in late, they couldn't do their jobs. If it's unavoidable that you'll be late, talk to your instructor beforehand and explain. Also remember that repeatedly coming to class late makes a poor impression and may lower your grade.

YOUR PERSONAL JOURNAL

Here are several things to write about. Choose one or more. Or choose another topic related to personality and learning styles.

1. As best you can determine, what is your true psychological type/learning style? What specific experiences and characteristics lead you to believe that this one is yours?

2. What sorts of learning style behaviors come most easily to you? Which are most difficult?

3. How sure are you about what major and career you want to choose? What strengths from your psychological type will help you in this, and what potential weaknesses will you have to address?

4. What behaviors are you willing to change after reading this chapter? How might you go about changing them?

5. What else is on your mind this week? If you wish to share it with your instructor, add it to this journal entry.

READINGS

Accommodating Students' Learning Styles*

Professors want their lessons to stimulate all of their students' senses. Here are some of the latest innovations that turn an ordinary classroom into a multimedia event.

By Amy Milshtein

While there are many types of learning styles, people are generally grouped into one of three sensory categories: auditory (prefer to learn by hearing), tactile (prefer to learn by doing) and visual (prefer to learn by seeing or writing). No single way is good or bad, or right or wrong. The styles simply reflect our individual brain wiring and the way we absorb and store information.

That doesn't mean, however, that each person is locked into one style that was assigned in the cradle and is taken to the grave. We may favor one sense, but we are not ruled by one. "We are not born with one specific learning style," explains Dr. Mike Atwood, professor at Philadelphia's Drexel University College of Information Science and Technology. "We process information using a mixture of cues."

In fact, a 1971 study called Silent Messages conducted by Professor Albert Mehrabian asks how people communicate. His research reveals: only 7 percent of communication comes from the actual dictionary meaning of what was said; 35 percent comes from verbal inflection; while a whopping 58 percent comes from visual cues like eye contact, gestures, and body language.

College Planning & Management, March 2003, v6, i3, p. 30(2). Reprinted with permission from the author.

What does this mean to the professor trying to reach all of those differently wired brains? "We have gotten away from the 'sage on the stage' model where the lecturer drones on and the students take notes," says Atwood. "We've moved to a mode where students need to reach out and touch the material."

What are some of the important technologies that have aided in this effort? They run the gamut from state-of-the-art to low-tech yet surprisingly innovative. Here are some of the learning tools showing up in campuses across the country.

CAN YOU HEAR ME NOW?

While no longer the sole star of the show, the professor is still the facilitator. But what good is it if that facilitator cannot be heard? "The spoken voice gets weary, and strain sets in," explains Roscoe Anthony, vice president of marketing at Califone International, Inc., Chatsworth, Calif.

Since teachers are not trained to project to the back of the room like Celine Dion, products like Califone's Classroom Amplification Systems allow even the most soft-spoken to get their points across. "Studies suggest that amplifying the voice increases student material retention," says Anthony.

Systems range from simple boom boxes with microphones to more complex wireless headsets that allow teachers to move about the classroom effortlessly. When students break into groups, an amplified teacher can get everyone's attention at once. When students don their own headsets to work in computer or music labs, a teacher can break in on the lesson and instruct further.

"As multimedia labs develop, this technology has grown more sophisticated," Anthony interjects. "Don't expect to see cassettes." Instead, today's auditory aids are MP3 and CD driven.

THE IDIOT BOX GROWS UP

"Television used to be called 'the boob tube,' " says Bob Bauman, sales manager for Contemporary Research Corp. in Dallas. "Today it's a highly regarded learning tool."

Video applications have replaced such standard teaching tools as 16 mm films, filmstrips, and even overhead projections. Companies like Contemporary Research and VBrick Systems, Inc., Wallingford, Conn., offer the gamut from basic media retrieval systems to the bells and whistles of real-time, on-demand, DVD-quality video and CD-quality audio.

"A system like ours allows visual images from other locations to enter the classroom," says Rich Mavrogeanes, president and founder of VBrick Systems. "For instance, if a professor is lecturing on dinosaurs, the class can instantly connect to and interact with a museum curator holding a bone." For a visual learner, this beats any illustration in a book.

IT'S OKAY TO WRITE ON THE WALL

Even the old standard chalkboard has been polished up. "Whiteboards transform walls into a clean, bright, highly readable surface," says Erica Weaver, marketing assistant for Walltalkers in Fairlawn, Ohio. She says that whiteboards and colored markers are easier to see and more stimulating than chalkboards.

Interactive and smart whiteboards take the concept even further. "I've heard that using interactive whiteboards improves collaboration, decreases teaching time, and actually increases attention," explains Alfred Basilicato, president and CEO for Numonics Corp., Montgomeryville, Pa.

An interactive whiteboard uses a computer stylus instead of ink. The resulting writing can be saved, manipulated, and sent out to laptops instantly. This tool can also let teachers and students replay the entire lesson and even access the Internet.

"For auditory learners, it's wonderful because they can just sit back and listen without having to take notes," says Basilicato. "But it's great for the tactile learner too. He or she can come up to the board, grab the pen, and start writing."

All of these tools aim to help students learn in any style. But more important, they help them interact. Atwood stresses the importance of collaborative learning: "They need to be active participants in the process. Learning has become a collaborative effort. One in which technology is key."

Texas Tech U.:
Students Should Adapt
Study Habits to Learning Styles*
By Lauren Clonts

Students who spend hours cramming the night before a test only to forget half of the material come test time are not uncommon. Not to worry, however; several approaches aid in remembering.

Ruth Maki, professor of psychology, said how well people learn and remember depends upon the way they learn the information.

"There are a number of things we know from the study of human memory that improve speed of learning and retention," she said. "The main thing is levels of processing—when students read, hear, or study information, they need to be thinking about how things relate to each other and the meaning of

---

The America's Intelligence Wire, September 21, 2004. Copyright 2004 M2 Communications Ltd. Reprinted with permission.

things." Maki said good strategies for learning include making visual images and tying information to things you already know. As opposed to just hearing or reading the surface of things, think about how they all relate, she said.

"Tie things to personal experiences and make diagrams instead of just reading about them," Maki said. "Ask yourself questions about the material." The key to remembering information is remembering things different ways, Maki said.

"The more ways you can get things into your memory, the better you will remember it," she said.

Some students read a textbook ten times, but cannot recall the information, Maki said.

Reading things repeatedly is not effective, but making diagrams, taking good notes, and creating questions for yourself is a good approach, she said.

"Often students learn material very specifically, so if a test question is exactly how they learned it, they can pull it out [of memory]," she said. "But if a test question is different than the students learned it, they may not remember the information." Nathan Harkey, a senior agricultural communications major from Petersburg, said he usually starts studying the night before a test.

"I can never find time," he said. "I know I should study a lot more, but if I can get by, I'd rather do that." Harkey said his method of studying is to read the notes from class and any handouts professors give.

"If there is a lot of information or anything with formulas, I'll make flash-cards," he said.

Maki said when students just memorize information, they will not remember the information if the test question is not exactly as they read it.

Students must think of information in different ways and aspects, she said. "Link information together, and you will be able to retrieve it better," Maki said. The best method to remember material for the long term is to study it not all at once, but to study it now, then next week and the next week and so on, she said.

"If you spread studying out over time, you will remember it much longer," Maki said.

If someone remembers facts for a long enough period of time, it will become ingrained in their mind, she said."Information that is learned over long periods of time basically becomes unforgettable," she said.

Robin Hilsabeck, assistant professor of neuoropsychiatry and behavioral science at Texas Tech Health Sciences Center, said students usually discover their own learning techniques before coming to college.

"Students have different strengths and weaknesses," she said. "Some are visual learners, some have to write things down, and some have to do it to learn it." Hilsabeck said the personality of a student often determines his/her learning strategies. Some students have to write material down fifteen different ways, and some have to only write it down once, she said.

"Mnemonic techniques, such as acronyms, help students remember the information by encoding it better," she said. "They process it more deeply." A lot of research shows the context in which people learn information helps them remember it better, Hilsabeck said.

"If you are used to drinking coffee while you study, you should drink coffee before taking a test," she said. "Figure out what learning techniques work for you, and stick with those."

DISCUSSION

1. Discuss how what you've learned about your psychological type and your learning style may affect your choice of a major and a career. Discuss this with other students.

2. Think of some examples of how your learning style preferences may or may not explain why you select certain kinds of people as friends—or why you would prefer certain types to be your supervisor or teacher. Compare your observations with those of some students in this class.

3. What is the connection between your learning style preferences and the fact that you seem to learn more from some instructors than others? As a group, share some coping skills to use with teachers whose teaching styles aren't the best fit with your learning style preferences.

4. The first reading, "Accommodating Students' Learning Styles," offers strategies for creating a more stimulating classroom learning environment. Discuss which of these suggestions you think would be appropriate to suggest to one or more of your professors in a course evaluation and explain why you would learn better under these recommended conditions.

5. In the second reading, the author states: "Some students read a textbook 10 times, but cannot recall the information." Talk about this in a small group and find out how many in the group are facing this problem. Then come up with a number of ideas for overcoming it.

Active Learning

Because many college teachers emphasize critical thinking, they offer you the chance to move from a pattern of being taught *passively* to one of learning *actively*.

What is active learning, how does it take place, and why do many teachers believe it's the best way to learn? Active learning is simply a method that involves students in an active manner. It happens whenever your teacher asks you a question in class, puts you in groups to solve a problem, requires you to make an oral presentation to the class, or does anything else that gives you and other students a voice in the learning process.

The Many Benefits of Active Learning

In addition to placing you "in the center" of learning, active learning teaches you a variety of skills employers want most: thinking, writing, oral communication, goal setting, time management, relationship building, problem solving, ethical reasoning, and more. All these skills are an important part of leadership.

A teacher who urges students to collaborate on an assignment is aware that two or more heads may be far more productive than one. Each student turns in an original piece of work but is free to seek advice and suggestions from another student.

More than likely, this is how you will be working after college, so it makes sense to learn how to collaborate when you can, rather than compete. Students who embrace active learning not only learn better but enjoy their learning experiences more. Even if you have an instructor who lectures for an entire period and leaves little or no time for questions, you might form a study group with three or four other students so that each of you can benefit from what the others have learned. Or you might ask the teacher for an appointment to discuss unanswered questions from the lecture. By doing so, you can transform a passive learning situation into an active one. In a passive classroom, where you listen and take notes, you are less likely to retain information or put it to use.

Active learners are willing to try new ideas and discover new knowledge by exploring the world around them instead of just memorizing facts. Here are some things you can do to practice learning actively:

- Try to find out which teachers will actively engage you in learning. Ask friends, your advisor, and other teachers.
- Even in a large class, sit as close to the front as you can and never hesitate to raise your hand if you don't understand something. Chances are, the other students didn't understand it either.
- Put notes into your own words instead of just memorizing the book or the lecture.
- Study with other students. Talking about assignments and getting other points of view will help you learn the material faster and more thoroughly.
- Follow the suggestions in Chapters 2 and 3 and Chapters 6–8 about managing your time, optimizing your learning preferences, taking class notes, reading texts, and studying for exams.
- If you disagree with what your instructor says, politely challenge him or her. Good teachers will listen and may still disagree with you, but they may think more of you for showing you can think and that you care enough to challenge them.
- Stay in touch with teachers, other students, and your academic advisor. One great way is through email. Or call and leave a voice mail if the person is out.

Why Active Learners Can Learn More Than Passive Learners

Active learning puts students in charge of their own education. Although you may acquire knowledge listening to a lecture, you may not be motivated to think about what that knowledge means. Through active learning, you will learn not only the material in your notes and textbooks, but also how to:

- Work with others
- Improve your critical thinking, listening, writing, and speaking skills
- Function independently and teach yourself

- Manage your time
- Gain sensitivity to cultural differences

Asking a question in class has as much to do with developing assertiveness as with knowing the answer to a question. And keeping a journal will help you learn *how* you learn so that you can teach yourself.

Becoming an Active Learner

Active learning requires preparation before and after every class, not just before exams. Active learning also can include browsing the Internet for credible Web sites related to the subjects you are studying, searching for more information in the library, making appointments to talk to faculty, making outlines from your class notes, going to cultural events, working on a committee, asking someone to read something you've written to see if it's clear, or having a serious discussion with students whose personal values are different from yours.

Yet with all its benefits, some students resist active learning out of fear of trying something new and challenging. One student described an active learning class as "scary" and a more traditional class as "safe." The traditional class was safe because the teacher did not invite students to sit in a semicircle, and he used a textbook and lectures to explain ideas. On the other hand, discussions in the active learning class were scary because of the process, the uncertainty, and the openness.[1]

Studies have indicated that the larger the class, the less most students want to speak out. As one student explains, "If I give the wrong answer in a large class, students will see me as a dunce." Yet when the instructor creates an atmosphere where such participation is comfortable and makes it clear that even reasonable "wrong" answers are better than no answers at all, you probably will want to participate more often.

According to student development theory, an active approach to learning and living has the potential to produce individuals who are well-rounded in all aspects of life. The hexagon in Figure 4.1 depicts seven aspects of development, with intellectual development at its center. Optimal personal development depends on each area's supporting every other area. For example, with good active learning skills, you likely will feel more comfortable socially, gain a greater appreciation for diversity and education, and be better able to make decisions about your college major and future career. Staying physically active

[1]Adapted from Russell A. Warren, "Engaging Students in Active Learning," *About Campus,* March–April 1997.

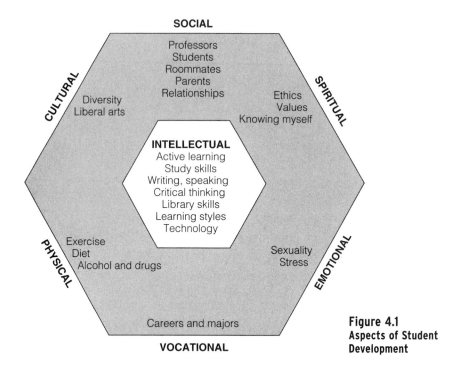

Figure 4.1
Aspects of Student Development

can reduce stress and keep your mind alert while you study. Developing a sense of values can help you choose your friends more carefully and decide how you choose to manage your time.

One way to practice active learning daily is through a process called the "one-minute paper." In a major study of teaching at Harvard University, one of many suggestions for improving learning was a simple feedback exercise. At the end of each class, students were asked to write what they thought was the main issue of that class and what their unanswered questions were for the next class.

Even if your instructors don't require it, try writing your one-minute paper each day at the end of class. Use it to think about the main issues discussed that day, and save it so that you can ask good questions at the next class meeting.

Teachers Who Embrace Active Learning Love to Teach

For a teacher, it's probably much easier to write and deliver a lecture than to engage students in discussion. But those who favor the latter probably do so because they believe it's a better way to learn and because sometimes it's more exciting to hear students demonstrate how much they've learned.

And just as some teachers go the extra mile to make classes interesting, so should you. Instead of blending in with your peers—as many new students seem to do—ask the questions in class others probably want to ask but don't. Try to do something genuinely innovative with every paper and project. Be certain it is "on track" with the assignment. Sure, you'll make some mistakes, but your instructor probably will appreciate your inquisitive nature, reward you for it, and be more willing to help you improve your work.

As friendly and understanding as they are, teachers will set deadlines for work and stick to them. This should instill in you an appreciation of time management: If one thing isn't done on time, the whole plan can fall apart. So if you're not sure of a deadline, ask.

Just as good teachers invite you to speak out in class, they also keep lines of communication open. They not only grade your work but may ask you how you're learning, what you're learning, and how clearly their teaching is coming across to you. In fact, some of the best learning may take place one-on-one in the instructor's office. Research shows that students who interact with their teachers outside of class have a greater chance of returning to college for their second year. Remember, this isn't high school, where it wasn't cool to speak to a teacher.

Your college instructors will encourage you to develop new ways of thinking, to realize there may be many acceptable answers as opposed to only one, to question existing knowledge, to take issue with something they might say, to ask questions in class, and to offer possible solutions to problems. You may be surprised to find that most college teachers do not fit the stereotype of the ivory tower scholar. Though many college instructors still must spend some of their time doing scholarly research and performing service for the institution, a majority of them say they love teaching most of all, and for good reason: Motivating students like you can be deeply rewarding.

Instructors may also do things your high school teachers never did, such as:

- Supplementing textbook assignments with other information
- Giving exams covering both assigned readings and lectures
- Questioning conclusions of other scholars
- Accepting several different student opinions on a question
- Leaving it up to you whether to take notes or read the text
- Demanding more reading of you in a shorter period of time
- Giving fewer quizzes or many more quizzes
- Expecting you to be familiar with topics related to their field
- Being sympathetic to difficulties you may have while at the same time holding firm to high standards of grading.

You may be on friendly terms with your instructor and find you have received a low grade because you missed too many classes, did not complete all required work, or simply failed to produce acceptable work. A college teacher may tell you that although your grades may be unacceptable, this is not necessarily a reflection on your character or potential abilities.

Making the Most of the Student-Instructor Relationship

1. **Make it a point to attend class regularly and on time.** And participate in the discussion; you'll learn more if you do. If you miss a class, you might get another student's notes, but that isn't the same thing as being present during class. Learning is simply easier when you're there every day.

2. **Save your cuts for emergencies.** When you know you will be absent, let your instructor know in advance, even if the class is a large one. It could make a big difference in your teacher's attitude toward you. And if the class is really large, it's one way of introducing yourself.

3. **Sit near the front.** Studies indicate that students who do so tend to earn better grades.

4. **Speak up.** Ask questions when you don't understand or need clarification, and voice your opinion when you disagree.

5. **See your instructor outside class when you need help.** Instructors are required to keep office hours for student appointments. Make an appointment by phone, email, or at the end of class. You will likely be pleasantly surprised at how much your instructor is willing to work with you. Get your instructor's email address and use it.

6. **Share one or more "one-minute papers" with your instructor.** You can do this either in writing or through email. It could be the start of an interesting dialogue.

Teachers, Students, and Academic Freedom

College instructors possess and believe in the freedom to speak out, whether in a classroom discussion about economic policy or at a public rally on abortion or gay rights. What matters more than what instructors believe is their right to proclaim that belief to others without fear. Colleges and universities have promoted the advancement of knowledge by granting scholars virtually unlimited freedom of inquiry (academic freedom), as long as human lives, rights, and privacy are not violated.

Some teachers may speak sarcastically about a politician you admire. Although you need not accept such ideas, you must learn to evaluate them for yourself, instead of basing your judgments on what others have always told you is right.

Academic freedom also extends to college students. This means you will have more freedom than in high school to select certain research topics or to pursue controversial issues. You will also have the right to disagree with the instructor if you feel differently about an issue, but be certain you can support your argument with reliable published or personal evidence.

Above all, discuss—never attack. Cite something you've read or heard, and ask what the instructor thinks about your approach to the issue. Done respectfully, such queries can enrich learning for the entire class.

"Great teachers know their subjects well. But they also know their students well," says Dr. Eliot Engel of North Carolina State University. "In fact," he continues, "great teaching fundamentally consists of constructing a bridge from the subject taught to the student learning it. Both sides of that bridge must be surveyed with equal care if the subject matter of the teacher is to connect with the gray matter of the student. But great teachers transcend simply knowing their subjects and students well. They also admire both deeply."[2]

As an active learner, you should find it easier to admire both your teacher and your subject deeply, just as your teacher will learn to admire you.

If Things Go Wrong between You and a Teacher

What if you can't tolerate a particular instructor? Arrange a meeting to try to work things out. Getting to know the teacher as a person may help you cope with the way he or she teaches the course. If that fails, check the "drop/add" date, which usually falls at the end of the first week of classes. You may have to drop the course altogether and pick up a different one. If it's too late to add classes, you may still want to drop by the drop date later in the term and avoid a penalty. See your academic advisor or counselor for help with this decision.

If you can't resolve the situation with the instructor and need to stay in the class, see the head of the department. If you are still dissatisfied, move up the administrative ladder until you get a definite answer. Never allow a bad instructor to sour you on college. Even the worst course will be over in a matter of weeks.

What if you're not satisfied with your grade? First, make an appointment to see the instructor and discuss the assignment. Your teacher may give you a second chance because you took the time to ask for help. If you get a low grade on an exam, you might ask the instructor to review certain answers with you. Never directly insist on a grade change, as this will most likely backfire.

What if you're dealing with sexual harassment or sexism? Sexual harassment is a serious offense and a cause for grievance. If an instructor makes inappropriate or threatening remarks of a sexual nature, report this to the

---

[2]From a column in the *Dickens Dispatch,* the newsletter of the North Carolina Dickens Club, January 1989.

instructor's department chair. No instructor should ask for a date or otherwise pressure students to become involved in personal relationships, because the implied threat is that if you refuse, you may fail the course.

Sexism refers to statements or behaviors that demonstrate a belief in the greater general worth of one gender over the other. Comments such as "I don't know why girls take chemistry" are not only insulting but may cause women to lose confidence in their abilities. The same rules apply to defamatory remarks about one's ethnic group. Your campus has specific procedures to follow if you believe you are being harassed sexually; make use of them.

Collaborative Learning Teams

Besides "teaming" with your teachers to enhance your learning, you can also team with your fellow students as a collaborative learning team.

How does such collaboration improve learning? Joseph Cuseo of Marymount College, an expert on collaborative learning, points to these factors:

- Learners learn from one another as well as from the instructor.
- Collaborative learning is by its very nature active learning, and so tends to increase learning by involving you more actively.
- "Two heads are better than one." Collaboration can lead to more ideas, alternative approaches, new perspectives, and better solutions.
- If you're not comfortable speaking out in larger classes, you will tend to be more comfortable speaking in smaller groups, resulting in better communication and better ideas.
- You will develop stronger bonds with other students in the class, which may increase everyone's interest in attending.
- An environment of "positive competition" among groups develops when several groups are asked to solve the same problem—as long as the instructor clarifies that the purpose is for the good of all.
- Through the group experience, you may develop leadership skills.
- You will learn to work with others, a fact of life in the world of work.

When students work effectively in a supportive group, the experience can be a highly powerful way to enhance academic achievement and meaningful learning. Interviews with college students at Harvard University revealed that nearly every senior who had been part of a study group considered this experience to be crucial to his or her academic progress and success.

Making Learning Teams Productive

Not all learning groups are equally effective. Sometimes teamwork is unsuccessful or fails to reach its potential because no thought was given to how the group should be formed or how it should function. Use the following strategies to develop high-quality learning teams that maximize the power of peer collaboration:

1. **Remember that learning teams are more than study groups.** Don't think that collaborative learning simply involves study groups that meet the night before major exams. Effective student learning teams collaborate regularly on other academic tasks besides test review sessions.

2. **In forming teams, seek students who will contribute quality and different points of view to the group.** Resist the urge to include people just like you. Look for fellow students who are motivated, attend class regularly, participate actively while in class, and complete assignments. Include both men and women, and select teammates from different ethnic, racial, or cultural backgrounds, different age groups, and different personality types and learning styles. Choosing only your friends can often result in a learning group that is more likely to get off track.

3. **Keep the group small (four to six teammates).** Smaller groups allow for more face-to-face interaction and eye contact and less opportunity for any one individual to shirk responsibility to the team. Also, it's much easier for small groups to meet outside class. Consider choosing an even number of teammates (four or six), so you can work in pairs in case the team decides to divide its work into separate parts.

4. **Hold individual team members personally accountable for their own learning and for contributing to the learning of their teammates.** Research on study groups indicates that they are effective only if each member has done the required work in advance of the group meeting (for example, completing required readings and other assignments). One way to ensure accountability is to have each member come to group meetings with specific information or answers to share with teammates as well as questions to ask the group. Or have individual members take on different roles or responsibilities, such as mastering a particular topic, section, or skill to be taught to others.

The Many Uses of Learning Teams

1. **Note-taking teams.** Team up with other students immediately after class to share and compare notes. One of your teammates may have picked up something you missed, or vice versa. By meeting immediately after class, your group may still have a chance to consult with the instructor about any missing or confusing information.

2. **Reading teams.** After completing reading assignments, team with other students to compare your highlighting and margin notes. See if all agree on what the author's major points were and what information you should study for exams.

3. **Library research teams.** Forming library research teams is an effective way to develop a support group for reducing "library anxiety" and for locating and sharing sources of information. (*Note:* Locating and sharing sources of information isn't cheating or plagiarizing as long as the final product you turn in represents your own work.)

4. **Team/instructor conferences.** Have your learning team visit the instructor during office hours to seek additional assistance in study or completing work. You may find it easier to see an instructor in the company of other students. And the feedback from your instructor is also received by your teammates, so that useful information is less likely to be forgotten. Your team visit also tells your instructor that you are serious about learning.

5. **Team test results review.** After receiving test results, the members of a learning team can review their individual tests together to help one another identify the sources of their mistakes and to identify any answers that received high scores. This provides each team member with a clearer idea of what the instructor expects. You can use this information for subsequent tests and assignments.

YOUR PERSONAL JOURNAL

Here are several things to write about. Choose one or more. Or choose another topic related to this chapter.

1. We've stated that college teachers are different from high school teachers. Can you give an example or two of those differences, based on one of your high school teachers and one of your current college teachers? Whose style are/were you more comfortable with? Why? In which class do you believe you'll learn more? Why?

2. If you've tried collaborative learning, write about how that went. If you haven't tried it yet, write about why you haven't and whether you plan to do so in the near future.

3. An important part of active learning is student participation. What if some students are reticent about speaking in class? (Their learning styles may indicate they are introverted.) Should the teacher be flexible about this? If so, how? If not, what should he or she do?

4. What behaviors are you thinking about changing after reading this chapter? How will you go about changing them?

5. What else is on your mind this week? If you wish to share it with your instructor, add it to this journal entry.

READINGS

Ten Strategies for Getting Students to Take Responsibility for Their Learning*

By Sara Jane Coffman

Abstract. *This article presents ten strategies instructors can use to get their students to take more responsibility for their learning. Suggestions are given about the importance of getting students to verbalize why they are taking the course, helping students get into the proper mind-set for each class, and structuring assignments so students will be more likely to come to class prepared. Other suggestions include teaching students to look out for each other, behave responsibly when working in groups, and analyze their learning experiences. By teaching responsibility, as well as content in our classrooms, we can enhance learning, raise the level of our classrooms, and produce more responsible members of society.*

Wouldn't it be great if our students came to class prepared—not just having read the assignment, but mentally prepared as well—alert and ready to debate, challenge, interact, and contribute?

Unfortunately, it often seems that when students walk into our classrooms their brains are set on the lowest possible setting. One reason students may not feel compelled to prepare (or be in the proper mind-set for learning) is that they don't mind being shortchanged. In our consumer-driven society, where more is supposedly better, education is the one area where people are content to settle for less: Want to make a class happy? Let them out early.

Are there some things we can do to get our students to read the assignment, come to class ready to participate, and be responsible learners? Absolutely! Not only are there things we could be doing, we should be doing them, according to Marcia Magolda in her article "Helping Students Make Their Way to Adulthood: Good Company for the Journey." Magolda believes that instructors are in a unique position to help students learn two important lessons: (*a*) to be less dependent on external authorities, and (*b*) to take ownership and responsibility for their own lives.

College Teaching, Winter 2003, v51, i1, p. 2(3). Copyright 2003 Heldref Publications. Reprinted with permission.

By teaching our students to be responsible learners, we can change our classrooms in dramatic ways. The following is a list of ten strategies you can use to bring your students to become more responsible.

1. Ask your students why they are taking the course. Many students enter the classroom without having thought out why they are there—they signed up for the class because their advisors told them to. Make your students put their reasons for taking your course in writing. This will get them to think about their commitment to the course and give you some valuable information about their needs, expectations, and goals.

One instructor makes the following assignment on the first day of class: "Please read the syllabus carefully and skim through the textbook. Then, write a short essay describing your expectations for the course, given what you know about yourself as a student and relating your experiences to what you see in the syllabus and in the textbook." In this way, he gets his students to read the syllabus, buy the textbook, and begin making a connection to the course.

If you have your students put their reasons for taking the course in writing, you can ask them to revisit their answers on the last day of class. This lets your students see if they achieved their goals, and it gives the class a nice sense of closure.

2. Get your students to come to class prepared. There are several ways to get your students to come to class prepared. First, when choosing a textbook for the course, select one with study questions (or an accompanying study guide) and require students to complete assignments (that you collect and respond to). Second, put study questions in the course syllabus under the heading "Be prepared to answer the following questions." Third, design interesting and unusual homework assignments so your students will want to come to class to discuss their answers. And, fourth, start class with a quick quiz (graded or ungraded).

Decide if you need every student to be prepared at every class session. It may be unrealistic to expect everyone to be prepared every time. Also, redefine your idea of "being prepared." Being prepared may be as simple as having them bring in a question that they'd like to have answered.

3. Help your students attain the proper mind-set for class. Can you imagine what would happen if students brought the same level of concentration to our classes that they use when playing a computer game or watching "Friends" on TV? Instructors can help their students get into the proper mind-set by making clever use of the time before class begins. Some have music playing when their students enter the classroom. Others show intriguing clips from relevant videos.

Studies have shown that students are most alert and attentive during the first ten minutes of a class (Hartley and Davies, 1978); so pay particular attention to how you use this time. Students enjoy classes that start in unusual and interesting ways. Put an engaging question on the board. Start with a surprise, a mystery, or a table full of props (for your visual learners). Set up a problem that you'll solve during the lecture (for your logical learners). The idea is to not begin the meat of the lesson until you have your students hooked.

4. Make participation and interaction integral parts of the course. According to Magolda, classrooms can be a place for young people to learn to defend their views, hear alternative perspectives, and redefine their belief systems. Use discussions and questions as often as possible. Explain to your students that it's important for you to hear what they're thinking so that you know whether or not they're processing the information.

A positive classroom climate can greatly facilitate learning. Have your students learn each other's names and get to know each other as quickly as possible. One professor asks her students to sit in a different seat each time so that they'll meet everyone in the class by the end of the semester. If it's a large class, have them use name tents. And, from the very first day, don't just take volunteers when you ask a question. Go ahead and call on your students! It adds a much-welcomed element of suspense to the classroom.

5. Make your students responsible for each other. Students learn at different speeds, so use your students who master the material more quickly to help the others. Have students pair up with a study buddy who can fill them in if they have to miss a class. Assign students to study groups and give them class time to prepare for the first exam together.

Make an announcement at the beginning of the semester that everyone in the class is in the same boat and that no one is going to be left behind. (But make sure your students know it's their responsibility for getting on the boat.)

6. Teach your students to behave responsibly in groups. Group work can be extremely frustrating because some students don't know how to behave in groups. Before using group work, ask your class to brainstorm a list of rules they think they should follow (e.g., respect other's opinions, don't interrupt each other, stay on track, etc.). Once the groups begin, spend time with each group and monitor their progress and behavior.

Let your students know that for a group to work well, everyone must contribute equally. Group members (no matter how shy) who have special information have an obligation to share it. And every member of the group is responsible for seeing that the group achieves its goals.

7. Model higher cognitive skills. Students can expand their curiosity and learn to ask questions by watching you be curious and ask questions. Teach your students not to skim over the top of a topic like a jet skier, but to put scuba diving equipment on and go down to examine underlying causes and relationships. When you ask a question, don't let students who give one-word answers off the hook. Ask them to elaborate.

8. Have your students analyze their learning experiences. Give your students a learning styles inventory to help them understand how they process information. Your teaching style may differ from their learning styles, and this will give you a chance to discuss what you both might do to bridge the gap.

In addition, give your students several opportunities throughout the course to give you feedback on how the course is going and to suggest changes that would help them learn better. According to Magolda, giving students a chance to evaluate the course is another way for them to challenge their reliance on external authority.

Finally, make your students give each other feedback (either formative or summative) on speeches and papers. Most students are hesitant to give their classmates feedback—they don't want to get involved, or they don't know how to give feedback. But giving feedback is a skill they'll use on the job and in every aspect of their lives. The classroom is a good place for them to learn to do it.

9. End class in a meaningful way. The last ten minutes of a class can be as important as the first ten. Make your students responsible for the lecture by having them write a short summary or take a short quiz before they leave. Another good way to end class is to ask, "Why did we do this?" "Why did we study this?" or "Why is this important?"

10. Don't try to save your students. Having compassion and extending a deadline when a student has a crisis is one thing; trying to save a student by extending a deadline because of his or her lack of planning is quite another. Even something as insignificant as bringing pencils for your students to borrow on exam days teaches students that they don't need to be responsible for bringing them.

SUMMARY

Whose responsibility is it for learning to occur in the classroom? The responsibility belongs to both the instructor and the students. Responsibility can (and should) shift, depending on the time in the semester and the level of the students. Faculty working with freshmen may take more of the responsibility for learning to occur than faculty working with seniors or graduate students. Likewise, instructors may take more of the responsibility at the beginning of the semester. As the class progresses, they can slowly relinquish control and prepare their students to take over, so that by the end of the semester, the students are shouldering most of the responsibility.

By teaching responsibility, we not only enhance learning and raise the level of our classrooms, but we help produce responsible citizens and productive members of society.

Class Participation:
Report from Beijing*

By Peter Phillips Simpson

Thanks to a Fulbright scholarship, I am teaching political philosophy at Beijing's Renmin (People's) University of China this year [2002]. My students are all rather silent in class. I attribute this mostly to difficulty in understanding English or diffidence with respect to speaking English. Among those students whose English is quite good, I think this diffidence has something to do with speaking one's mind in a country where people are understandably fearful of government surveillance and retribution. But it probably also has something to do with speaking with a foreigner, especially an American. Chinese students expect me to be biased against China. Whatever the reason, they only talk when one-on-one in my office or after class over coffee. When they get a chance to speak reasonably freely, they show themselves to be very bright and amusing kids.

Occasionally I try to get them to speak about life in China, but they are reluctant to do so. One-party rule inhibits discussion, but so does the traditional closeness of Chinese families. The parents of some of my students have sacrificed to enable their children to go to a good university and the kids are expected to repay the kindness by raising the family's status and economic standing. China does not have much of a welfare system and the old communist system, where one's factory provided housing, medical care, and retirement, has long since gone. So if your kids don't help you out, who will? Of course, the kids are grateful to their parents and feel duty bound to them. Family pressures can force students to forgo further study, either in China or abroad.

Surprisingly, a form of Marxism is still a powerful influence here. It is taught in the high schools and universities, and attendance at a certain number of classes in Marxist theory is compulsory. But it is taught mainly through textbooks, not from Marx's work itself. Consequently, what students know about Marxism is quite limited. When the subject has come up in class, I'm the one who introduces all the relevant concepts: labor theory of value, class struggle, proletariat, etc. Maybe the kids don't care about Marxism anymore or they've forgotten it or they don't trust me and just let me blabber on. I make no attempt to be cautious in what I say about communism, Marxism, or Chairman Mao. I imagine my students put up with this as the price to be paid

---

*Commonweal, April 5, 2002, v129, i7, p. 11. © 2002 Commonweal Foundation. Reprinted with permission. For subscriptions, www.commonwealmagazine.org.

to have free teaching (the U.S. government pays for Fulbright lecturers; the host university just provides accommodation).

Recently, I was giving an invited lecture on war and terrorism at another university in Beijing. In answer to a question about the Vietnam War, I remarked that it was in general a good thing to oppose communism and stop its spread. Since this occasioned some surprise, I explained that while communism professed noble enough aims (the improvement of the people, especially the poor), it actually produced greater poverty by means of brutal tyranny. My translator thought this too controversial and declined to translate (though some in the audience knew enough English to have caught on). I did not press him. After all, he has to live here; I can go when I please.

My translator was again surprised (though he did translate this time) when in answer to a question about Taiwan, I said that if China tried to invade, any American president who refused to defend Taiwan would face the wrath of the American people. The surprise for my translator was the word "invade." How could China invade what is, after all, its own territory? he reasoned. I hastily added that I was speaking from the American perspective and went on to explain the special relationship that has long existed between the United States and the one part of China that did not succumb to communism.

Whenever I challenge students to explain why Tibet or Taiwan should belong to China, or what is so important about such supposed issues of "territorial integrity," they respond with distorted history (Tibet has always been part of China and ruled by China) or tu quoque arguments (What would you do if Georgia broke away from the United States?). When I ask if they would be willing to accept the results of a referendum in either place, they are not at all keen to say yes. My guess is that students just repeat the party line, which no one has ever seriously challenged before in their hearing. I suspect that patriotism is also a factor.

I think the same patriotism is behind the generally favorable opinion that most people have of Chairman Mao. After all, Mao did preside over China's restoration to national independence and international prominence. That Mao was at least by one measure three times worse than Stalin (Stalin killed 20 million of his own people while Mao killed 60 million) and six times worse than Hitler (who killed 10 million) does not seem to matter. When I make this comparison, as I did on a number of occasions at the English Corner (which meets weekly for anyone who wants to practice English), the listeners gasp with astonishment, not unmixed with amusement (Did he really say that?). But the worst gasps, unmixed by any amusement, are reserved for any Chinese who agrees with me or voices the same opinion—which has, surprisingly, happened on more than one occasion.

The Chinese, whether students, faculty, or others, tend to have a pretty jaundiced attitude toward American foreign policy. A typical feeling about the attacks of September 11, for instance—apart from shock and sympathy, of course—was that America somehow brought them on itself by its bullying approach to international questions. "America is always using force to settle problems; America runs the UN according to its own interest; America wants to keep China weak and dependent" (code for American military support for Taiwan); and so on.

Beyond the rather crude nationalism, I think there is a certain defensiveness behind the respect people show for Mao. After all, the tyrant tormented China for some thirty years, and to think there was nothing good in what he did, that nothing at all about his rule redeems it from being murderous insanity, that those thirty years were a complete waste, is just too much to bear. One has to think otherwise just to preserve a bit of sanity. Those who lived through that period are the most defensive, but I'm puzzled about why younger Chinese often share this view. (All of my students were born after Mao died.) Was there really something good about Mao's rule? Sometimes my students suggest as much. Here is what one of them wrote (English uncorrected):

> *It's more difficult to understand China by American than to understand America by Chinese. Because China is just like an old grandmother who have experienced much, and America is just like a young gal who is very beautiful but can't understand the full wrinkles and scars on the face of an old woman. As for the concrete affairs, I can't explain them clearly. But I'm sure that you have not known China well, for example, Taiwan affairs and Tibet problems. The difficulty is we (not only you) can't separate the Chinese government with China and Chinese people!*

Perhaps I do not know China well. But I make no apology for being controversial. It's part of a teacher's task to provoke students into thought. So far, no one in authority has complained or suggested I cool it or told me to leave the country. I suppose that says something too—about both China and my students.

DISCUSSION

1. Discuss your understanding of the core idea of this chapter: active learning. How does this notion of active learning compare with how you think you learn best? Can you identify teachers who encourage active learning—and with what results?

2. Discuss successful—or unsuccessful—ways you have addressed problems or differences with any of your college teachers. If you have not had any—and we hope you haven't—speculate on how you think you would handle such a challenge. Share what you know about your campus's official

procedures for filing a formal grievance against or appeal of an instructor's action.

3. Discuss how you work with other students on group assignments. What have you done to make this successful?

4. Experts have long known that students who take more responsibility for their own learning are more successful in college (and life). Discuss the recommendations in the first reading, "Ten Strategies for Getting Students to Take Responsibility for Their Learning," and consider how these would apply to you successfully and why.

5. The second reading is a firsthand account of an American professor's attempts to nudge his Chinese students in Beijing to participate in class. What can you infer about the Chinese students' learning process? Does lack of participation imply that the students aren't active learners? Or does it merely reflect a different style of interaction? Or are there other reasons?

Critical Thinking

In college, one of the most important lessons has less to do with *what* you're learning and more to do with *how* you're learning. For example, imagine that your instructor tells you on the first day of class:

I'm going to fill your minds with lots of important facts, and I expect you to take extensive notes and to know those facts in detail when you take your quizzes. The important thing in my class is how well you learn the material and how frequently you choose the right answers. And remember, while there are lots of wrong answers, there is one answer that always is correct.

In another class, the instructor introduces the course quite differently:

Although I've taught this course many times, it's never quite the same. Each time a new group of students begins the course, they bring their own values, ideas, and past knowledge to the material. The important thing in my class is that you use your heads. You certainly will need to read the assignments and take notes on the material in class. But that's only the beginning. What's most important is that you learn to analyze facts, decide which facts are supportable by evidence, and know how to convince others of your beliefs. And remember, while there are lots of wrong conclusions, there also may be more than one right conclusion.

When you earn your college degree and land a better job, chances are your employer is going to be more interested in how well you can think than in how well you can memorize minute bits of information. The second instructor

71

seems to be moving in that direction. She admits that many possibilities may exist. She may even confess that the class may come up with a better answer—or answers—if each student gathers his or her own information on the topic, if students discuss it in small groups, and if they share what they have learned with the teacher, who may then react to what she hears.

The first instructor will *tell you what you should know;* the second instructor wants you—through class discussion, small group sessions, problem solving, research, and other methods—*to seek the truths yourself.* If you do, you will probably have more faith in your conclusions and remember the information much more easily. What's most important, you will surely learn something!

From Certainty to Healthy Uncertainty

If you have just completed high school, you may be experiencing an awakening as you enter college. (If you're an older, returning student, discovering that your instructor trusts you to find valid answers may be somewhat stressful.) In high school you may have been conditioned to believe that things are either right or wrong. If your high school teacher asked, "What are the three branches of the U.S. government?" you had only one choice: "legislative, executive, and judicial." What you might have learned were the names of the three branches, but knowing names doesn't necessarily help you understand what the branches do, or how they do it, even though these three names suggest certain basic functions.

A college instructor might ask instead, "Under what circumstances might conflicts arise among the three branches of government, and what does this reveal about the democratic process?" Certainly, such questions have no simple—or single—answer. Most likely, your instructor is attempting not to embarrass you for giving a wrong answer but to engage you in the process of critical thinking.

Critical thinking is a process of choosing alternatives, weighing them, and considering what they suggest. Critical thinking involves understanding why some people believe one thing rather than another—whether you agree with their reasons or not. Critical thinking is learning to ask pertinent questions and testing your assumptions against hard evidence.

A Skill to Carry You through Life

Employers hiring college graduates often say they want an individual who can find information, analyze it, organize it, draw conclusions from it, and present it convincingly to others. One executive said she looked for superior communication skills "because they are in such short supply these days." These skills are the basic ingredients of critical thinking, which includes the ability to:

- Manage and interpret information in a reliable way.
- Examine existing ideas and develop new ones.
- Pose logical arguments, arguments that further the absorption of knowledge. In college, the term *argument* refers not to an emotional confrontation but to reasons and information brought together in logical support of some idea.
- Recognize reliable evidence and form well-reasoned arguments.

Walking through the Process

When thinking about an argument, a good critical thinker considers questions like the following:

- Is the information given in support of the argument true? For example, let's say that you and your fellow students are debating the pros and cons of the electoral college system and the popular vote system. Could it be possible that both systems might be equally representative?
- Does the information really support the conclusion? If you determine that each system has its merits (the electoral college gives more voting power to the less populated states, whereas the popular vote represents how the majority of voters feel), can you conclude that there may be a more judicious way to employ both systems in presidential elections?
- Do you need to withhold judgment until better evidence is available? Maybe you haven't any proof that a system that counted both the electoral vote and the popular vote would be more equitable because it has never been tried. Maybe it's time to set up a trial using a small sample.
- Is the argument really based on good reasoning, or does it appeal mainly to your emotions? You may think the electoral vote can alter the results of elections in a way that undermines the intentions of the voters, as evidenced in the 2000 presidential election. But you need to ask if your emotions, rather than relevant information that supports the argument, are guiding you to this conclusion.
- Based on the available evidence, are other conclusions equally likely (or even more likely)? Is there more than one right or possible answer? Perhaps there is a third or fourth way to count the vote by replacing the electoral college concept with something else.
- What more needs to be done to reach a good conclusion? You may need to do more reading about the election process and find some evidence that the system didn't work as planned in earlier presidential elections. Then you might try to find out how people felt about the voting system. Since

you are far from an expert on this, perhaps you should hold a forum with local voters to gain more views on the pros and cons of the electoral college system. Good critical thinking also involves thinking creatively about what assumptions may have been left out or what alternative conclusions may not have been considered. When communicating an argument or idea to others, a good critical thinker knows how to organize it in an understandable, convincing way in speech or in writing.

Four Aspects of Critical Thinking

Critical thinking cannot be learned overnight or always accomplished in a neat set of steps. Yet as interpreted by William T. Daly, professor of political science at The Richard Stockton College of New Jersey, the critical thinking process can be divided into four basic steps. Practicing these basic ideas can help you become a more effective thinker.

Step 1. Abstract Thinking: Using Details to Discover Some Bigger Idea

From large numbers of facts, seek the bigger ideas or the abstractions behind the facts. What are the key ideas? Even fields like medicine, which involve countless facts, culminate in general ideas such as the principles of circulation of the blood or the basic mechanisms of cell division.

Ask yourself what larger concepts the details suggest. For example, you read an article that describes how many people are using the Internet now, how much consumer information it provides, and what kinds of goods you can buy cheaply over the Internet, and also reports that many low-income families are still without computers. Think carefully about these facts, and you might arrive at several different important generalizations.

One might be that as the Internet becomes more important for shopping, the lack of computers in low-income households will put poor families at an even greater disadvantage. Or your general idea might be that because the Internet is becoming important for selling things, companies will probably find a way to put a computer in every home.

Step 2. Creative Thinking: Seeking Connections, Finding New Possibilities, Rejecting Nothing

Creative thinking and logical thinking seem opposed to each other. So how can creative and imaginative thinking help you solve a logical problem? Use the general idea you have found to see what further ideas it suggests. The important thing at this stage is not to reject any of your ideas. Write them all down. You'll narrow this list in step 3.

This phase of thinking can lead in many directions. It might involve searching for ways to make the Internet more available to low-income households. Or it might involve searching out more detailed information on how much interest big companies really have in marketing various goods to low-income families. In essence, the creative thinking stage involves extending the general idea—finding new ways it might apply or further ideas it might suggest.

Step 3. Systematic Thinking: Organizing the Possibilities, Tossing Out the Rubbish

Systematic thinking involves looking at the outcome of the second phase in a more demanding, critical way. This is where you narrow that list from step 2. If you are looking for solutions to a problem, which ones really seem most promising after you have conducted an exhaustive search for materials? Do some answers conflict with others? Which ones can be achieved? If you have found new evidence to refine or further test your generalization, what does that new evidence show? Does your original generalization still hold up? Should it be modified? What further conclusions do good reasoning and evidence support? Which notions should be abandoned?

Step 4. Precise Communication: Being Prepared to Present Your Ideas Convincingly to Others

Intelligent conclusions aren't very useful if you cannot share them with others. Consider what your audience will need to know to follow your reasoning and be persuaded. Remember to have "facts in hand" as you attempt to convince others of the truth of your argument. Don't be defensive; instead, just be logical.

How College Encourages Critical Thinking

Many college students believe that their teachers will have all the answers. Unfortunately, most important questions do not have simple answers, and you discover there are numerous ways to look at important issues. In any event, you must be willing to challenge assumptions and conclusions, even those presented by experts.

Critical thinking depends on your ability to evaluate different perspectives and to challenge assumptions—your own and those made by others. To challenge how you think, a good college teacher may insist that how you solve a problem is as important as the solution, and even may ask you to describe that problem-solving process.

Because critical thinking depends on discovering and testing connections between ideas, your instructor may ask open-ended questions that have no clear-cut answers, questions of "Why?" "How?" or "What if?" For example: "In these essays we have two conflicting ideas about whether bilingual education is effective in helping children learn English. What now?" Your instructor may ask you to break a larger question into smaller ones: "Let's take the first point. What evidence does the author offer for his idea that language immersion programs get better results?"

She or he may insist that more than one valid point of view exists: "So, for some types of students, you agree that bilingual education might be best? What other types of students should we consider?" Your instructor may require you to explain concretely the reason for any point you reject: "You think this essay is wrong. Well, what are your reasons?" Or he or she may challenge the authority of experts: "Dr. Fleming's theory sounds impressive. But here are some facts he doesn't account for . . ." You may discover that often your instructor reinforces the legitimacy of your personal views and experiences: "So something like this happened to you once, and you felt exactly the same way. Can you tell us why?" And you also will discover that you can change your mind.

It is natural for new college students to find this mode of thinking difficult, to discover that answers are seldom entirely wrong or right but more often somewhere in between. Yet the questions that lack simple answers usually are the ones most worthy of study.

We hope you won't toss aside these rules once you finish this chapter. If you hang on to them, we promise that your classes may not be easier but certainly will be more interesting, for now you know how to use logic to figure things out instead of depending purely on how you feel about something. The best way to learn, practice, and develop critical thinking skills is to take demanding college courses that provide lots of opportunities to think out loud, discuss and interact in class, and especially to do research and write, write, write. Take courses that use essay examinations as opposed to multiple choice, true/false, and short answer—the latter three are much less likely to develop your critical thinking skills. A good class becomes a critical thinking experience. As you listen to the teacher, try to predict where the lecture is heading and why. When other students raise issues, ask yourself whether they have enough information to justify what they have said. And when you raise *your* hand to participate, remember that asking a sensible question may be more important than trying to find the elusive "right" answer.

YOUR PERSONAL JOURNAL

Here are several things to write about. Choose one or more, or choose another topic related to this chapter.

1. Based on the definitions in this chapter, do you believe you already are a critical thinker? If so, tell why. If not, tell how you plan to become more of one.
2. Some students will complain that "the teacher should have all the answers." They resent it when a teacher says, "I'm not sure. What do you think about that, Mary?" How would you characterize these students' attitudes?
3. Think about one or more careers you hope to pursue. They don't have to correlate with your academic major at this point, but they should be fields for which you have a passion. How might you use critical thinking in those fields? How would it help you do a better job?
4. What behaviors are you willing to change after reading this chapter? How might you go about changing them?
5. What else is on your mind this week? If you wish to share it with your instructor, add it to this journal entry.

READINGS

Rethinking Thinking*

College classes that make one think—it's a basic concept assumed as a given. But many grads walk away with a diploma yet still lack critical thinking skills. That's why some educators are asking students to close their textbooks and do a little more reflecting.

By Mark Clayton

While pondering a problem in a plant biology course at Ohio University one semester, John Withers suddenly realized something unusual was going on: This class was actually requiring him to think.

---

*Reproduced with permission from the October 14, 2003 issue of the *Christian Science Monitor* (www.csmonitor.com). © 2003 The Christian Science Monitor. All rights reserved.

Thinking is presumed to be the bread and butter of higher education. Beyond simply getting a diploma to land a job that pays well, the promise of sharpening thinking skills still looms as a key reason millions apply to college. Yet some say there is a remarkable paucity of critical thinking taught at the undergraduate level, even though the need for such skills seems more urgent than ever.

Americans can now expect to change jobs as many as a half-dozen times in their lives, a feat requiring considerable mental agility. The ability to sift, analyze, and reflect upon large amounts of data is crucial in today's information age. Yet a major national report released last year entitled "Greater Expectations: A New Vision for Learning as a Nation Goes to College" raises serious questions as to whether undergraduates are absorbing these essential skills. "Outsiders who find college graduates unprepared for solving problems in the workplace question whether the colleges are successfully educating their students to think," the report notes.

Critical thought certainly receives considerable lip service on many campuses. College Web sites beckon students to "learn to think critically." Classes with "critical thinking" in the title are abundant. But Carol Schneider, president of the Association of American Colleges and Universities in Washington, isn't convinced. "Critical thinking, social responsibility, reflective judgment, and evidence-based reasoning . . . are the most enduring goals of a first-rate liberal education," says Ms. Schneider. Yet research shows that "many college graduates are falling short in reaching these goals." That's why some college faculty are leading the charge to move the teaching of thinking skills out of isolated courses and into all classes. Much as writing is now often taught as part of every discipline, they argue, learning to think ought to be the goal of every class.

In the case of Mr. Withers's biology class, that's exactly what his professor, Sarah Wyatt, was aiming at. Inspired by an initiative at Ohio University in Athens, where she was teaching, to focus harder on teaching students critical thinking skills, she directed her class to turn away temporarily from the usual round of textbooks, lectures, notes, and tests. She asked them instead to break into teams and work to develop original hypotheses of a plant's development.

As Withers and his group began designing an experiment to test their hypothesis, they were forced to reconsider methods and conclusions. What flaws and limits might be embedded in their approach? What could they know with certainty? What could they not know? It was a challenging mental exercise, and as a result, Withers found he began thinking about biology outside class with more clarity, precision, and reflection than ever before.

At the University of Massachusetts in Boston, Esther Kingston-Mann is interested in training her students to think like historians rather than biologists. But her goal of encouraging her students to do their own thinking is similar to that of Professor Wyatt's. Like Wyatt, she has her students occasionally close their textbooks. In her course on the cold war, she asks them to read newspaper accounts instead. They scan articles dating from the "red scare" in the 1920s on through World War II and then read further new accounts of relations between the U.S. and the Soviet Union in later decades. Later they collaborate in small groups, trying to identify in the newspaper clippings the voices being used to tell the story at a particular moment—and to note which perspectives and voices are missing.

"They're looking directly at the newspapers and not at a textbook," she says. "They find it difficult, but they end up liking it, and they feel more confident intellectually." It's all part of asking students to hone their own thinking skills, rather than simply allowing them to absorb and repeat the material they find in their textbooks or get from lectures.

Unless the professor creates a situation where students are required to reflect explicitly on an issue, says Professor Kingston-Mann, "they don't necessarily carry it anywhere else; it's just 'something I took in that class.' " Yet some say efforts like these are still the exception on many campuses, despite a decades-long discussion on the need for critical thought in higher education.

BUZZWORD OF THE '80S

At least since the 1970s, some college faculty have been calling for higher education to refocus on the "liberal learning" model espoused by John Dewey. The philosopher argued that teaching students to be learners was the whole point of education. His belief that good thinkers make good citizens also seemed an apt message for the times. Indeed, many seemed ready, even eager, to inject critical thinking much more deliberately into higher education. Critical thinking became a 1980s buzzword in academe. Sometime in the 1990s, it lost its buzz—not because it was rejected, but because it was adopted wholesale.

Professors today often believe erroneously that they are already teaching critical thinking in their courses and that students are absorbing it. But that's not necessarily the case, says Richard Paul, president of the Center for Critical Thinking and author of *Critical Thinking: How to Prepare Students for a Rapidly Changing World*. At the request of California's Commission on Teacher Credentialing, Dr. Paul and his colleagues in 1995 conducted interviews with faculty at 83 public and 28 private colleges and universities in California. The professors were asked specifically how they taught students to think critically.

"The basic conclusion we came to is that while everyone claims to be teaching critical thinking . . . the evidence is that very few can articulate what they mean by it or explain how they emphasize it on a typical day," Dr. Paul says. "It's something everyone wants to believe they are doing."

But if not teaching thinking, then what are colleges doing?

Patricia King and her colleagues in educational psychology at the University of Michigan have spent the last 25 years conducting experiments to assess the degree to which college produces "reflective judgment" and higher-order thinking skills in undergraduates. The good news, she says, is that an increase in critical thinking appears to be a direct outcome of attending college. The bad news is that even by the time they graduate, most college students don't reach the higher levels of critical thinking involving true reflective judgment.

"They're making what we call quasi-reflective judgments," she says. "Even four years of college only brings traditional-age college students to a very low level of critical thinking and judgment." Seniors do have the ability to understand that a controversial problem can and should be approached from several perspectives, she says. But they are often unable to come to a reasoned conclusion even when all the facts to solve a problem are present. "They're left on the fence," she says. "They say, 'Look how open-minded I am.' But when pressed to say, 'What do you think about this? What suggestions would you make and what are they based on?'—that's when the process falls apart. They are unable to reach or defend a conclusion that's most reasonable and consistent with the facts."

Pressure for colleges to cultivate critical thinking is growing, however, as state legislatures interested in accountability press educators to determine what kind of learning an undergraduate diploma represents. Margaret Miller, a University of Virginia professor and director of the National Forum on College Level Learning, is leading the charge to measure what students at state-funded colleges know and can do, including an assessment of intellectual skills. She worries that critical-thinking skills are not truly valued by many state schools and their students.

"Students and institutions are more and more focused on the vocational—at a high level, but vocational nonetheless," she says. "But producing a group of non-reflective highly competent technicians is something we want to avoid if we want a functioning society." Because the curriculum is so fragmented across many narrow disciplines, students have a greater challenge in making sense of it. That means colleges can't just ghettoize critical thinking in a few courses, but need to spread the focus on thinking across the curriculum. "All disciplines need to become more liberal-arts-like in their focus on the intellectual skills that underlie what they do," Miller says. "Some of that is critical thinking, some of it is broader and encompasses that."

CULTIVATING OPEN-MINDEDNESS

If undergraduates aren't learning to think, one major reason may be that most higher education institutions don't know how to systematically teach it, says

Elizabeth Minnich, professor of philosophy at the Union Institute and University in Cincinnati. In an article last month entitled "Teaching Thinking: Moral and Political Considerations" in *Change* magazine, a higher-education publication, she argues that thinking can and should be taught more deliberately and intentionally in college courses.

She then goes on to describe the kind of thought process she most values. "Thinking is neither coerced nor coercive," she writes. "It is exploratory, suggestive; it does not prove anything, or finally arrive anywhere. Thus, to say people are 'thoughtful' or 'thought-provoking' suggests that they are open-minded, reflective, challenging—more likely to question than to assert, inclined to listen to many sides, capable of making distinctions that hold differences in play rather than dividing in order to exclude, and desirous of persuading others rather than reducing them to silence by refuting them."

Rather than trying to "cover the material" in a class and force-feed terms and concepts to undergraduates, she says in an interview that she tries to cultivate open-mindedness, reflection, and a questioning attitude. She might, for instance, begin a class using Plato's *Republic* as an occasion for "thinking practice." Before the students are even assigned to read the *Republic,* she explains to her class the confusing mixture of tongues and nationalities Socrates and his friends would encounter at the port of Athens. For help, they turned to an old man, Cephalus, to ask questions.

"Then I ask the students, 'To whom would you take a question raised for you by an encounter with people(s) whose differences suddenly make you unsure of your own, hitherto unquestioned, values? Would you take it to an old person? A religious authority? A political leader? Your mother or father? A scientist? A friend?' "

Rather than just downloading content of the *Republic,* she wants to be sure "the students are bringing something to it." The idea is that the students then begin to read Plato as if reading it through the lens of their own experience. She often asks at some point: "What would you do if you were an Aristotelian? How would you see that tree, or how would you listen to your friends when they are trying to tell you their problem?"

"HEY, I'M ALREADY DOING THAT"

There are, of course, a number of liberal arts colleges and a few public universities that consciously pursue critical thinking across the curriculum. George Nagel is a professor of communications at Ferris State University, just north of Grand Rapids, Michigan. "I was pretty skeptical, probably a little cynical, like a lot of our faculty," he says. "I had the attitude [three years ago], 'Hey, I'm already doing that and doing it well.' But it's funny, when you ask [the faculty] what they're doing so well, they can't really explicate it for you." Now he and a growing number of faculty on campus are warming to the idea of specifically and intentionally teaching critical thinking in every discipline. Professor Nagel has received training from the Center for Critical Thinking in Dillon, Calif., and is now teaching others at Ferris to do the same.

But such notions are not always immediately welcomed on campus.

At Ohio University, Wyatt at first had to buck the tide of opinion among some colleagues when she retooled her courses to focus on critical thinking. "What I'm doing is different than what normally is done," she says. "When I first started, people said that's going to be a lot more work and students won't get it. This is the way you do lab: You run the lab, the cookbook, and this is what you get."

Today, instead of being in the academic doghouse, Dr. Wyatt finds her thinking-based classes are a hit, popular with both students and a growing number of faculty who believe she offers something of genuine value. "They like the product we're turning out," she says—"kids who are actually thinkers."

Judging Authority*

We are often required to accept the word of another person,
but how can we best judge whether or not that person
is a legitimate authority?

By Jere H. Lipps

Living well requires that we be able to evaluate our environment rationally. Simple things, like crossing the street, shopping, eating, and listening to our doctors, involve three skills: critical thinking, evidential reasoning, and judging authority. Many people, including previous authors writing for the *Skeptical Inquirer* (Lett, 1990; Wade and Tavris, 1990), have discussed the first two of these. Here I focus on the last of them, judging authority, but I must revisit the other two first because they are central to it. These same skills are fundamental to scientific reasoning as well, since the ordinary person and the scientist both need to understand our personal or scientific surroundings. Indeed this short article is an outgrowth of material I present to science students first learning the methods of science, but this should not discourage the nonscience reader, for science and everyday life are far closer in function than most would suppose.

There may be little here not fairly obvious to those of you long involved in issues of science and skepticism, but perhaps it can be of some use in your dealings with students, friends, colleagues, and the wider public.

Skeptical Inquirer, January-February 2004, v28, i1, p. 35(3). Copyright 2004 Committee for the Scientific Investigation of Claims of the Paranormal. Reprinted with permission.

CRITICAL THINKING

Critical thinking involves eight skills. These skills require that you understand the problem clearly, consider all possible views about the problem, set emotion aside, and be willing to be flexible when solutions are imperfect. The skills will aid you in dealing with the problem.

The first three critical skills in Table 1 may be self-evident, but the others are often difficult for people to practice because of human nature. The analysis of assumptions and biases requires a certain amount of personal insight. We all have biases based on our past experiences and personal beliefs, but we must try to set them aside when we need to understand the way the world works. This is often very difficult to do, because we are not even aware of many of our personal biases. One way to identify bias is to make a list of your feelings and knowledge about the subject. Then apply the evidence. If it does not support your feeling, perhaps the feeling is unjustified. Later, after examining other factors, you can return to this issue with a better understanding of your own emotional biases. If in conflict, your feelings should probably be suppressed in favor of evidence.

The last three items are particularly difficult. We all need explanations, and we tend to jump to conclusions based on too little evidence. Again, an analysis of the evidence is required to determine if it is sufficient. Alternative interpretations should always be sought, even if the evidence seems compelling. In science, this process is known as the "method of multiple working hypotheses," an especially powerful way of approaching the truth (Chamberlain, 1897; Platt, 1964; Lipps, 1999). Does the evidence allow for other possible

Table 1   Skills Involved in Critical Thinking (Wade and Tavris 1990) and Simple Techniques for Achieving Them.

SKILLS	SIMPLE TECHNIQUES
1. Ask questions: be willing to wonder	Start by asking "Why?"
2. Define the problem.	Restate the issue several different ways so it is clear.
3. Examine the evidence.	Ask what evidence supports or refutes the claim. Is it reliable?
4. Analyze assumptions and biases.	List the evidence on which each part of the argument is based. The assumptions and biases will be unsupported and should be eliminated from further consideration.
5. Avoid emotional reasoning.	Identify emotional influence and "gut feelings" in the arguments and exclude them.
6. Don't oversimplify.	Do not allow generalization from too little evidence.
7. Consider other interpretations.	Make sure alternate views are included in the discussion.
8. Tolerate uncertainty.	Be ready to accept tentative answers when evidence is incomplete, and new answers when further evidence warrants them.

interpretations? Try to think of other ways to account for the observation or phenomenon you are interested in.

And last, tolerate uncertainty. No one likes uncertainty in our lives—we all want, perhaps need, to know things such as what is before us, why things happen to us, and what happens when we die. Although difficult, tolerating uncertainty can be done by simply setting aside the uncertainties and, for the moment at least, accepting them and moving forward.

EVIDENTIAL REASONING

Evidential reasoning should be used in our daily lives, as it is in science, to evaluate various problems and claims that confront us. We might even make such claims ourselves. All claims should, ideally, be subjected to an analysis like that outlined in Table 2.

Of these points, perhaps the most critical is the last one. Any claim must be sufficient. In other words, you do not have to prove that the claim is false in order to test it; the claimant must provide sufficient proof himself. Second, the more extraordinary a claim, the more extraordinary the evidence must be to test it. For example, if a person claims that some herb has cured his cancer, you would be well advised to seek a good deal of further supporting evidence before risking your own life. Or if a person claims to have an extraterrestrial being in her garage, do not accept a photograph as proof—demand a piece of it for further study. And last, the word of someone is never sufficient to establish the truth of a claim. This article addresses this last issue, judging whether or not that authority is worth considering.

JUDGING AUTHORITY

The evaluation of authority requires special consideration because all of us must depend on authorities for information almost daily. In science, too, we

Table 2 Rules for Evidential Reasoning (Lett 1990), or a Guide to Intelligent Living and the Scientific Method (Lipps 1999).

All claims, whether scientific or not, should be subjected to these rules in order to ensure that all possibilities are considered fairly.

RULES FOR EVIDENTIAL REASONING	WHAT TO DO
1. Falsifiability	Conceive of all evidence that would prove the false claim
2. Logic	Argument must be sound
3. Comprehensiveness	Must use all available evidence
4. Honesty	Evaluate evidence without self-deception
5. Replicability	Evidence must be repeatable
6. Sufficiency	A. Burden of proof rests on the claimant
	B. Extraordinary claims require extraordinary evidence
	C. Authority and/or testimony is always inadequate

scientists rely on other scientists for certain kinds of information or data, simply because we cannot know enough about everything. Scientific papers are scattered through with references to the work of others. The evaluation of those works and their authors are part and parcel of science. It should be so in general life too.

Who can we trust to help us in our daily lives? That question is not easy to answer. A scientist dealing with auto insurance may be as susceptible to pseudo-authority in that area as anyone else. A politician listening to a case for particular legislation may be incapable of judging the claimant, and thus vote incorrectly. A housewife may listen to glamorous stars pitching a particular useless household product on television, and buy it. Everyone is vulnerable to incorrect judgment of authority.

I present some general guidelines for judging authority, but each case may differ and so require additional methods. These additional techniques usually take the form of further probing questions. We all judge authority but sometimes in the emotions or heat of the moment, we forget to question authority. If the authority cannot pass the general guidelines below, don't believe him (or her). Of course, these are not the only ways a person needs to judge authority, for the skilled charlatan will find ways around any such guidelines. Be alert.

1. Most important, does the authority use [the] skills of critical thinking and evidential reasoning [listed in Tables 1 and 2]? If not, question him using those very skills yourself, and don't believe him until he produces the evidence required.

2. Does the authority have proper credentials? Considerable study or experience in a subject along with the appropriate learning tools is required to become an expert in any field. Does the authority have degrees from a recognized college or university that has the faculty, libraries, and other facilities for proper education in the subject? Has the authority worked in the field for some time for an organization that is known for and equipped for competent dealings in the field?

3. Does the authority have proper affiliations? Is she identified closely with a reliable organization, such as a university, museum, government agency, hospital, or corporation that practices the subject? If not, ask how she makes a living.

4. Does that organization have a stake in the claims made by the claimant? Be suspicious of anyone making claims that support the position or product of their own organization. Seek independent evidence that the claim is correct. This may be hard to do for even relatively common decisions we face, but in its essence, this is simply "comparative shopping." A good comparative shopper is interested not merely in relative costs, but also in the range of products or services available, the quality of the products or magnitude of the services, warranties, and service contracts. Does the

expert provide this information, or does he pressure you to decide before you are ready? Be careful of those who will not allow you the time for a carefully reasoned decision.

5. Has the authority subjected his or her work to peer review? In other words, have other experts evaluated the work so that some independent assessment has been made positively? If not, seek that evaluation yourself or find another authority. In our day-to-day dealings, such information is available on the Internet, Better Business Bureaus, and consumer affairs magazines and agencies.

6. Is the authority a demonstrated expert in the relevant field? Other trust-worthy people should rely on this person's expertise. Do other experts cite their conclusions? If not, find another authority others do rely on. Do people you know who have used this person's expertise recommend him?

7. Does the authority present arguments without undue call on unsupported or untenable claims? Does the authority present sufficient evidence to evaluate? If not, find an authority that can provide evidence supporting the claims.

8. Does the authority have a past record of making rational claims backed by evidence or not? Check the usual business sources and your friends.

Even when an authority passes these tests, be aware of lapses that may reveal the degree of knowledge possessed by an expert. Well-known or highly honored people are commonly asked to comment on subjects outside their own field of expertise. We are plagued by testimonials provided by actors, sports figures, television personalities, and a host of others, but do they possess any particular knowledge that would make them an authority on what they are pitching? Probably not. These people should be subjected to exactly the same questions as an unknown authority to determine how much you should rely on their statements. Does a Nobel Prize winner in physics, for example, have any credibility when making pronouncements about evolution? It seems unlikely because the evidence and hypotheses about evolution are very far removed from the usual literature and knowledge base of physics. Be suspicious. Question authority. Use critical thinking and evidential reasoning.

In our daily lives, pseudo-authorities are always making one claim or another to sell you something. Ask questions of your insurance salesman, your plumber, your doctor, your housekeeper, or anyone else that you may depend on for important or essential services and products. Proper judgment of authority can save you money and perhaps a good deal of grief too. So critical thinking, evidential reasoning, and judging authority are essential to living an intelligent, full, happy, and good life. These are worth considering carefully in our daily lives!

DISCUSSION

1. Think of a compelling issue in our society today for which you think there is a "right" answer. If so, what are the underlying questions that would lead to the right answer? Discuss those with some other students.
2. In like manner, think of a question you hear friends, family, students, and/or the news media discussing for which there seems to be no "right" answer. Discuss this with other students and practice some of the principles from this chapter on critical thinking.
3. Drawing on your reactions to the article "Rethinking Thinking," discuss with your friends what you think the impact of college so far has been on your "thinking" skills. What can you do to make the impact greater?
4. The article "Judging Authority" provides you with eight suggestions for deciding for yourself the legitimacy of the authority of some of your teachers, required readings, and prominent people in our society. Discuss how you could use some of the suggestions to evaluate an authoritative source.

CHAPTER 6

Listening, Note Taking, and Participating

Jeanne L. Higbee of the University of Minnesota, Twin Cities, contributed her valuable and considerable expertise to the writing of this chapter.

IN THIS CHAPTER, YOU WILL LEARN

- How to assess your note-taking skills and how to improve them
- Why it's important to review your notes as soon as reasonable after class
- How to listen critically and take good notes in class
- Why you should speak up in class
- How to review class and textbook materials after class

In virtually every college class you take, you'll need to master two skills to earn high grades: listening and note taking. Taking an active role in your classes—asking questions, contributing to discussions, or providing answers—will help you listen better and take more meaningful notes. That in turn will enhance your ability to learn: to understand abstract ideas, find new possibilities, organize those ideas, and recall the material once the class is over.

Listening and note taking are critical to your academic success because your college instructors are likely to introduce new material in class that your texts don't cover, and chances are that much of this material will resurface on quizzes and exams. Keep these suggestions in mind as you read the rest of this chapter:

1. Since writing down everything the instructor says is probably not possible and you are not sure what is important to remember, ask questions in class, go over your notes with a tutor or someone from your campus learning center, or compare your notes with a friend's.

2. Don't record a lecture unless you can concentrate on listening to the tape while commuting. Instead, consider asking the instructor to speak more slowly or to repeat key points, or meet with a study group to compare notes. If there is a reason you do need to tape-record a lecture, be sure to ask the instructor's permission first. But keep in mind that it will be difficult to make a high-quality recording in an environment with so much extraneous noise. And even though you're recording, take notes.

3. Instead of copying an outline from the board, wait until the instructor covers each point in sequence. Write down the first point and listen. Take notes. When the next point is covered, do the same, and so on.

4. Take notes on the discussion. Your instructors may be taking notes on what is said and could use them on exams. You should be participating as well as taking notes.

5. Choose the note-taking system that works for you.

6. If something is not clear, ask the instructor in class or after class.

7. Instead of chatting with friends before class begins, use the time to review your study notes for the previous class.

8. Make it a habit to review notes with one or two other students.

9. Be aware that what the instructor says in class may not always be in the textbook, and vice versa.

10. Speak up! People tend to remember what they have said more than what others are saying to them.

Short-Term Memory: Listening and Forgetting

Ever notice how easy it is to learn the words to a song? We remember songs and poetry more easily in part because they follow a rhythm and a beat, in part because we may repeat them—sometimes unconsciously—over and over in our heads, and in part because they often have a personal meaning for us—we relate them to something in our everyday lives. We remember prose less easily unless we make an effort to relate it to what we already know. And, because it is the most unstructured form of communication, and virtually impossible to relate to previous knowledge, we can hardly remember gibberish or nonsense words (see Figure 6.1).

Because most forgetting takes place within the first 24 hours after you see or hear something, it may be difficult to retrieve the material later. In two weeks, you will have forgotten up to 70 percent of the material! Forgetting can be a serious problem when you are expected to learn and remember a mass of different facts, figures, concepts, and relationships. Many instructors draw a significant proportion of their test items from their lectures; remembering what is presented in class is crucial to doing well on exams.

Using Your Senses in the Learning Process

You can enhance memory by using as many of your senses as possible while learning. How do you believe you learn most effectively?

1. **Aural.** Do you learn by listening to other people talk, or does your mind begin to wander when listening passively for more than a few minutes?

2. **Visual.** Do you learn best when you can see the words on the printed page? During a test, can you actually visualize where the information appears in your text? Can you remember data best when it's presented in the form of a picture, graph, chart, map, or video?

3. **Interactive.** Do you enjoy discussing course work with friends, classmates, or the teacher? Does talking about information help you remember it?

4. **Tactile.** Do you learn through your sense of touch? Does typing your notes help you remember them?

5. **Kinesthetic.** Can you learn better when your body is in motion? Do you learn more effectively by doing it than by listening to or reading about it?

6. **Olfactory.** Does your sense of taste or smell contribute to your learning process? Do you cook following a recipe or by tasting and adding ingredients? Are you sensitive to odors?

Figure 6.1 Learning and Forgetting

Psychologists have studied human forgetting in many laboratory experiments. Here are the forgetting curves for three kinds of material: poetry, prose, and nonsense syllables. The shallower curves for prose and poetry indicate that meaningful material is forgotten more slowly than nonmeaningful information. Because poetry contains internal cues such as rhythm and rhyme, we tend to forget it less quickly than prose.

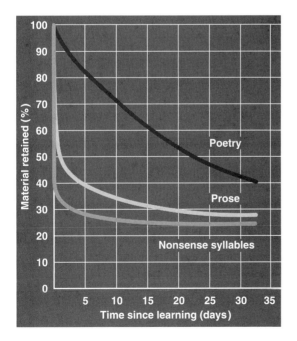

Source: Used with permission from Wayne Weiten, *Psychology: Themes and Variations* (Pacific Grove, CA: Brooks/Cole, 1989, p. 254. Based on data from D. van Guilford, Van Nostrand, 1939).

In college, many faculty members share information primarily through lecture and the text. However, many students learn best through visual and interactive means, creating a mismatch between learning and teaching styles. This is a problem only if you do not learn how to adapt material conveyed by means of lecture and text to your preferred modes of learning. Following a system will help you remember and understand lecture material better and relate information to other things you already know. The approach we recommend consists of preparing to listen before class, listening and taking notes during class, and reviewing and recalling information after class.

Before Class: Prepare to Remember

Even if lectures don't allow for active participation, you can take a number of active learning steps to make your listening and note taking more efficient. Remember that your goals are improved learning in the classroom, a longer attention span, improved retention of information, clear, well-organized notes for when it's time to study for exams, and better grades.

Because many lectures are demanding intellectual encounters, you need to be intellectually prepared before class begins. You would not want to walk in cold to give a speech, interview for a job, plead a case in court, or compete in sports. For the same reasons, you should begin active listening, learning, and remembering before the lecture.

1. **Do the assigned reading.** Unless you do, you may find the lecturer's comments disjointed, and you may not understand some terms he or she uses. Some instructors refer to assigned readings for each class session; others may hand out a syllabus and assume you are keeping up with the assigned readings. Completing the readings on time will help you listen better, and critical listening promotes remembering.

   As an experiment, don't take notes, but listen for the main points of a lecture. Then write down those main points and, with the permission of your instructor, compare them in small groups with other students. How many groups remembered all the main points? Why was there some forgetting?

2. **Warm up for class.** Read well and take good notes, or annotate (add critical or explanatory notes), highlight, or underline the text. Then warm up by reviewing chapter introductions and summaries and by referring to related sections in your text and to your notes from the previous class period.

3. **Keep an open mind.** Every class holds the promise of discovering new information and uncovering different perspectives. One of the purposes of college is to teach you to think in new and different ways and to provide

support for your own beliefs. Instructors want you to think for yourself. They do not necessarily expect you to agree with everything they or your classmates say, but if you want people to respect your values, you must show respect for them as well by listening with an open mind to what they have to say.

4. **Get organized.** Develop an organizational system. Decide what type of notebook will work best for you. Many study skills experts suggest using three-ring binders because you can punch holes in syllabi and other course handouts and keep them with class notes. Create a recording system to keep track of grades on all assignments, quizzes, and tests. Retain any papers that are returned to you until the term is over and your grades are posted on your transcript. That way, if you need to appeal a grade because an error occurs, you will have the documentation you need to support your appeal.

During Class: Listen Critically

Listening in class is not like listening to a TV program, listening to a friend, or even listening to a speaker at a meeting. Knowing how to listen in class can help you get more out of what you hear, understand better what you have heard, and save time. Here are some suggestions:

1. **Be ready for the message.** Prepare yourself to hear, to listen, and to receive the message. If you have done the assigned reading, you will know what details are already in the text so that you can focus your notes on key concepts during the lecture. You will also know what information is not covered in the text, and will be prepared to pay closer attention when the instructor is presenting unfamiliar material.

2. **Before taking notes, listen to the main concepts and central ideas, not just to fragmented facts and figures.** Although facts are important, they will be easier to remember and make more sense when you can place them in a context of concepts, themes, and ideas.

3. **Listen for new ideas.** Even if you believe you are an expert on the topic, you can still learn something new. Do not assume that college instructors will present the same information you learned in a similar course in high school.

4. **Really hear what is said.** Hearing sounds is not the same as hearing the intended message. Sit near the front and focus on the instructor. As a critical thinker, make a note of questions that arise in your mind as you listen, but save the judgments for later.

5. **Repeat mentally.** Words can go in one ear and out the other unless you make an effort to retain them. If you cannot translate the information into your own words, ask for further clarification.

6. **Decide whether what you have heard is not important, somewhat important, or very important.** If it's really not important, let it go.
7. **Ask a question.** Early in the term, determine whether the instructor is open to responding to questions as they arise during lecture. If so, do not hesitate to ask if you did not hear or understand what was said. It is best to clarify things immediately, if possible, and other students are likely to have the same questions. If you can't hear another student's question, ask that the question be repeated.
8. **Listen to the entire message.** Concentrate on "the big picture," but also pay attention to specific details and examples that can assist you in understanding and retaining the information.
9. **Respect your own ideas and those of others.** You already know a lot of things. Your own thoughts and ideas are valuable, and you need not throw them out just because someone else's views conflict with your own. At the same time, you should not reject the ideas of others too casually.
10. **Sort, organize, and categorize.** When you listen, try to match what you are hearing with what you already know. Take an active role in deciding how best to recall what you are learning.

During Class: Use The Cornell Format to Take Effective Notes

You can make class time more productive by using your listening skills to take effective notes. Here's how.

1. **Use a recall column.** One method for organizing notes is called the Cornell format, in which you create a "recall" column on each page of your notebook by drawing a vertical line about 2 to 3 inches from the left border. As you take notes during lecture, write only in the wider column on the right and leave the recall column on the left blank.

   You may also want to develop your own system of abbreviations. For example, you might write "inst" instead of "institution" or "eval" instead of "evaluation." Just make sure you will be able to understand your abbreviations when it's time to review.
2. **Identify the main ideas.** Good lectures always contain key points. The first principle of effective note taking is to identify and write down the most important ideas around which the lecture is built. Although supporting details are important as well, focus your note taking on the main ideas.

   Some instructors announce the purpose of a lecture or offer an outline, thus providing you with the skeleton of main ideas, followed by the details. Others develop overhead transparencies or PowerPoint presentations, and may make these materials available on a class Web site before the lecture. If so, you can enlarge them, print them out, and take notes right on the teacher's outline.

Some lecturers change their tone of voice or repeat themselves for each key idea. Some ask questions or promote discussion. If a lecturer says something more than once, chances are it's important.

Ask yourself, "What does my instructor want me to know at the end of today's session?"

3. **Stop being a stenographer.** Some first-year students try to do just that. If you're an active listener, you will ultimately have shorter but more useful notes (see Figure 6.2).

As you take notes, leave spaces so that you can fill in additional details later that you might have missed during class. But remember the forgetting curve—do it as soon as possible.

4. **Don't be thrown by a disorganized lecturer.** When a lecture is disorganized, it's your job to try to organize what is said into general and specific frameworks. When the order is not apparent, you'll need to indicate in your notes where the gaps occur. After the lecture, you will need to consult your reading material or classmates to fill in these gaps.

You might also consult your instructor. Though most instructors have regular office hours for student appointments, it is amazing how few students use these opportunities for one-on-one instruction. You can also raise questions in class. Asking such questions may help your instructor discover which parts of his or her presentation need more attention and clarification.

5. **Return to your recall column.** The recall column is essentially the place where you write down the main ideas and important details for tests and examinations as you sift through your notes as soon after class as feasible, preferably within an hour or two. It can be a critical part of effective note taking and becomes an important study device for tests and examinations. In anticipation of using your notes later, treat each page of your notes as part of an exam-preparation system.

Look at the recall column while you cover the rest of the page, and recite out loud in your own words what you remember from your notes. Keep in mind that you want to use as many of your five senses as possible to enhance memory. The recall column is a powerful study device that reduces forgetting, helps you warm up for class, and promotes understanding during class.

Taking Notes in Nonlecture Courses

Always be ready to adapt your note-taking methods to match the situation. Group discussion is becoming a popular way to teach in college because it involves active learning. On your campus you may also have Supplemental

Figure 6.2 **Sample Lecture Notes**

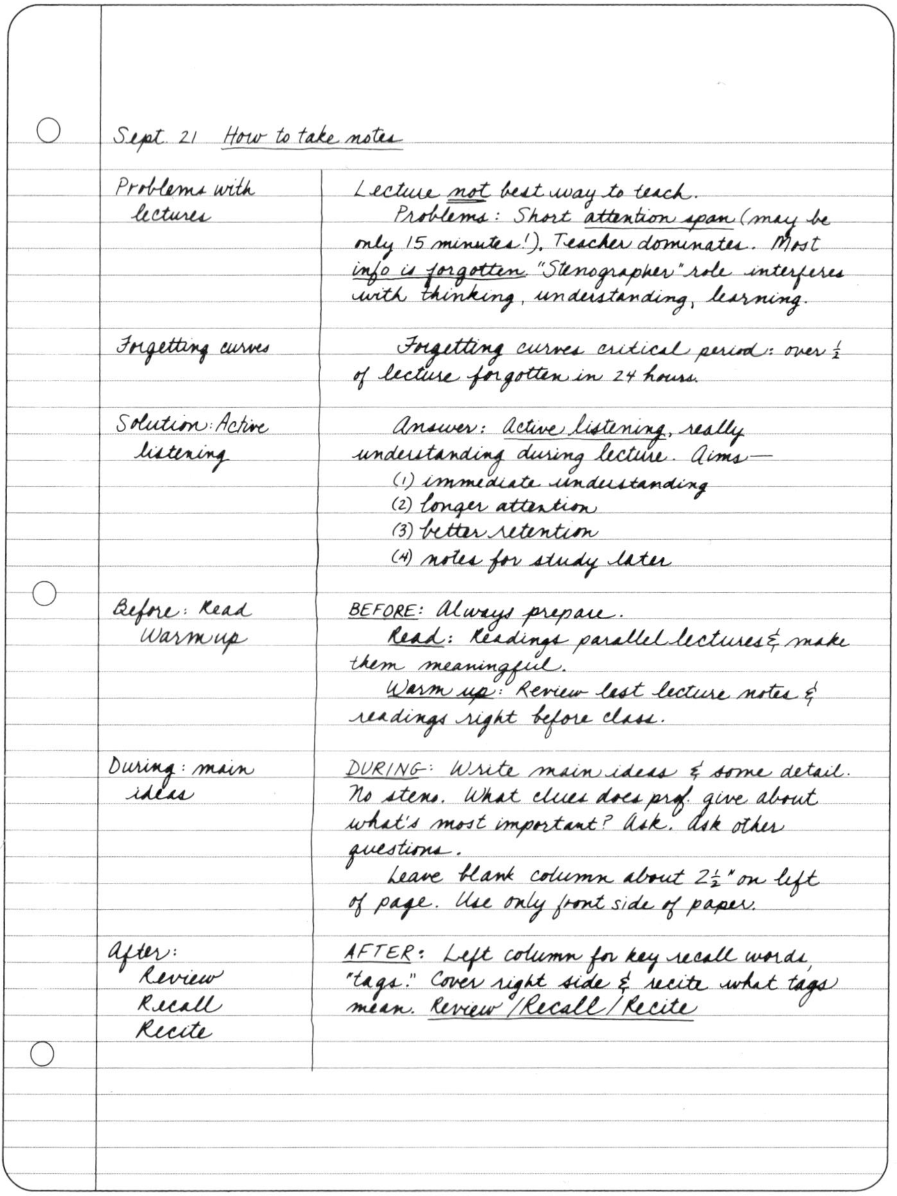

Sept. 21 How to take notes

Problems with lectures	Lecture _not_ best way to teach. Problems: Short attention span (may be only 15 minutes!). Teacher dominates. Most info is forgotten. "Stenographer" role interferes with thinking, understanding, learning.
Forgetting curves	Forgetting curves critical period: over ½ of lecture forgotten in 24 hours.
Solution: Active listening	Answer: Active listening, really understanding during lecture. Aims— (1) immediate understanding (2) longer attention (3) better retention (4) notes for study later
Before: Read Warm up	BEFORE: Always prepare. Read: Readings parallel lectures & make them meaningful. Warm up: Review last lecture notes & readings right before class.
During: main ideas	DURING: Write main ideas & some detail. No steno. What clues does prof. give about what's most important? Ask. Ask other questions. Leave blank column about 2½" on left of page. Use only front side of paper.
After: Review Recall Recite	AFTER: Left column for key recall words, "tags." Cover right side & recite what tags mean. Review/Recall/Recite

Instruction (SI) classes that provide further opportunity to discuss the information presented in lectures.

How do you keep a record of what's happening in such classes? Assume you are taking notes in a problem-solving group assignment. You would begin your notes by asking yourself "What is the problem?" and writing down the answer. As the discussion progresses, you would list the solutions offered. These would be your main ideas. The important details might include the positive and negative aspects of each view or solution.

The important thing to remember when taking notes in nonlecture courses is that you should record the information presented by your classmates as well as from the instructor and consider all reasonable ideas, even though they may differ from your own.

When a course has separate lecture and discussion sessions, you will need to understand how the discussion sessions augment and correlate with the lectures. How to organize the notes you take in a class discussion depends on the purpose or form of the discussion. But it usually makes good sense to begin with a list of issues or topics that the discussion leader announces. Another approach is to list the questions that the participants raise for discussion. If the discussion is exploring reasons for and against a particular argument, it makes sense to divide your notes into columns or sections for pros and cons. When conflicting views are presented in discussion, it is important to record different perspectives and the rationales behind them.

Class Notes and Homework

Good class notes can help you complete homework assignments. Follow these steps:

1. **Take 10 minutes to review your notes.** Skim the notes and put a question mark next to anything you do not understand at first reading. Draw stars next to topics that warrant special emphasis. Try to place the material in context: What has been going on in the course for the past few weeks? How does today's class fit in?

2. **Do a warm-up for your homework.** Before doing the assignment, look through your notes again. Use a separate sheet of paper to rework examples, problems, or exercises. If there is related assigned material in the textbook, review it. Go back to the examples. Cover the solution and attempt to answer each question or complete each problem. Look at the author's work only after you have made a serious effort to remember it.

   Keep in mind that it can help to go back through your course notes, reorganize them, and highlight the essential items, thus creating new notes that let you connect with the material one more time and are better than the originals.

3. **Do any assigned problems and answer any assigned questions.**
   Now you are actually starting your homework. As you read each question
   or problem, ask: What am I supposed to find or find out? What is essential
   and what is extraneous? Read the problem several times and state it in
   your own words. Work the problem without referring to your notes or the
   text, as though you were taking a test. In this way, you'll test your knowledge and will know when you are prepared for exams.

4. **Persevere.** Don't give up too soon. When you encounter a problem or
   question that you cannot readily handle, move on only after a reasonable
   effort. After you have completed the entire assignment, come back to those
   items that stumped you. You may need to mull over a particularly difficult
   problem for several days. Let your unconscious mind have a chance.

5. **Complete your work.** When you finish an assignment, talk to yourself
   about what you learned from this particular assignment. Think about how
   the problems and questions were different from one another, which
   strategies were successful, and what form the answers took. Be sure to
   review any material you have not mastered. Seek assistance from the
   teacher, a classmate, study group, learning center, or tutor to learn how to
   answer any questions that stumped you.

   You may be thinking, that all sounds good, but who has the time to do
   all that extra work? In reality, this approach does work and can actually
   save you time. Try it for a few weeks. You will find that you can diminish
   the frustration that comes when you tackle your homework cold, and that
   you will be more confident going into exams.

Computer Notes in Class?

Laptops are often poor tools for taking notes. Computer screens are not conducive to making marginal notes, circling important items, or copying diagrams. And although most students can scribble coherently without watching
their hands, few are really good keyboarders. Entering notes on a computer
after class for review purposes may be helpful, especially if you are a tactile
learner. Then you can print out your notes and highlight or annotate just as
you would handwritten notes.

After Class: Respond, Recite, Review

Don't let the forgetting curve take its toll on you. As soon after class as possible, review your notes and fill in the details you still remember, but missed
writing down, in those spaces you left in the right-hand column.

   Relate new information to other things you already know. Organize your
information. Make a conscious effort to remember. One way is to recite impor-

tant data to yourself every few minutes; if you are an aural learner, repeat it out loud. Another is to tie one idea to another idea, concept, or name, so that thinking of one will prompt recall of the other. Or you may want to create your own poem, song, or slogan using the information.

Use these three important steps for remembering the key points in the lecture:

1. **Write the main ideas in the recall column.** For five or ten minutes, quickly review your notes and select key words or phrases that will act as labels or tags for main ideas and key information in the notes. Highlight the main ideas and write them in the recall column next to the material they represent.

2. **Use the recall column to recite your ideas.** Cover the notes on the right and use the prompts from the recall column to help you recite *out loud* a brief version of what you understand from the class in which you have just participated.

   If you don't have a few minutes after class when you can concentrate on reviewing your notes, find some other time during that same day to review what you have written. You might also want to ask your teacher to glance at your recall column to determine whether you have noted the proper major ideas.

3. **Review the previous day's notes just before the next class session.** As you sit in class the next day waiting for the lecture to begin, use the time to quickly review the notes from the previous day. This will put you in tune with the lecture that is about to begin and will also prompt you to ask questions about material from the previous lecture that may not have been clear to you.

These three engagements with the material will pay off later, when you begin to study for your exams.

What if you have three classes in a row and no time for recall columns or recitations between them? Recall and recite as soon after class as possible. Review the most recent class first. Never delay recall and recitation longer than one day; if you do, it will take you longer to review, make a recall column, and recite. With practice, you can complete your recall column quickly, perhaps between classes, during lunch, or while riding a bus.

Participating in Class: Speak Up!

Participation is the heart of active learning. We know that when we say something in class, we are more likely to remember it than when someone else does. So when a teacher tosses a question your way, or when you have a question to ask, you're actually making it easier to remember the day's lesson.

Naturally, you will be more likely to participate in a class in which the teacher emphasizes discussion, calls on students by name, shows students signs of approval and interest, and avoids shooting you down for an incorrect answer. Often, answers you and others offer that are not quite correct can lead to new perspectives on a topic. To take full advantage of these opportunities in all classes, try using these techniques:

1. **Take a seat as close to the front as possible.** If you're seated by name and your name is Zoch, plead bad eyesight or hearing—anything to get moved up front (the only time in this book we encourage you to avoid the truth!).
2. **Keep your eyes trained on the teacher.** Sitting up front will make this easier to do.
3. **Raise your hand when you don't understand something.** But don't overdo it. The instructor may answer you immediately, ask you to wait until later in the class, or throw your question to the rest of the class. In each case, you benefit in several ways. The instructor gets to know you, other students get to know you, and you learn from both the instructor and your classmates.
4. **Never feel that you're asking a "stupid" question.** If you don't understand something, you have a right to ask for an explanation.
5. **When the instructor calls on you to answer a question, don't bluff.** If you know the answer, give it. If you're not certain, begin with, "I think . . . but I'm not sure I have it all correct." If you don't know, just say so.
6. **If you've recently read a book or article that is relevant to the class topic, bring it in.** Use it either to ask questions about the piece or to provide information from it that was not covered in class. Next time you have the opportunity, speak up.

Listening, note taking, and participating are the three essentials for success in the classroom. If you think of the classroom as a workplace, where it's essential that you listen, jot down things to remember, and ask others for guidance, you'll understand why.

YOUR PERSONAL JOURNAL

Here are several things to write about. Choose one or more. Or choose another topic related to this chapter.

1. Think of one of your courses in which you're having trouble taking useful notes. That must be frustrating! Now write down some ideas from this chapter that may help you improve your note taking in that course.

2. How might a study group help you improve your note taking and other study habits? Is there a possibility that you might join one? Jot down the names of students in your classes whom you admire for their academic achievements. Ask one of them if he or she is interested in forming a group. If that person already belongs to a group, ask if you might join.
3. What behaviors are you willing to change after reading this chapter? How might you go about changing them?
4. What else is on your mind this week? If you wish to share it with your instructor, add it to your journal entry.

READINGS

Why Do I Have to Take this Class?*
A Lesson in making the required course relevant.
By Chad M. Hanson

Today, students enrolled in required courses are more likely than ever to ask, Why do I have to take this class? I teach required social science courses exclusively, so I face the question a lot. But instead of giving students a sermon about why they need to take Introduction to Sociology, I use the "why" question as an opportunity to engage students in a round of Socratic dialogue about the relevance and value of general education.

In fact, I ask the "why" question myself, if students don't beat me to it. I ask, "Why is this class required? Why do we bother?" In response, I often receive comments like that of a former student who said, "These classes make us well rounded." The answer suits me, of course, but even when I get good, positive responses like that one I continue turning questions back to the group. In this case I said, "Excellent! I think that's true," but I continued, "By the way, what does it mean to be well rounded?"

At points like these, depending on how students respond, I make a spur-of-the-moment decision about whether to continue or change the format. If students are responding well, I continue with the entire class. If they are reticent, I form small groups to give them more time to think. Either way, I try to lead people toward ideas found in the literature on the role of social science in general education.

For example, I emphasize the idea that social science courses are a chance for students to explore how their own thoughts and feelings are determined in part by their society and their place in history. I ask them, "What do you want to become?" After listening to a round of reasonable career choices I ask, "How come no one wants to be a blacksmith?" Faces light up as students begin to see how their own choices are determined by the structure of opportunities in the United States.

I also question them along lines that show how their own personal decisions help maintain the structure of society. I ask, "How many of you came to school by yourself in an automobile?" When everyone raises their hand it is possible to see how individual decisions lie at the base of our broadest social patterns.

In my experience, acknowledging the "Why do I have to take this class?" question in the open has improved students' morale, improved their perfor-mance, and had a positive impact on the way they evaluate my classes. If, despite my efforts, students miss the relevance of my course at some point, they know the "why" question is a fair one to ask. Every time they do, I seize the opportunity. I believe it is my duty to honor students' doubt and to lead them past asking, Why do I have to take this class? and toward a genuine appreciation of general education.

Making the Grade*

Ace your college classes with this advice on choosing courses,
selecting a major, writing papers, and dealing with professors.
By Tracey Randinelli

Swarthmore College? One of the toughest liberal arts schools in the country? No sweat, thought Esther Zeledon. After all, the Miami resident graduated sixth in her class from Braddock High School, the largest secondary school in the U.S., with more than 5,400 students. In high school, she took 10 AP courses and pulled mostly A's. She figured work at Swarthmore would be more of the same. "I thought college was going to be like high school: Do some homework, a test here and there," she says. "I thought I would be able to get straight A's."

It didn't take long for Zeledon to realize she wasn't in high school any-more. The environmental science major soon discovered the workload was staggering. "I got about one paper a week for English and one every other week for history, as well as 800 pages a week to read," she says. That did not include a five-hour chemistry lab and four hours of pre- and post-lab work, as well as stuff like eating and sleeping.

Careers & Colleges, March-April 2004, v24, i4, p. 12(5). Reprinted with permission.

But the worst part, says 20-year-old Zeledon, was that despite long hours of studying, she couldn't manage to pull the top-notch grades that came so easily in high school. "It was so difficult to get an A," she says. "I didn't see that pretty letter my first year."

Zeledon's story isn't unique. Even the most successful high school students can find their academic world turned upside down at college. The problem: They haven't been prepared for the vast differences between high school and college academia.

"Students find that the strategies that served them in high school are not good enough for college," says Pat Grove, campus director of the Learning Resource Center at Rutgers University in New Brunswick, New Jersey. "The volume and complexity of the material is so vastly different, and the expectations of the faculty are entirely different from the expectations of their high school teachers."

In high school, says Grove, students are required to memorize and recall information. But in college, professors expect students to truly analyze and understand concepts.

Colleges are just beginning to recognize that graduating high school students need more guidance to make the transition. Many schools now require freshmen to take orientation courses designed to teach them time management, communication dynamics, and other skills they need to be successful in the brand-new world of college.

CHOOSING COURSES

In high school, choosing your courses is easy—most are requirements and very few are electives. At many colleges, however, it's a little more complicated. You get a course book that may contain several hundred pages of classes. Which classes you take, the times you take them, the days you take them—it's more or less all up to you.

It doesn't have to be overwhelming, though. You most likely will have an academic advisor to help you. "Your advisor is your university resource broker," says Elizabeth Teagan, director of the University Transition Advising Center at Texas Tech University in Lubbock. The college advisor is familiar with faculty, knows what's needed to fulfill requirements within the university and in your major, and he or she can spot problems that you are likely to miss.

For many students, one of those problems is filling general education, or gen-ed, requirements. In order to graduate, many colleges require that you take a number of credits in liberal arts disciplines—English, math and science, a foreign language.

"Gen-ed courses teach a lot of skills that students will need in their other courses—working in groups, critical thinking, analysis," says Dave Meredith, director of enrollment management for the honors programs at the University of Cincinnati. It's important to balance your schedule with a required math or foreign language course as well.

Getting gen-ed requirements out of the way early can be particularly beneficial to students who are still undecided about their major, adds Meredith. "If you can say I'm wiping off my history requirement,' that can make you feel like you're progressing."

Plan a Balanced Schedule

Consider courses that are extra-challenging and courses that require less effort. "You shouldn't take biology, calculus, physics, and chemistry together the first semester—that's ridiculous," says Rutgers University's Grove.

Robin Diana, associate director of the Center for Student Transition and Support at Rochester Institute of Technology in New York, suggests meeting with your advisor early in the course selection process. Take a look at the course sequence for your major with an eye toward the next four years, not just the coming semester. Then agree on what courses you should be taking, says Diana, "so that four years down the road you don't realize you need two that are not being offered that semester." Other points to remember:

Be Flexible

At many universities, first-year students are the last to register. That means that many of the more popular classes and class times have already been filled. "Know that the days and times that you want will probably not be the days and times you get," says Diana. "Have a plan A, a plan B, and a plan C ready to go."

Keep Your Own Personality in Mind

If you're a morning person, schedule your classes early in the day. (Early birds are at an advantage, since the competition for an 8 a.m. class is much less fierce than for a class at a later hour.) If you know you can't function before 10 a.m., however, don't force yourself to take early-morning classes.

Make Sure You're Prepared

Some classes have prerequisites. An introductory class in chemistry, for example, may require that you have had several years of chemistry in high school.

GET TO KNOW YOUR PROFESSOR

You'll find that one of the biggest differences between school and college academics is the relationship you have with the person standing in front of the class. "In high school, teachers pretty much tell you what your responsibilities are," says Bonnie B. Gorman, director of first-year programs at Michigan

Technological University in Houghton. "In college, you have to figure that out." It's your job—not the professor's—to make sure you are keeping up with assignments and progressing through the class.

What's more, a college professor is often less accessible than a high school teacher. In high school, you saw your teachers every day; in college, you may spend only an hour or two with a professor each week. And that hour or two is far from intimate: In an introductory class, it may well be you, the professors, and several hundred other students.

"In a lecture hall, it's not likely a professor is going to know you one on one," says Diana. "You need to take the initiative to get to know your professors and have them know who you are."

Classroom Impressions

Start in the classroom environment itself. That means showing up—and on time. (An interesting side note, says Victoria McGillin, dean for academic advising at Wheaton College in Norton, Massachusetts: Depending on a college's costs, each class you cut costs between $70 and $150. Ouch.)

Sit as close to the front as you can, and particularly in larger classes, try to sit in the same seat or area of the room for each session. The professor may not immediately know your name, but he or she will begin to recognize your face. Show that you're attentive by making eye contact on a consistent basis. "It's about being present versus that vague stare students get after the first 20 minutes," says Texas Tech University's Teagan.

In smaller, less lecture-driven sessions, class participation can also help get you noticed by a professor, particularly when you've done the assigned reading or writing. While raising your hand to make a point is great, don't forget that asking probing questions can be an effective way to participate in class discussions.

Communication Is Key

If participating is difficult because of class size, see if available alternatives exist. "Some faculty are increasingly playing around with Web-based email discussions," says McGillin. "They'll consider that comparable to having raised your hand in class." If all else fails, drop the professor an email with questions or comments on the day's lecture. "If it's clear to a professor that a student is making an effort in their class," says Gorman, "that's what's important."

The Office Visit

One of the best ways of getting to know a professor is also one of the most underutilized. At most colleges, professors designate several hours a week as "office hours": times when students can talk to them about grades, assignments, and problems they have with the class material. But if you ask most professors, you'll find that office hours are often very quiet. "We have several professors who use our center for their office hours," says Rutgers University's Grove, "and they get lonely sitting there."

The University of Cincinnati's Meredith suggests visiting a professor early in the semester to say hello and introduce yourself. "If you only see the professor after you've bombed the midterm, they may look at it as, 'Oh they're just trying to save their grade.' " Meredith stresses that taking advantage of office hours throughout the semester can definitely help your final grade. "If it's a difference between a B-plus and an A, maybe if you've been to his office a couple of times he'll remember it and you'll get the A."

Facing Problems

It's also important to remember that professors are people, too. Sure, they might have Ph.Ds, but as Teagan says, "They're dads and moms and aunts and uncles just like anybody else. If you're having a problem, most will do whatever they can to help." Becky Libby, a student at the University of Southern California, found herself floundering in a first-year writing class. To her surprise, her professor noticed something was bothering her and came to her rescue. "She met with me every day for literally two weeks to bring my writing up to par," Libby remembers.

TAKE NOTES

In high school, studying is a day-to-day process. You go to class, you get homework, you do it. Your teacher tells you you're having a test next Friday, you study, you take the test. You might know a paper is due in two weeks, but that's about as far into the future as you get.

In college classes however, your semester is usually mapped out from day 1. Most professors hand out a syllabus on the first day of class. The syllabus tells you when to expect quizzes and tests, when papers are due, what you'll be expected to read in time for each class, even the topics that will be covered in each day's lecture. The syllabus makes it easier to see how you'll be progressing throughout the semester, but it also puts more responsibility on you to make sure you're getting the work done—and doing it well.

Taking good notes is a vital step in the process. Again, you'll probably find it was easier in high school. A high school class environment is usually more interactive, while a college-level introductory class can consist of 90 minutes of lecture. Trying to copy the lecture verbatim isn't very smart, unless you happen to be a court reporter or stenographer. Taping a lecture helps, but it takes valuable time to transcribe the tape.

Instead, make sure you've read the assigned material before class—that way, you'll have some idea of what the professor is going to say before he or she says it. During the lecture, don't try to take down every word the professor says. Instead, look or listen for clues that will tell you what topics or ideas the professor thinks matter. Did he or she write something on the board? Mention something more than once? Illustrate an idea with examples? Chances are, those are things the professor considers important—and will probably include on an exam. "You want to synthesize and identify the main points," says Michigan Technological University's Gorman.

Many high school students find their note-taking strategies—if in fact they have any—have to change once they get to college. There's no one "right" way to take notes; different strategies work for different people. Some prefer an outline. Others favor some variation of the Cornell, or "one-third, two-thirds" method, in which you record specific notes from the lecture on the right two-thirds of the page, and later, in your own words, summarize the main ideas on the left side of the page. Still other students prefer mapping out ideas on the page and linking relationships visually. You may even find you need to use several different strategies, depending on the subject.

EXAM TIME

College and high school exams are similar in that they measure what you've learned. What's different is the learning process itself. "A lot of learning in high school is memorization," explains Texas Tech's Teagan. "In college, memorization may be part of a body of investigation, but it's really just the first step." College learning isn't just about knowing concepts—it's about understanding the relationships between those concepts.

In high school, you're usually tested on a few chapters or concepts every couple of weeks. Many college classes, on the other hand, hold just two exams—a midterm and a final—that measure your knowledge of weeks of lectures, dozens of pages of notes, and hundreds of pages of text. Obviously, this is not a process that happens overnight.

"Studying for an exam is really an extended review period you should be doing every day," says Ken Miller, director of student affairs at Pennsylvania State University at Erie. "Day by day the material may not be difficult, but over 12 weeks, it will be more difficult to absorb and recall all the material. Students who keep up are more prepared than those who try to cram."

When you're faced with prepping for an exam, your first step is to find out what kind of exam it's going to be. A closed-ended (i.e., multiple choice, true/false) will stress concepts: Was Robert E. Lee a southern or northern general? An open-ended (i.e., essay) exam will stress relationships between concepts: Compare Lee's battle strategy to Grant's. Knowing the type of exam you're facing will give you a better idea of how you'll need to study for it.

If you've kept up with the reading, paid attention during class, and practiced good note taking, you probably have a good idea of what material is going to be on the exam. "A professor is not going to put together a final that doesn't look like anything you've seen during the semester," says Rochester Institute of Technology's Robin Diana. Many professors also keep copies of previous exams on file; while they won't tell you the exact questions you'll be facing, they will give you an idea of what to expect. In any case, it's your right to ask for guidance, says Teagan.

YOU WILL SURVIVE!

You know the academic strategies—but you still feel like you can barely keep your head above water. What can you do? Nearly all campuses have academic advisement centers you can turn to if you're feeling the crunch. Also, take comfort from the fact that even the most successful high school students go through much of the college academic process with some difficulty. "It is just getting used to the whole process," says Swarthmore freshman Esther Zeledon. "It's hard, but at least there are a lot of support groups that really make things easier. Just don't give up!"

8 STEPS (AND A WARNING*) TO A GREAT PAPER

Chuck Guilford, associate professor of English at Boise State University, author of *Beginning College Writing* (Little, Brown), and creator of the Paradigm Online Writing Assistant (www.powa.org), offers these tips:

1. Own the topic. Ask yourself, "What about this topic do I care about? What about it has value to me?" Make the subject your own.
2. "Problematize" the topic. Mold the topic into a core question or problem that must be solved using research and investigation.
3. Survey what's out there. Your professor, former students in the class, or other faculty may have suggestions for finding sources.
4. Get the information. Use the library, Internet, and even interviews, when appropriate.
5. Come up with the solution. Propose a hypothesis to your research problem, which you can use to help structure the paper.
6. Start writing. Divide the problem into the main points, and then plug in your information. The final solution or answer to the research problem should be the conclusion of the paper.
7. Document your sources. Note that departments within a university often have different requirements for citing sources.
8. Write it again . . . and again. Be prepared to do at least three drafts, plus a final edit.

*And here's that warning. Don't be tempted to buy an essay off the Web. "Plagiarized papers lack the voice that students bring to their writing," says Guilford. Having someone else write your paper for you may save you a few days or weeks of work, but the reward may end up being an F for the paper or even the course.

MAJOR DECISIONS

For many students, their first academic dilemma arrives in the form of that little box on the college application labeled "desired major." Most students do not have a clear idea of what they want to do for the next 40 years—and that can cause some "major" stress. Students also feel pressure to choose, says Texas Tech's Teagan. "[Not having a major] has a negative connotation. The first question people ask after 'What college are you going to?' is 'What's your major?' "

If you fall into the undecided category, you're not alone. According to Ablongman.com, a college-planning Web site, one-third of high school students haven't a clue what they want to do for a living, and more than half change their major during their freshman year. Eventually, you will have to choose your course. These tips can help:

- **Get to know yourself.** Pinpointing the qualities that make you who you are can often help you narrow down career choices that best coincide with those qualities. What type of personality do you have? What do you enjoy doing? What are your values?
- **Take advantage of campus facilities.** Career counseling or resource centers are not just for seniors arranging job interviews. Schedule an appointment with a career counselor. "Talk about what you like, what you don't like, your interests, your dreams," says Wheaton College's McGillin. Your academic advisor can also be useful in helping you determine the major that will best prepare you for what you want to do.
- **Talk to everyone you know.** Everyone has a story about how they got into their field. Get the scoop first-hand from adults you know—and pay special attention to people whose career path took an unlikely turn.
- **Investigate internships.** Many companies offer internships to high school as well as college students. If you have an idea of what you want to do, find an internship in that field to solidify—or negate—that interest.
- **Take advantage of gen-ed requirements.** "We encourage students to think of general education courses as potential career avenues," says McGillin. If you haven't decided on a major by the time you matriculate, use your gen-eds to get a taste of several different job fields. You might not be excited about taking a required government course, but three weeks of the class might convince you that politics is your calling.
- **Don't be afraid to go in undecided.** At most schools, you're not even required to settle on a major until sometime during your sophomore year. "Undecided students are a step ahead of those who declare and change," says Teagan.

DISCUSSION

1. One of the authors of this book couldn't do any better than C work (and often much worse) on most college exams until he learned how to take notes from a very successful upperclass student who let him see his notebook for comparison purposes. Interview several upperclass students who are making above-average grades, and then discuss in class what you have learned.

2. In a small group of fellow students, exchange your notebooks for any course and take a look at how other students literally "take" notes. Then discuss strategies for successful note taking. Make sure you define how you know what "successful" note taking is. As you listen to others, rate your own effectiveness.

3. In a group of five or six students, work out a division of labor whereby each of you agrees to interview faculty members representing such different subjects as math, physical and biological sciences, a social science such as history, humanities, and so forth. Ask these faculty members how they would advise students in their courses to take good notes. Discuss your findings with others in your group.

4. Why is the commonly asked question "Why do I have to take this class?" so relevant to students and so repugnant to teachers?

5. What does the teacher who wrote the article "Why do I have to take this class?" do to engage his students in their course work? As a student, how might you participate in this class? Would your listening and note taking skills improve? Why?

6. After describing what a tough time a bright student had during her first year of college, the author of "Making the Grade" writes, "You will survive." As you make your way through classes this year, tell yourself, "I will survive" as you plan strategies for doing so. Exchange those strategies with others in your class and reach a consensus on the best ways to survive college.

Reading to Remember

Jeanne L. Higbee of the University of Minnesota, Twin Cities, contributed her valuable and considerable expertise to the writing of this chapter.

IN THIS CHAPTER, YOU WILL LEARN
- How to "prepare to read"
- How to preview reading material
- How to mark your textbooks
- How to review your reading
- How to develop a more extensive vocabulary

College texts are loaded with concepts, terms, and complex information that you are expected to learn on your own in a short period of time. To do this, you will need to learn and to use a reading method such as the one described in this chapter.

The following plan for textbook reading is based on four steps: previewing, reading, marking, and reviewing.

Previewing

The purpose of previewing is to get "the big picture." Begin by reading the title of the textbook chapter. Ask yourself, "What do I already know about this subject?" Next, quickly read through the introductory paragraphs, and then read the summary at the beginning or end of the chapter (if there is one). Finally, take a few minutes to page through the chapter headings and subheadings. Note any study exercises at the end of the chapter.

As part of your preview, note how many pages the chapter contains. It's a good idea to decide in advance how many pages you can reasonably expect to cover in your first 50-minute study period. This can help build your concentration as you work toward your goal of reading a specific number of pages. Before long, you'll know how many pages is practical for you. Also keep in mind that different types of textbooks may require more or less time to read.

Mapping

Mapping the chapter as you preview it provides a visual guide to how different chapter ideas fit together. Because about 75 percent of students identify themselves as visual learners, visual mapping is an excellent learning tool for test preparation as well as reading (see Chapter 3, Learning Styles and Personality).

How do you map a chapter? While you are previewing, use either a wheel or a branching structure (Figure 7.1). In the wheel structure, place the central idea of the chapter in the circle, place secondary ideas on the spokes emanating from the circle, and place offshoots of those ideas on the lines attached to the spokes. In the branching map, the main idea goes at the top, followed by supporting ideas on the second tier, and so forth. Write in the title first. Then, as you skim through the rest of the chapter, use the headings and subheadings to fill in the key ideas.

Alternatives to Mapping

Perhaps you prefer a more linear visual image. Then consider making an outline of the headings and subheadings in the chapter. You can fill in the outline after you read. Or make a list. Set up the list with the terms in the left column and fill in definitions, descriptions, and examples on the right after you read. Divide the terms on your list into groups of five, seven, or nine, and leave white space between the clusters so that you can visualize each group in your mind. This practice, known as "chunking," will help you learn the material more easily.

If you are an interactive learner, make lists or create a flash card for each heading and subheading. Then fill in the back of each card after reading each section in the text. Use the lists or flash cards to review with a partner, or to recite the material to yourself. As you preview the text material, look for connections between the text and the related lecture material. Call to mind the related terms and concepts that you recorded in the lecture. Use these strate-

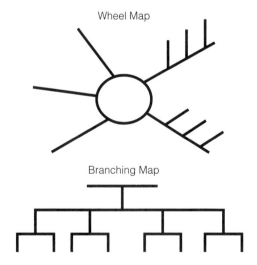

Figure 7.1   **Wheel and Branching Maps**

gies to warm up. Ask yourself, "Why am I reading this? What do I want to know?"

Reading Your Textbook

Read before you highlight. With your skeleton map or outline, you should be able to read more quickly and with greater comprehension. Read without using your pencil or highlighter. When you have reached the end of a section, stop and ask yourself, "What are the key ideas in this section? What do I think I'll see on the test?" Then, and only then, decide what to underline or highlight.

Learn to concentrate. Consider these suggestions, and decide which ones would help you concentrate on your material:

- Find a study location, preferably in the library if you are on campus, that is removed from traffic and distracting noises.
- Read in 50-minute blocks of time, with short breaks in between. By reading for 50 minutes more frequently during the day instead of cramming all your reading in at the end of the day, you should be able to process material more easily.
- Set goals for your study period, such as "I will read 20 pages of my psychology text in the next 50 minutes." Reward yourself with a 10-minute break after each 50-minute study period.
- If you are having trouble concentrating or staying awake, take a quick walk around the library or down the hall. Stretch or take some deep breaths and think positively about your study goals. Then resume studying.
- Jot study questions in the margin, take notes, or recite key ideas. Reread parts of the text that you find confusing, and make a note to ask your instructor for clarification.
- Focus on the important portions of the text. Pay attention to the first and last sentences of paragraphs and to words in italics or bold print.
- Use the glossary in the text for definitions of unfamiliar terms.

Marking Your Textbook

Some students report that marking is an active reading strategy that helps them focus and concentrate on the material as they read. In addition, most students expect to use their text notations when studying for tests. To meet these goals, some students like to underline, some prefer to highlight, and others use margin notes or annotations. Look at Figure 7.2 on pages 114–115 for examples of different methods of marking.

Figure 7.2 Sample Marked Pages

Source: Pages adapted with permission from James W. Kalat, *Introduction to Psychology*, 4th ed. (Pacific Grove, CA: Brooks/Cole, 1996).

CONCEPT CHECKS

7. *Some students who read a chapter slowly get very good grades; others get poor grades. Why?*
8. *Most actors and public speakers who have to memorize lengthy passages spend little time simply repeating the words and more time thinking about them. Why? (Check your answers on page 288.)*

People need to monitor their understanding of a text to decide whether to keep studying or whether they already understand it well enough. Most readers have trouble making that judgment correctly.

SELF-MONITORING OF UNDERSTANDING

Whenever you are studying a text, you periodically have to decide, "Should I keep on studying this section, or do I already understand it well enough?" Most students have trouble monitoring their own understanding. In one study, psychology instructors asked their students before each test to guess whether they would do better or worse on that test than they usually do. Students also guessed after each test whether they had done better or worse than usual. Most students' guesses were no more accurate than chance (Sjostrom & Marks, 1994). Such inaccuracy represents a problem: Students who do not know how well they understand the material will make bad judgments about when to keep on studying and when to quit.

(why)

Even when you are reading a single sentence, you have to decide whether you understand the sentence or whether you should stop and reread it. Here is a sentence once published in the student newspaper at North Carolina State University:

He said Harris told him she and Brothers told French that grades had been changed.

(How)

Ordinarily, when good readers come to such a confusing sentence, they notice their own confusion and reread the sentence or, if necessary, the whole paragraph. Poor readers tend to read at their same speed for both easy and difficult materials; they are less likely than good readers to slow down when they come to difficult sentences.

Although monitoring one's own understanding is difficult and often inaccurate, it is not impossible. For example, suppose I tell you that you are to read three chapters dealing with, say, thermodynamics, the history of volleyball, and the Japanese stock market.

Later you will take tests on each chapter. Before you start reading, predict your approximate scores on the three tests. Most people make a guess based on how much they already know about the three topics. If we let them read the three chapters and again make a guess about their test performances, they do in fact make more accurate predictions than they did before reading (Maki & Serra, 1992). That improvement indicates some ability to monitor one's own understanding of a text.

SPAR
Survey
Process
Ask
Review

A systematic way to monitor your own understanding of a text is the (SPAR) method: Survey, Process meaningfully, Ask questions, and Review and test yourself. Start with an overview of what a passage is about, read it carefully, and then see whether you can answer questions about the passage or explain it to others. If not, go back and reread.

THE TIMING OF STUDY

(Also decide about larger units?)

Other things being equal, people tend to remember recent experiences better than earlier experiences. For example, suppose someone reads you a list of 20 words and asks you to recall as many of them as possible. The list is far too long for you to recite from your phonological loop; however, you should be able to remember at least a few. Typically, people remember items at the beginning and end of the list better than they remember those in the middle.

That tendency, known as the serial-order effect, includes two aspects: The primacy effect is the tendency to remember the first items; the recency effect refers to the tendency to remember the last items. One explanation for the primacy effect is that the listener gets to rehearse the first few items for a few moments alone with no interference from the others. One explanation for the recency effect is that the last items are still in

Cause of primacy effect

Figure 7.2 Sample Marked Pages (continued)

Cause of recency effect

the listener's phonological loop at the time of the test.

The phonological loop cannot be the whole explanation for the recency effect, however. In one study, British rugby players were asked to name the teams they had played against in the current season. Players were most likely to remember the last couple of teams they had played against, thus showing a clear recency effect even though they were recalling events that occurred weeks apart (Baddeley & Hitch, 1977). (The phonological loop holds information only for a matter of seconds.)

So, studying material—or, rather, *reviewing* material—shortly before a test is likely to improve recall. Now let's consider the opposite: Suppose you studied something years ago and have not reviewed it since then. For example, suppose you studied a foreign language in high school several years ago. Now you are considering taking a college course in the language, but you are hesitant because you are sure you have forgotten it all. Have you?

Harry Bahrick (1984) tested people who had studied Spanish in school 1 to 50 years previously. Nearly all agreed that they rarely used Spanish and had not refreshed their memories at all since their school days. (That is a disturbing comment, but beside the point.) Their retention of Spanish dropped noticeably in the first 3 to 6 years, but remained fairly stable from then on (Fig-

ure 7.18). In other words, we do not completely forget even very old memories that we seldom use.

In a later study, Bahrick and members of his family studied foreign-language vocabulary either on a moderately frequent basis (practicing once every 2 weeks) or on a less frequent basis (as seldom as once every 8 weeks), and tested their knowledge years later. The result: More frequent study led to faster learning; however, less frequent study led to better long-term retention, measured years later (Bahrick, Bahrick, Bahrick, & Bahrick, 1993).

The principle here is far more general than just the study of foreign languages. If you want to remember something well for a test, your best strategy is to study it as close as possible to the time of the test, in order to take advantage of the recency effect and decrease the effects of retroactive interference. Obviously, I do not mean that you should wait until the night before the test to start studying, but you might rely on an extensive review at that time. You should also, ideally, study under conditions similar to the conditions of the test. For example, you might study in the same room where the test will be given, or at the same time of day.

However, *if you want to remember something long after the test is over,* then the advice I have just given you is all wrong. To be able to remember something whenever you want, wherever you are, and whatever you are doing, you should study it under as varied circumstances as possible. Study and review at various times and places with long, irregular intervals between study sessions. Studying under such inconsistent conditions will slow down your original learning, but it will improve your ability to recall it long afterwards (Schmidt & Bjork, 1992).

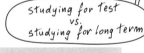

studying for test vs. studying for long term

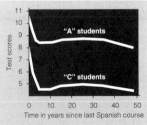

FIGURE 7.18
(Left) Spanish vocabulary as measured by a recognition test shows a rapid decline in the first few years but then long-term stability. (From Bahrick, 1984.) (Right) Within a few years after taking your last foreign-language course, you may think you have forgotten it all. You have not, and even the part you have forgotten will come back (through relearning) if you visit a country where you can practice the language.

CHAPTER 7
MEMORY

284

No matter what method you prefer, remember these important guidelines:

1. **Read before you mark.** Finish reading a section before you decide which are the most important ideas and concepts.
2. **Think before you mark.** If you just mark pages, you are committing yourself to at least one more viewing of all the pages that you have already read—all 400 pages of your anatomy or art history textbook. Instead, take notes, create flash cards, make lists, or outline textbook chapters. These methods are also more practical if you intend to review with a friend or study group.
3. **Don't let highlighting or underlining give you a false sense of security.** When you force yourself to put something in your own words when taking notes, you are not only predicting exam questions but assessing whether you can answer them. Write as you read. Taking notes on your reading helps you focus on the key ideas and summarize as you go.
4. **Annotate.** You may want to try a strategy known as annotating the text. In your own words, write key ideas in the margins of the text.

Monitor Your Comprehension

An important step in textbook reading is to monitor your comprehension. As you read, ask yourself, "Do I understand this?" If not, stop and reread the material. Look up words that are not clear. Try to clarify the main points and how they relate to one another.

Another way to check comprehension is to try to recite the material aloud to yourself or your study partner. Using a study group to monitor your comprehension gives you immediate feedback and is highly motivating. One way that group members can work together is to divide up a chapter for previewing and studying and get together later to teach the material to one another.

Recycle Your Reading

After you have read and marked or taken notes on key ideas from the first section of the chapter, proceed to each subsequent section until you have finished the chapter.

After you have completed each section—and *before* you move on to the next section—ask again, "What are the key ideas? What will I see on the test?" At the end of each section, try to guess what information the author will present in the next section. Good reading should lead you from one section to the next, with each new section adding to your understanding.

Reviewing

The final step in effective textbook reading is reviewing. Many students expect the improbable—that they will read through their text material one time and be able to remember the ideas four, six, or even twelve weeks later at test time. More realistically, you will need to include regular reviews in your study process. Here is where your notes, study questions, annotations, flash cards, visual maps, or outlines will be most useful. Your study goal is to review the material from each chapter every week.

Consider ways to use your many senses to review. Recite aloud. Post diagrams, maps, or outlines around your living space so that you will see them often and will likely be able to visualize them while taking the test.

Adjusting Your Reading Style

With effort, you can improve your reading dramatically, but remember to be flexible. How you read should depend on the material. Assess the relative importance and difficulty of the assigned readings, and adjust your reading style and the time you allot accordingly. Connect one important idea to another by asking yourself, "Why am I reading this? Where does this fit in?" When the textbook material is virtually identical to the lecture material, you can save time by concentrating mainly on one or the other. It takes a planned approach to read textbook materials and other assigned readings with good understanding and recall.

Developing Your Vocabulary

Textbooks are full of new terminology. In fact, one could argue that learning chemistry is largely a matter of learning the language of chemists and that mastering philosophy or history or sociology requires a mastery of the terminology of each particular discipline.

If words are such a basic and essential component of our knowledge, what is the best way to learn them? Follow these basic vocabulary strategies:

- During your overview of the chapter, notice and jot down unfamiliar terms. Make a flash card for each term, or a list of all terms.
- When you encounter challenging words, consider the context. See if you can predict the meaning of an unfamiliar term using the surrounding words.
- If context by itself is not enough, try analyzing the term to discover the root or other meaningful parts of the word. For example, *emissary* has the root "to emit" or "to send forth," so we can guess that an emissary is

someone sent forth with a message. Similarly, note prefixes and suffixes. For example, *anti-* means "against" and *pro-* means "for."

- Use the glossary/index of this text, a dictionary, or **http://www.m-w.com/ netdict.htm** (*The Merriam-Webster Dictionary Online*) to locate the definition. Note any multiple definitions and search for the meaning that fits this usage.

- Take every opportunity to use these new terms in your writing and speaking. If you use a new term, then you'll know it! In addition, studying new terms on flash cards or study sheets can be handy at exam time.

YOUR PERSONAL JOURNAL

Here are several things to write about. Choose one or more. Or choose another topic related to this chapter.

1. How can you use the suggestions in this chapter, along with those in the previous chapter on taking notes in class, to improve your study skills? What should you do first?
2. This chapter makes a number of suggestions for reading textbooks. Which ones strike you as most important? Which will be toughest for you to follow? Explain.
3. Try following some of the suggestions in this chapter the next time you are reading a homework assignment. Then write how it felt to use them.
4. What behaviors are you willing to change after reading this chapter? How might you go about changing them?
5. What else is on your mind this week? If you wish to share it with your instructor, add it to this journal entry.

READINGS

New Words, 7 Drops at a Time*
Vocabulary boosts can energize writing—or overload it
By Arthur Plotnik

The label on my Schultz Plant Food, a sea-blue slosh of nutrients in a bottle, reads: "7 drops per qt water every time you water."

---

*This article appeared in *The Writer,* June 2003, v116, i6, p. 15(3). Copyright 2003 Arthur Plotnik. Reprinted courtesy of *The Writer* magazine and Arthur Plotnik.

Years ago, I tossed a grapefruit seed in a pot, and the rest is limp-leaved history—except when I pump an eye-dropper-full of Schultz into the plant's water. Overnight, foliage snaps to. Jessant shoots erupt like green starbursts.

This is not a product plug, but a Schultzy spin on infusing a writer's vocabulary. Writing piece after piece exhausts the loam of expression. Sentences, descriptive passages, lines of poetry start to droop. The brain cries for invigoration, and the eye-dropper approach—seven new words or so weekly—may be just the ticket.

Who has not resolved to master a dictionary or jumbo vocabulary-builder? Most such enterprises fizzle—which may not be a bad thing for readers. An overdose of new words can create a garden of monstrous locutions. Drop-by-drop enrichment allows one to savor and test a word, integrate it into one's style before sounding like Thomas Pynchon on Miracle-Gro.

WRITERS' WORDS

The planet groans with word resources, many of them targeting language hobbyists or "logophiles." In *The New York Times Dictionary of Misunderstood, Misused, Mispronounced Words,* lexicographer Laurence Urdang wisecracks that an "enchiridion of arcane and recondite sesquipedalian items will appeal to the oniomania of an eximious Gemeinschaft"—and who could disagree? Translation: Certain admirable types like to buy collections of big, unusual words.

Writers appreciate recondite items as much as the next word junkie, but they don't want to gag readers on them. An asphyxiating vocabulary flirts with what Jonathan Franzen calls the "status model" of authorship: the uncompromising artiste who disdains broad appeal and for whom "difficulty tends to signal excellence." In the opposing "contract model," Franzen says, the author makes a deal with readers, a promise to connect with them for their efforts. When contract readers "crack a tooth on a hard word," maybe they oughtta sue.

Those who want to connect, then, stock their journals with writers' words—not always the plainest or best-known, but somehow rewarding to the reader. Franzen himself uses words such as "pemmican" and "solipsistic" in his article ("Mr. Difficult," *The New Yorker,* Sept. 30, 2002), but they turn out to be pretty good chaws in context.

For special purposes, a writers' word can be anything from firkin to floccinaucinihilipilification. But to earn a place in one's general writing vocabulary, the word should meet at least one of these criteria:

Precise: e.g., *tor* (hilltop rock heap)
Concise: *mulct* (defraud, as of money)
Euphonious: *fanfaronade* (bluster)
Onomatopoetic: *williwaw* (violent squall)

Forceful: *fulgent* (dazzlingly bright)
Evocative: *mojo* (charmed object)
Fun: *cachinnate* (laugh immoderately)
Fresh alternative: *nimiety* (an abundance, instead of "plethora")

A word outside the reader's active or half-known vocabulary should have some seductive aura, like majesty or mystery. Perhaps it reveals itself in context—"steam purled up from the pavement" (flowed in curls)—or begs to be looked up, like scumble (to soften brilliant color).

Where does one find writers' words not yet trampled to death? Self-help compilations such as Word Smart or 1000 Most Important Words house a few, but big lists can be overwhelming. I favor collections with narrative to slow things down—e.g., Word Watch, Anne H. Soukhanov's riffs on modern coinages such as "mamou" (something big and important).

Swarms of writers' words appear in thesauruses and specialized glossaries, especially in the sciences (see *Syntax*, October and December 2002); in obscure and antiquated works, including old slang dictionaries; and in such loopy Web sites as the Rap Dictionary http://www.rapdict.org. Desk novelties like The Mavens' Word of the Day Block Calendar deliver a few winners among their daily doses, but it's hard to pay attention as days and desktops pile up.

Choice items are more likely to surface in the world's flow of expression—literary, journalistic, ethnic, and subcultural. So what if Sunday pundits and other word mavens snap up the lunkers? Individual writers with keen eye and notebook will net their share. Anyone is free to snatch isolated words from what they read and hear. Outside of trademarked names, no one owns a word, not even poets associated with, say, "darkling" or "diverged."

My recent pickings include "flense" (to skin a whale or, figuratively, to flay) from Michael Chabon, "peridot" (green transparent gemstone) from Sandra McPherson, and "camorra" (secret society) from Anne Fadiman. I'll keep them handy for some inspired use.

WEB OF WORDS

These days, the most overwhelming word source is the Internet, where some sites offer useful vocabulary in delayed-release doses, and others overwhelm the frontal lobes with Scrabble babble, blogger chat, and link madness.

Among daily infusions, the most renowned is A.Word.A.Day http://wordsmith.org/awad/index.html. Loaded with features and claiming more than half a million devotees, it produced a bestselling book, *A Word a Day*, from its archives last fall. Subscriptions for a selected word and commentary emailed each weekday are free.

In most word-a-day services, many selections will be technical, silly, arcane, or ordinary (though with interesting background). Only a few each month will be writers' words; but here's the point: You will see them, and see them at a reasonable pace for building your vocabulary. When eager for more, you can dive into the sites' archives of prior words and swim among the momes (boors) and bonces (heads).

The big-mamou question: Should you use a word you fear will stump your readers? Absolutely—if you adore it, believe it to be what Mark Twain would call the "intensely right word," and haven't used too many puzzlers elsewhere. After all, what sweeter lagniappe for readers than a new word for their delectation?

Internet Word-a-Day Sources

Vocabulary sort of spavined (over the hill)? Get some revitalizing words each day from sites like these personal favorites. Each offers emailed words by free subscription unless otherwise noted. Sample words (*in italics*) are only partly defined.

A Definition a Day
http://www.vocabula.com
Selects words with "an aura of fun or majesty." Stellar columns, quizzes, and random words.
Weanling (a newly weaned child or animal).

Merriam-Webster's Word of the Day
http://m-w.com
Solid, informative. Etymology, usage examples. Archive. Free e-mail delivery.
Quidnunc (a busybody).

Spizzerinctum: The Quiz of Breaking News & Obscure Words
http://www.spizzquiz.net/index.html
Cool site that retrieves juicy forgotten words, lets you guess meanings from three choices, and then uses the word in a rewrite of current (linked) news. Archive. Free e-mail delivery.
Creachy (dilapidated, sickly).

A Vocabulary Word of the Day
http://www.americanliterature.com
Created by the late Aaron Rene Ezis. Superior words and partial backlist.
Gobbet (a fragment or piece of raw flesh).

A.Word.A.Day
http://www.wordsmith.org/words
By Anu Garg. The granddaddy of word-a-day sites. Free e-mail delivery.
Hobbledehoy (an awkward young fellow).

Word of the Day from Lexico Publishing
http://dictionary.reference.com/wordoftheday
Well organized; archives, quotes. Free e-mail delivery.
Wayworn (travel-weary).

The Word Spy
http://www.wordspy.com
Paul McFedries' sharp-eyed collection of recent coinages; context, background, sightings, quotes, indexed archives.
Invacuate (to hold people in a building for safety).

Worthless Word for the Day
http://home.mn.rr.com/wwftd
Anything but worthless. Its exchange of "obscure, abstruse, and/or recondite words" are often writers' words. Archive. Free e-mail delivery.
Muzzy (muddled, confused).

How to Study*

*Even though she claims she hates studying, consultant anaesthetist
Leyla Sanai has passed all her many exams at the first sitting. In this
article she shares her tips for success.*
By Leyla Sanai

Studying for exams is a nightmare. There is no easy way of doing it—it is a relentless grind. Two of the worst things about medical school are the frequency and enormity of the exams. No sooner have you finished one and had a breather for a couple of months when another looms forebodingly on the horizon, with its whispered threats of doom. . .

When I was a student there seemed to be people who could breeze effort-lessly through all their exams with minimal effort. Some of these people boasted about how they had barely picked up a textbook, and bragged about nights spent in the pub instead of studying. These individuals were telling huge porkies. It's impossible to make it through medical school without work-ing hard—the sheer volume of facts to be learnt mitigates against luck or brains as passports to exam success. Any successful medical student who pre-tends that they have never studied in their life deserves an Oscar. I think that their motivation for spinning these webs of fiction is, firstly, a wish to be seen as a genius who never needs to study; secondly, a wish to be viewed as a life and soul type who rarely stops partying, and, thirdly, it is a desperate insur-ance scheme. So if they fail, despite their secretive hours of cramming, they can swagger in and drawl that it is no surprise they failed since they did no work, and exclaim about what miserable swots everyone else is.

Once you have accepted that, sadly, your desk is not just somewhere to park your butt when looking out the window, and the library is not just a place to meet your pals before the midweek night out at the union, it is essential to devise a method of study which is effective for you.

MAKE A TIMETABLE

Plan your study carefully. There is no point in flicking through your anatomy book with such lack of enthusiasm and boredom that you get through only one chapter in three months. On the other hand, do not be ridiculously overambi-tious in your aims: setting yourself two hours to learn the entire physiology of the respiratory and cardiovascular systems is a trifle optimistic. Once you have made your plan, try and stick to it—if you keep taking a week longer for each chapter than you had intended you will have a huge panic at the end. Remember, it is better to know everything moderately well than to be an expert in only 1 percent of the syllabus. It is futile knowing the anatomy of the dorsum of the upper limb digits like the, er, back of your hand, if you would not recognise a lower limb if you fell over one.

THINK IN TERMS OF AMOUNT LEARNT, NOT HOURS

As a student, I wasted many, many months sitting staring at the same page of some vast volume, daydreaming about what I would buy from the supermar-ket, or where I would go that weekend. I equated being miserable and tortur-ing myself with virtuous study, surmising that if I was having a hideously dull time then it must be doing me some good. Sadly, the adage "no pain, no gain" is not necessarily true in reverse—that is, pain does not automatically lead to gain. I was also envious of my best mate, who could sit and study intensively for hours at a time, then pack her books up and go and have fun. My method involved self-punishment. When I caught myself daydreaming, I would forgo little treats like the late night drink in a pub or the movie at the weekend and spend these times staring at the same page. Again. This was not constructive.

GIVE YOURSELF REWARDS

If you have something to aim for it is far easier to motivate yourself. Tell yourself that if you learn the chapter really well, then you will allow yourself a treat. Whether this is a night out, some new clothes, a day off at the weekend, or whatever is up to you. But be strict with yourself. If you spend the day skiving off instead of studying, then you must forgo your treat. No cheating.

DON'T BE TEMPTED TO TRY FADDY METHODS

I found studying so immensely painful that I always believed there was some secret trick that would suddenly render it all easy. This was not the case then, nor tragically, is it now. My flatmate and I amassed many different systems that would miraculously change our lives, making studying a doddle. Highlighter pens were one—the idea was that you would go through your notes or the textbook, highlighting salient points so that they would lodge themselves stubbornly in your memory.

Unfortunately, my highlighter pen did not stop me from daydreaming, and I ended up with many textbooks in which every second word would be religiously highlighted, whether it was a key word or just "and" or "a." My flatmate fared no better. She spent hours poring over filing cards on which she wrote important facts, but ended up with a floor littered with hundreds of little cards and little else.

RELATE FACTS TO FUNCTION

The best way of remembering something is to understand it. Okay, so this is not always possible as some things need to be memorised parrot fashion—the Krebb's cycle, for instance. The friendly biochemist will not wave you through the viva just because you understand its concept, he still wants the mind-numbing details of the numbers of adenosine triphosphates, etc. However, in many other areas, facts are far more easily remembered if they are understood. Anatomy is one example. In my experience ploughing through *Cunningham's Anatomy* (a manual for dissection) was like the worst form of self-flagellation. Never has a book been written before or since that was so dull, verbose, opaque, difficult to plough through, unimaginative, unenlightening, tedious, and unrelated to function. Some of the sentences would drone on for what seemed like days, veiling any potentially memorable facts in a surfeit of heavy medical terminology and Latin. It was a great cure for insomnia but carried the risk of inducing narcolepsy. Far, far better are the books which explain things in as simple a way as possible, and, better still, relate dry fact to function. It is much easier to remember the effects of different muscle groups if you have visualised the results of their malfunction. Similarly, textbooks that show pictures of patients with particular medical conditions make it far easier to recall the sequelae of these conditions. A picture is worth a thousand words, especially if they are cloaked in pompous medical terminology.

DO NOT COMPARE YOURSELF WITH OTHERS

People who claim that they have done no work will try and convince you that the clavicle will come up, the first rib is a "dead cert." Do not listen. Others will work but for a fraction of the time you need to. They may have partially photographic memories. They may have far better concentration. Their neurons may be more supple and adept. However, you cannot hone your brain by sending it to the gym. You are stuck with your grey cells. They may be greyer and more dingy than your best mate's, but deal with it.

CATEGORISE AND COMPARTMENTALISE

When a chapter is fresh in your mind, 10 minutes after reading it for the 67th time, it may seem as if all the facts contained within it will spring forth effortlessly the next time you summon them. However, three months down the line, your only memories of it may be that it was a large and fact-filled chapter of which you have no recollection. Because of this, it is a good idea to categorise and compartmentalise whenever you can. If the chapter gives you a load of different drugs that can be used in a particular disorder, categorise them into their different methods of action. Then, if you just understand these different modes, you will be able to recollect the categories at a later date and give an example of a drug in each group. Similarly, if a particular disease has effects on many different parts of the body, try and compartmentalise these into different organ systems. If you remember the headings the small print will follow. And the headings are much easier to recall if they are filed away in some logical order.

TEST YOURSELF

As studying is so unpleasant, it is tempting to just cram facts into your cerebrum without testing whether they can be retrieved. My motives for not testing recall were an ostrich-like reluctance to face the possibility of retrieval failure. This is not a good approach. You want to make sure the traffic is two-way. Trying to extract stringy bits of knowledge from your brain for the first time in the exam is stressful and doomed to failure.

PRACTICE THE RELEVANT FORM

If the exam will include multiple choice questions (MCQs)/essays/short answers/vivas/spot dissections, make sure you practise these endlessly. When I started swotting for my part 1 MRCP [Membership of the Royal Colleges of

Physicians of the United Kingdon], I read and learnt *Kumar and Clarke,* my favourite textbook, three times. Then I attempted an MCQ and got about 20 percent. For the next few months, I abandoned the textbooks and practised MCQs endlessly. It was the right thing to do.

As a final word of encouragement, despite my loathing of study, I have passed all parts of the MRCP and the FRCA (fellowship of the Royal College of Anaesthetists) the first time simply by sticking to the rules above, in particular the last one—that is, practising the relevant type of questions over and over. The only test I have ever failed is my driving test. I did not practise the format I was tested on—that is, driving!

DISCUSSION

1. Using this textbook as a point of contrast to the required texts in other courses, discuss the following with your classmates:
   a. Did you actually purchase the text?
   b. When do you use it—frequently and in conjunction with class meetings?
   c. What suggestions do you have for other students on how to get more value out of this particular text?
2. Of the other texts you are using this term, which poses the greatest challenges for you? Which of the specific suggestions in this chapter can you use to improve your understanding and ability to use the textbook? Share these in discussion with other students.
3. Compare and contrast how your instructors are using their required texts in terms of material presented/discussed in class and the materials for which you are held accountable in examinations. What patterns did you discover? Bottom line: do your textbooks help you learn? Defend your answer.
4. The reading selection "How to Study" relates the experiences of a British student. Compare its advice to that contained in this chapter from your American authors and share your reactions with fellow students. Are your courses as dependent on "studying" text materials as this British student's would appear to be?

CHAPTER 8

Taking Tests

Jeanne L. Higbee of the University of Minnesota, Twin Cities, contributed her valuable and considerable expertise to the writing of this chapter.

IN THIS CHAPTER, YOU WILL LEARN

- How to prepare for an exam
- Study tips that will help improve your grades
- How to do better on essay exams
- Strategies for succeeding on various kinds of objective tests
- How to handle a take-home exam
- How cheating hurts you, your friends, and your college

Now that you've learned how to listen and take notes in class and how to read and review your notes and assigned readings, you're ready to use those skills to achieve high scores on tests and exams.

Many students entering college assume that every problem has a single right answer and the instructor or the text-book is always a source of truth. Actually, though, some questions may have more than one correct answer, and your teachers may accept a number of answers as long as they correctly answer the question.

Most college instructors expect you to use higher-level thinking skills like analysis, synthesis, and evaluation. They want you to be able to support your opinions, to see *how* you think. You can cough up a list of details from lecture notes or readings, but unless you can make sense of them, you probably won't get much credit.

Exams: The Long View

You actually began preparing for a test on the first day of the term. All of your lecture notes, assigned readings, and homework were part of that preparation. As the test day nears, you should know how much additional time you will need to review, what material the test will cover, and what format the test will take.

Three things will help you study well:

- **Ask your instructor.** Ask whether the exam will be essay, multiple-choice, true/false, or another kind of test. Ask if the test covers the entire term's worth of material, or just the material since the last test. Ask how long the test will last and how it will be graded. Some instructors may let you see copies of old exams, so you can see the types of questions they use. Never miss the last class before an exam, because your instructor may summarize valuable information.

- **Manage your time wisely.** Have you laid out a schedule that will give you time to review effectively for the exam, without waiting until the night before?
- **Sharpen your study habits.** Have you created a body of material from which you can effectively review what is likely to be on the exam? Is that material organized in a way that will enable you to study efficiently?

Planning Your Approach

Physical Preparation

1. **Maintain your regular sleep routine.** Don't cut back on your sleep in order to cram in additional study hours. Remember that most tests will require you to *apply* the concepts that you have studied, and you must have all your brain power available. Especially during final exam periods, it is important to be well rested in order to remain alert for extended periods of time.

2. **Maintain your regular exercise program.** Walking, jogging, swimming, or other aerobic activities are effective stress reducers, may help you think more clearly, and provide positive—and needed—breaks from studying.

3. **Eat right.** You really are what you eat. Avoid drinking more than one or two caffeinated drinks a day or eating foods that are high in sugar or fat. Eat a light breakfast before a morning exam. Greasy or acidic foods might upset your stomach. To maintain a good energy level, choose fruits, vegetables, and foods that are high in complex carbohydrates. Consider a banana, a slice of cantaloupe, or other foods high in potassium to help prevent muscle cramps. You also might take a bottle of water to the exam.

Emotional Preparation

1. **Know your material.** If you have given yourself adequate time to review, you will enter the classroom confident that you are in control. Study by testing yourself or quizzing one another in a study group so you will be sure you really know the material.

2. **Practice relaxing.** Some students experience upset stomachs, sweaty palms, racing hearts, or other unpleasant physical symptoms before an exam. See your counseling center about relaxation techniques.

3. Use positive self-talk. Instead of telling yourself "I never do well on math tests" or "I'll never be able to learn all the information for my history essay exam," make positive statements, such as "I have attended all the lectures, done my homework, and passed the quizzes. Now I'm ready to pass the test!"

Design an Exam Plan

The week before the exam, set aside a schedule of one-hour blocks for review, along with notes on what you specifically plan to accomplish during each hour.

Join a Study Group

Study groups can help students develop better study techniques. In addition, group members can benefit from differing views of instructors' goals, objectives, and emphasis; have partners to quiz them on facts and concepts; and gain the enthusiasm and friendship of others to help sustain their motivation.

Study groups can meet throughout the term, or they can review for midterms or final exams. Group members should complete their assignments before the group meets and prepare study questions or points of discussion ahead of time.

Before a major exam, work together to devise a list of potential questions for review. Then spend time studying separately to develop answers, outlines, and mind maps (discussed below). The group should then reconvene shortly before the test to share answers and review.

Tutoring and Other Support

Often excellent students seek tutorial assistance to ensure their A's. In the more common large lecture classes for first-year students, you have limited opportunity to question instructors. Tutors know the highlights and pitfalls of the course. Most tutoring services are free. Ask your academic advisor or counselor or campus learning center. Most academic support centers or learning centers have computer labs that can provide assistance for course work. Some offer walk-in assistance for help in using word processing, spreadsheet, or statistical computer programs. Often computer tutorials are available to help you refresh basic skills. Math and English grammar programs may also be available, as well as access to the Internet.

Now It's Time to Study

Through the consistent use of proven study techniques, you will already have processed and learned most of what you need to know. Now you can focus your study efforts on the most challenging concepts, practice recalling information, and familiarize yourself with details.

Review Sheets, Mind Maps, and Other Tools

To prepare for an exam covering large amounts of material, you need to condense the volume of notes and text pages into manageable study units. Review your materials with these questions in mind: Is this one of the key ideas in the chapter or unit? Will I see this on the test? You may prefer to highlight, underline, or annotate the most important ideas, or you may create outlines, lists, or visual maps containing the key ideas. Or you can use large pieces of paper to summarize main ideas chapter by chapter or according to the major themes of the course. Look for relationships between ideas. Try to condense your review sheets down to one page of essential information. Key words on this page can bring to mind blocks of information. A *mind map* is essentially a review sheet with a visual element. Its word and visual patterns provide you with highly charged clues to jog your memory. Because they are visual, mind maps help many students recall information more easily.

Figure 8.1 shows what a mind map might look like for a chapter on listening and learning in the classroom. See if you can reconstruct the ideas in the chapter by following the connections in the map. Then make a visual mind map for this chapter and see how much more you can remember after studying it a number of times.

In addition to review sheets and mind maps, you may want to create flash cards or outlines. Also, do not underestimate the value of using the recall column from your lecture notes to test yourself or others on information presented in class.

Summaries

A written summary can be helpful in preparing for essay and short-answer exams. By condensing the main ideas into a concise written summary, you store information in your long-term memory so you can retrieve it to answer an essay question. Here's how:

1. **Predict a test question from your lecture notes or other resources.** For example, one of the major headings in this chapter reads, "Join a Study Group." From this you might predict a question such as "Discuss the merits of joining a study group."
2. **Read the chapter, article, notes, or other resources.** Underline or mark main ideas as you go, make notations, or outline on a separate sheet.

Figure 8.1 Sample Mind Map on Listening and Learning in the Classroom

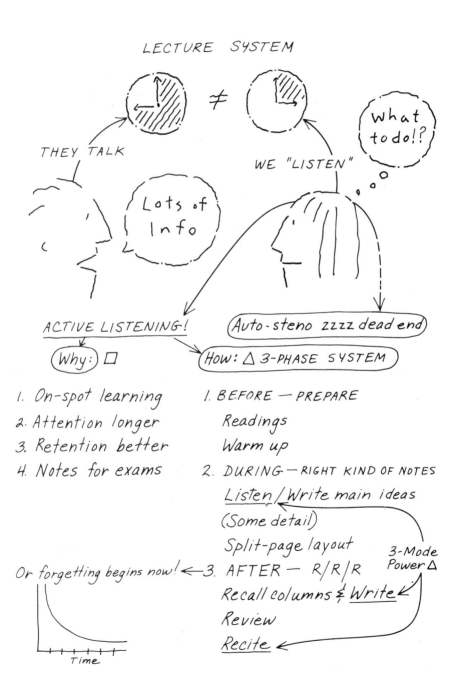

3. **Analyze and abstract.** What is the purpose of the material? Does it compare, define a concept, or prove an idea? What are the main ideas?
4. **Make connections between main points and key supporting details.** Reread to identify each main point and supporting evidence.
5. **Select, condense, and order.** Review underlined material and begin putting the ideas into your own words. Number in a logical order what you underlined or highlighted.
6. **Write your ideas precisely in a draft.** In the first sentence, state the purpose of your summary. Follow with each main point and its supporting ideas.
7. **Review your draft.** Read it over, adding missing transitions or insufficient information. Check the logic of your summary. Indicate the sources you used for later reference.
8. **Test your memory.** Put your draft away and try to recite the contents of the summary to yourself out loud, or explain it to a study partner who can provide feedback on the information you have omitted.
9. **Schedule time to review summaries and double-check your memory shortly before the test.** You may want to do this with a partner, but some students prefer to review alone.

Taking the Test

1. **Print your name on the test and answer sheet**—and sign it if your campus requires a signature.
2. **Analyze, ask, and stay calm.** Take a long, deep breath and slowly exhale before you begin. Read all the directions so that you understand what to do. Ask for clarification if you don't understand something. Be confident. Don't panic. Answer one question at a time. For an essay exam, read all questions first so that your mind can be thinking ahead.
3. **Make the best use of your time.** Quickly survey the entire test and decide how much time you will spend on each section. Be aware of the point values of different sections of the test. Are some questions worth more points than others?
4. **Answer the easy questions first.** Expect that you'll be puzzled by some questions. Make a note to come back to them later. If different sections consist of different types of questions (such as multiple-choice, short answer, and essay), complete the type of question you are most comfortable with first. Be sure to leave enough time for any essays.
5. **If you feel yourself starting to panic or go blank, stop whatever you are doing.** Take a long, deep breath and slowly exhale. Remind

yourself you will be okay and that you do know your stuff and can do well on this test. Then take another deep breath. If necessary, go to another section of the test and come back later to the item that triggered your anxiety.

6. **If you finish early, don't leave.** Stay and check your work for errors. Reread the directions one last time. If using a Scantron answer sheet, make sure that all answers are bubbled completely and correctly.

Essay Questions

Some types of exams tend to be exercises in memorization. Many college teachers, however, including the writers of this book, have a strong preference for the essay exam because it promotes higher-order critical thinking. Generally, the closer you are to graduation, the more essay exams you'll take. To be successful on essay exams, follow these guidelines:

1. **Budget your exam time.** Quickly survey the entire exam and note the questions that are the easiest for you, along with their point values. Take a moment to estimate the approximate time you should allot to each question, and write the time beside each number. Be sure you know whether you must answer all the questions or choose among questions. Start with the questions that are easiest for you, and jot down a few ideas before you begin to write. Wear a watch so you can monitor your time, including time at the end for a quick review.

2. **Develop a very brief outline of your answer before you begin to write.** Use your first paragraph to introduce the main points, and subsequent paragraphs to describe each point in more depth. If you find that you are running out of time and cannot complete an essay, at the very least provide an outline of key ideas. You will usually earn more points by responding to all parts of the question briefly than by addressing just one aspect of the question in detail.

3. **Write concise, organized answers.** Many well-prepared students write fine answers to questions that may not have been asked because they did not read a question carefully or did not respond to all parts of the question. Answers that are vague and rambling tend to be downgraded by instructors. You are less likely to ramble if you write an outline beforehand and stick to it.

4. **Know the key task words in essay questions.** Being familiar with the key word in an essay question will help you answer it more specifically. The following key task words appear frequently on essay tests. Take time to learn them, so that you can answer essay questions more accurately and precisely.

Analyze To divide something into its parts in order to understand it better.

Compare To look at the characteristics or qualities of several things and identify as well as define how the things are alike and how they are different.

Contrast To identify the differences between things.

Criticize/Critique To analyze and judge something. A criticism should generally contain your own judgments (supported by evidence) and those of other authorities who can support your point.

Define To give the meaning of a word or expression.

Describe To give a general verbal sketch of something, in narrative or other form.

Discuss To examine or analyze something in a broad and detailed way.

Evaluate To discuss the strengths and weaknesses of something. Evaluation is similar to criticism, but the word *evaluate* places more stress on the idea of how well something meets a certain standard or fulfills some specific purpose.

Explain To clarify something. Explanations generally focus on why or how something has come about.

Interpret To explain the meaning of something.

Justify To argue in support of some decision or conclusion by showing sufficient evidence or reasons in its favor.

Narrate To relate a series of events in the order in which they occurred.

Outline To present a series of main points in appropriate order. Ask the instructor what type of outline he or she wants.

Prove To give a convincing logical argument and evidence in support of some statement.

Review To summarize and comment on the main parts of a problem or a series of statements.

Summarize To give information in brief form, omitting examples and details.

Trace To narrate a course of events. Where possible, show connections from one event to the next.

Multiple-Choice Questions

Preparing for multiple-choice tests requires you to actively review all of the material covered in the course. Reciting from flash cards, summary sheets, mind maps, or the recall column in your lecture notes is a good way to review these large amounts of material.

Take advantage of the many cues that multiple-choice questions contain. Careful reading of each item may uncover the correct answer. Always question choices that use absolute words such as *always, never,* and *only.* These choices are often incorrect. Also, read carefully when terms such as *not, except,* and *but* are introduced before the choices. Often the most inclusive answer is correct. Generally, options that do not agree grammatically with the first part of the item are incorrect.

If you are totally confused by a question, leave it and come back later, but always double-check that you are filling in the answer for the right question. Sometimes another question will provide a clue for a question you are unsure about. If you have absolutely no idea, and there is no penalty for guessing (ask your instructor), look for an answer that at least contains some shred of correct information.

True/False Questions

Remember, for the question to be true, every detail of the question must be true. Questions containing words such as *always, never,* and *only* are usually false, whereas less definite terms such as *often* and *frequently* suggest that the statement may be true. Read through the entire exam to see if information in one question will help you answer another. Do not begin to second-guess what you know or doubt your answers because a sequence of questions appears to be all true or all false.

Matching Questions

The matching question is the hardest to answer by guessing. In one column you will find the term, in the other the description of it. Before answering any question, review all of the terms or descriptions. Match those terms you are sure of first. As you do so, cross out both the term and its description, and then use the process of elimination to assist you in answering the remaining items.

Fill-in-the-Blank Questions

First, decide what kind of answer is required. Be certain that your answer completes the sentence grammatically as well as logically (for example, don't use a verb when a noun is required). Look for key words in the statement that could jog your memory.

Machine-Scored Tests

Don't make extra marks or doodles on the answer sheet. The machine can't tell the difference. Make certain you're bubbling in the right dot in the right row. If you decide to change an answer, erase the original mark completely. Otherwise it may cancel out both choices.

Take-Home Tests

A take-home test, by its nature, is an open-book test. This means your instructor will expect precise and comprehensive answers, since you are (a) not under the pressure of time and (b) able to look up facts without penalty. Take-home tests usually require a lot more of your time than the one or two hours of an in-class exam, and grading standards are usually higher.

Academic Honesty

Colleges and universities have academic integrity policies or honor codes that clearly define cheating, lying, plagiarism, and other forms of dishonest conduct, but it is often difficult to know how those rules apply to specific situations. Is it really lying to tell an instructor you missed class because you were "not feeling well" (whatever "well" means) or because you were experiencing vague "car trouble"? (Some people think car trouble includes anything from a flat tire to difficulty finding a parking spot.)

Types of Misconduct

Institutions vary widely in how they define broad terms such as lying or cheating. One university defines cheating as "intentionally using or attempting to use unauthorized materials, information, notes, study aids, or other devices . . . [including] unauthorized communication of information during an academic exercise." This would apply to looking over a classmate's shoulder for an answer, using a calculator when it is not authorized, procuring or discussing an exam (or individual questions from an exam) without permission, copying lab notes, purchasing term papers over the Internet, watching the video instead of reading the book, and duplicating computer files.

Plagiarism, or taking another person's ideas or work and presenting them as your own, is especially intolerable in academic culture. Just as taking someone else's property constitutes physical theft, taking credit for someone else's ideas constitutes intellectual theft.

On most tests, you do not have to credit specific individuals. (But some instructors do require this; when in doubt, ask!) In written reports and papers, however, you must give credit any time you use (1) another person's actual words, (2) another person's ideas or theories—even if you don't quote them directly, and (3) any other information not considered common knowledge.

Many schools prohibit other activities besides lying, cheating, unauthorized assistance, and plagiarism. For instance, the University of Delaware prohibits intentionally inventing information or results; the University of North Carolina, Chapel Hill, outlaws earning credit more than once for the same piece of academic work without permission; Eastern Illinois University rules out giving your work or exam answer to another student to copy during the actual exam or to a student in another section before the exam is given in that section; and the University of South Carolina at Columbia prohibits bribing in exchange for any kind of academic advantage. Most schools also outlaw helping or attempting to help another student commit a dishonest act.

Reducing the Likelihood of Problems

To avoid becoming intentionally or unintentionally involved in academic misconduct, consider the reasons it could happen.

- **Ignorance.** In a survey at USC Columbia, 20 percent of students incorrectly thought that buying a term paper wasn't cheating. Forty percent thought using a test file (a collection of actual tests from previous terms) was fair behavior. Sixty percent thought it was all right to get answers from someone who had taken an exam earlier in the same or a prior semester.
- **Cultural and campus differences.** In other countries and on some U.S. campuses, students are encouraged to review past exams as practice exercises. Some campuses permit sharing answers and information for homework and other assignments with friends.
- **Different policies among instructors.** Ask your instructors for clarification. When a student is caught violating the academic code of a particular school or teacher, pleading ignorance of the rules is a weak defense.
- **A belief that grades—not learning—are everything,** when actually the reverse is true. This may reflect our society's competitive atmosphere. In truth, grades measure nothing if one has cheated to earn them.
- **Lack of preparation or inability to manage time and activities.** Before you consider cheating, ask an instructor for an extension of your deadline.

Here are some steps you can take to reduce the likelihood of problems:

1. **Know the rules.** Learn the academic code for your school. Study course syllabi. If a teacher does not clarify his or her standards and expectations, ask.

2. Set clear boundaries. Refuse to "help" others who ask you to help them cheat. You don't owe anyone an explanation for why you won't participate in academic dishonesty. In test settings, cover your answers, keep your eyes down, and put all extraneous materials away.

3. Improve time management. Be well prepared for all quizzes, exams, projects, and papers. This may mean unlearning habits such as procrastination.

4. Seek help. Get help with study skills, time management, and test taking. If your methods are in good shape but the content of the course is too difficult, see your instructor, join a study group, or visit your campus learning center or tutorial service.

5. Withdraw from the course. Your school has a policy about dropping courses and a last day to drop without penalty. You may decide only to drop the course that's giving you trouble. Some students may choose to withdraw from all classes and take time off before returning to school if they find themselves in over their heads, or some unexpected occurrence has caused them to fall behind. Before you withdraw, you should ask about campus policies as well as ramifications in terms of federal financial aid and other scholarship programs. See your advisor or counselor.

6. Reexamine goals. Stick to your own realistic goals instead of giving in to pressure from family or friends to achieve impossibly high standards. You may also feel pressure to enter a particular career or profession of little or no interest to you. If so, sit down with counseling or career services professionals or your academic advisor and explore alternatives.

YOUR PERSONAL JOURNAL

1. Assuming you have taken an exam, what strategies did you use to prepare? How did they work? If you haven't taken an exam, what strategies do you plan to use? Why?

2. It has been said that exams only measure how well you can memorize information, and because some people have a natural-born talent for memorization, exams aren't fair. Can you support or punch any holes in this argument?

3. Are you facing any issues related to academic honesty? What are they? What are you doing about them?

4. If you knew you could get away with cheating on an exam, would you do it? Explain your answer.

5. What behaviors are you thinking about changing after reading this chapter? How will you go about changing them?
6. What else is on your mind this week? If you wish to share it with your instructor, add it to this journal entry.

READINGS

How to Ace College*

A Harvard professor reveals secrets from his 10-year study
of successful students.

By Alisha Davis

There's so much focus on how to get into college these days, and not much advice about what to do once you get there. Back in the 1980s, the then Harvard president Derek Bok asked Richard J. Light, a professor at the Harvard Graduate School of Education, to study students on campus. The result of this 10-year survey is the book *Making the Most of College: Students Speak Their Minds,* which offers practical advice to school administrators, parents, and, most importantly, to the students themselves. In an interview with *Newsweek*'s Alisha Davis, Light discusses how to translate good intentions into practice.

DAVIS: What was the most surprising thing you discovered?

LIGHT: I had originally anticipated that most students would want the leaders of the college or the leaders of the school to treat them as grown-ups and get out of their way. The surprise is that student after student, 70 to 75 percent, said, "We need advice. We don't know what to do. How do we know which is the right history course to choose? How do we know how much time to spend on extracurriculars or homework?"

DAVIS: You talk a lot about the importance of finding a faculty mentor or a teacher. How should students do that?

LIGHT: It takes some initiative. If you don't have a reason to go talk to a teacher, invent one. I am a student advisor, and the first thing I ask my freshmen is, "What is your job this semester?" Students always say, "My job is to work really really hard." And I say, "Excellent, but that's not enough. Your job is to get to know at least one faculty member this semester. Just think, you're going to be here for eight semesters. Even if you succeed only half the time, four years later, you will now have four faculty members who can write a job recommendation or serve as a reference." Kids almost always say they never thought about it that way.

DAVIS: What mistakes do parents make?

LIGHT: Although parents obviously mean well, they generally give lousy advice when it comes to picking courses. In terms of academics, the students who were least happy tended to get the requirements out of the way before getting to the "good stuff." They took big courses, and then they said they felt their first years were too anonymous. The happiest students took a mix of courses that included small seminars. When I asked the unhappy students why they took so many requirements, almost all of them said that's what their parents suggested. It's counterintuitive for parents, but students should be taking small, specialized courses from the start.

DAVIS: What was one of the concrete differences between those students who prospered and those who struggled?

LIGHT: The one word that most sharply differentiated the two groups was the word "time." For a bunch of middle-aged professors like me, the idea of time management is a no-brainer, but for students sometimes it's not as obvious. Students really have to keep an eye on how they spend their time, and I have two suggestions for them. The first is to make a thorough evaluation of their schedule. I tell students to keep track of how they spend their time every day for a week. The most important change students need to make is often not how much they study, but when. Studying in a long uninterrupted block is much more effective than studying in short bursts. All students are pressed for time, and they need to be with their friends and participating in extracurriculars. It's how you divide up that time that makes the difference. One busy undergraduate told me, "Every day has three halves: morning, afternoon, and evening. And if I can devote any one of those blocks of time to getting my academic work done, I consider that day a success." Other students can learn from that.

DAVIS: Why do you emphasize extracurricular activities in your book?

LIGHT: Students who are involved in extracurriculars are the happiest students on campus and also tend to be the most successful in the classroom. They find a way to connect their academic work to their personal lives. For example, I spoke to a young woman who was a ballet dancer in high school. She joined the college ballet company, but she kept getting stress fractures and noticed that many of the other dancers were having the same problem. She began to wonder why and she decided to explore that in her coursework. That decision changed her life. She took science classes. She applied for a research grant. When she graduated, she applied to medical school to become an orthopedic surgeon. Her whole education was so much more meaningful because it connected to her life. If students can apply what they are learning to their real life, they are more engaged and tend to get more out of it.

How to Be a Great Test Taker*

Three simple words can help you replace test anxiety with test confidence: prepare, prepare, prepare.

By Mark Rowh

Sometimes it seems that life is just one big test. Pop quizzes. Chapter tests. Final exams. The daunting national examinations for those planning to go to college. You can't even get your driver's license without passing a test.

"Tests are a part of life," says Judy S. Richardson, professor of reading at Virginia Commonwealth University in Richmond, Virginia. "We take tests all of the time. I recently had to take one, even at my age, just to apply for a research grant. We may have to take them to apply for a job, or to join the armed forces."

IMPORTANCE OF TESTS

Tests are not just commonplace; they're also important. "Our society places an emphasis on test scores," says Maureen D. Gillette, associate dean of the College of Education at William Paterson University in New Jersey. "Most colleges and universities look at SAT or ACT tests as a measure of a student's potential for success in college. Students should realize that some people and institutions will make certain judgments about them, whether accurate or not, based on test scores."

Talk about pressure! With so much depending on the results, exams can be overwhelming. But they don't have to be. The right frame of mind and the use of smart test-taking strategies can help any student succeed.

Too often, people take a negative view of tests. Yet they actually have some positive features, according to Richardson. "Tests help us practice sharp, alert thinking," she says. "Answering test questions involves more than knowing a specific, literal answer. It also means knowing how to read between the lines, and then apply it to a situation. That is what we are expected to do every day, and so tests may help us be ready for that daily experience."

PROPER PREPARATION

In addition to these benefits, though, the primary goal in test taking is to do well. For some students, the objective might be a passing score. For others, the desired outcome might be an A grade. But what is the best guarantee of doing well in the testing process?

Career World, a Weekly Reader publication, September 2002, v31, i1, p. 8(8). Special permission granted. Published by Weekly Reader Corporation. All rights reserved.

The most basic factor, experts agree, is preparation. "Always be prepared for the test," Richardson advises. "Take notes, ask questions, read the material, guess what the teacher will be asking. Then when you see the test, you will have a confident reaction. You will be able to think clearly and do better on the test."

On the other hand, failing to prepare is the biggest mistake you can make. This may seem obvious. But in addition to lacking the necessary knowledge, lack of preparation can weaken your mental state.

"If you do not prepare all along, when you see the test, you may panic," Richardson notes. When fear creeps in, even the best student is unlikely to succeed.

Preparing for exams can include a variety of strategies. At a minimum, any important material should be read at least once, and preferably more, until you have absorbed the main points. Simply scanning over textbooks or notes is not enough.

"Reading it once is not studying," says Dr. Michael Epstein, professor of psychology at Rider University in New Jersey. He advocates taking a structured approach in which students review information both before a test and afterward.

Before taking an exam, you should commit important concepts to memory through focused study. Try using whatever memory techniques work best for you. This might mean writing notes, asking yourself questions and then answering them aloud, or employing clever memory devices.

MANAGING TIME

Key to the process is time management. Don't assume you can wait until the last minute and then make up for lost study time. Rather, be sure to prepare in advance. After all, you know tests will be coming up in virtually every course you take. Similarly, test dates for standardized tests are published months ahead of the actual dates.

"The most effective way to study for a test is to review briefly all along and then review some more before the test," Richardson says. "Cramming is not too effective."

Advance preparation need not be a solitary process. In fact, most teachers will work with you because they want students to succeed. So in the days or weeks preceding an exam, make sure to consult with your teacher and determine just what to expect. According to Dr. Douglas B. Reeves, author of *The 20-Minute Learning Connection: A Practical Guide for Parents Who Want to Help Their Children Succeed in School,* asking questions far in advance of a test is always a good idea.

"First, learn the rules of the game," he says. "It's OK to ask the teacher what the test covers. Teachers appreciate it when students express an interest and want to do well. You are not cheating [if you] ask about the material on the test and the types of questions that will be used."

Another strategy is to create practice test questions. "Put yourself in the teacher's shoes," Reeves says. "How would you test someone about this material? Of course, you can't create test questions unless you take time to read and learn the material."

Don't just mimic the efforts of other students. Analyze your own learning style, and employ methods that work best for you.

"Learn the ways you learn best," says Richardson. "I learn by taking notes and making charts. Some learn by making diagrams. Be active in listening to your teacher and reading the material. And try to summarize in your own mind what you learned each day. You can do this in the car on the way home, on the bus, and so forth—it takes just minutes to do."

Another tip is to hone your writing skills. "Of all the skills you can practice, the mastery of nonfiction writing is the one that will help you most in almost any test situation," says Reeves. "Even with a multiple-choice test, practice writing the reasons that a given answer is right or wrong."

STRENGTH IN NUMBERS

For some students, studying together can be helpful. "Study in groups," Gillette advises. "Most students retreat to individual spaces to study. If they have misconceptions or simply do not understand the material, they often study for hours but don't make any progress toward learning the material or preparing for a test."

To be effective, group study must include plenty of interaction. "When studying in small groups, use practice problems," Gillette says. "Discuss your answers together and share information. Then you'll have a greater understanding of why the correct answer is right and why incorrect ones are wrong."

When it comes time to sit down and take a test, make sure those giving the tests are aware of any special needs you might have. If you have a disability or your first language is not English, ask about measures such as a longer testing period or having a reader.

"If you need them, don't be afraid to utilize these supports," Gillette says. "A test should measure knowledge of the material tested, not the test taker's ability to use a particular format."

TACKLING STANDARDIZED TESTS

What about standardized tests such as the SAT? Many of the same strategies apply as for other types of examinations. In addition, it's wise to avoid getting caught up too much in the hype often associated with these exams.

"Prepare, but don't stress out," says Gillette. "If you study hard during the year, take appropriate courses in school, and do some test preparation, it is likely that you will do fine."

She adds that it can be worthwhile to take steps such as purchasing commercially made practice test material, studying in small groups as well as alone, doing practice problems, and using the answer key to discuss right and wrong answers.

"With measures like these, good students should have all the preparation they need," Gillette notes. "Many parents spend a lot of money on test preparation courses. Some people may value this route, but I really do not think it is necessary."

If you'd like to learn more about test-taking strategies, check out books on the subject along with Web sites such as the one provided by the National Council of Teachers of English at http://www.ncte.org. But don't depend too heavily on the World Wide Web.

"Remember, you can drown in Internet information," Reeves says. "When you are preparing for a test, you need focus, not 300 pages downloaded from the Web. Learn the rules of the game, get the information you need, and then write practice questions and practice responses. That's your best plan."

For More Information

For more information on test-taking strategies, check out these books:

No More Test Anxiety: Effective Steps for Taking Tests and Achieving Better Grades (includes audio CD) by Ed Newman. Learning Skills Publications.

The Student's Guide to Exam Success by Eileen Tracy. Open University Press.

Study Power: Study Skills to Improve Your Learning and Your Grades, by William R. Luckie. Brookline Books.

IF YOU DON'T DO WELL ON STANDARDIZED TESTS

What happens if you take the SAT or ACT exam and don't score as well as you would like? First, don't panic. You can always retake exams, and many students earn better scores with repeat efforts—especially after taking SAT preparation classes or otherwise focusing their efforts. Taking standardized tests two or three times may require some effort, but it can pay off.

At the same time, it's important to realize that colleges look at more than test scores when evaluating admission applications. Grades, extracurricular activities, leadership, and community service are all important. Special skills in areas such as music, athletics, or writing can also gain favorable attention. Of course, in the most competitive situations, students who have high test scores—along with other capabilities—will have the edge. But SAT or ACT scores are only part of the equation.

The kind of college you plan to attend makes a big difference too. Some schools—mainly community colleges—practice open admission. This means that anyone who can benefit is admitted. Many others admit students with less than stellar exam scores. If you're concerned about test scores, apply to several colleges with different admission standards. That way you'll be covered if you are not accepted by your first choice.

"Remember that a test score is not a measure of the worth of a person," says Maureen Gillette of William Paterson University. "I have known many students whose personal determination and drive for success are far greater predictors of academic achievement than their standardized test scores."

Five Steps for Test Success

Tests vary widely in approach and complexity. But these few basic steps will prove helpful for almost any type of exam.

1. **Be prepared.** It's simple but true: The better you know your subject, the more likely you are to succeed with any exam. Spend your time wisely, reading and rereading the material, answering practice questions, and so forth.

2. **Know how the test will be structured.** Before studying for a test, make sure you know how it will be set up. Will it include essay questions? True or false? Multiple choice? Ask your teacher just what to expect. If it is possible to preview some test questions in class well in advance of the actual test date, then do so. It may also help to compare notes with other students who have taken tests from the same teacher. In a way, taking a test is like running an obstacle course. The more you know about its layout, the better prepared you will be.

3. **Use your "test smarts."** While completing any exam, take full advantage of the time available. Don't just plow into answering questions. Read them carefully, and then answer each one with care. At the same time, be sure to pace yourself. Calculate how much time you have for each question, and make sure you don't run out of time before answering all the questions. If the test lists how many points are possible for each question, spend a greater proportion of your effort on those carrying the greatest weight.

4. **Stay calm.** When you're completing a test, try not to let your nerves get the best of you. Remember that even if you do not do well on a given exam, there will be more opportunities to improve your performance.

5. **Review results.** When a teacher returns a completed exam, don't make the mistake of looking only at your score. Instead, re-read any questions

you missed, and make sure you understand why they were wrong. By mastering the correct answer for such questions, you will increase your knowledge while also gaining a better understanding of what your teacher expects.

DISCUSSION

1. With a small group of your fellow students, decide which is more or less common in beginning college courses: objective (true/false, multiple choice, fill-ins, etc.) or subjective (essay) testing. Have each group member explain the difference between preparing for one type of test or the other.
2. In a discussion with fellow students, see if you can agree upon the common characteristics of an "easy" test versus a "hard" test. Then discuss whether it is the characteristics of the test or what students do to prepare for it, such as their listening, note taking, and exam preparation strategies as well as the instructors' teaching styles, that makes a test "hard" or "easy."
3. "How to Be a Great Test Taker" contains a number of memorable quotes, among them:

   "A test score is not a measure of the worth of a person."
   "Tests are a part of life."
   "Good writing skills can help you do better on tests."

   Divide your small group into three groups, with each one discussing the meaning behind each of these quotes. You are free to disagree with the quote as long as you can justify your argument.
4. Which tests do you perform best on? What seem to be the key variables: your attitude toward the course, how you prepare for it, the characteristics of the tests, or some combination of these?
5. In the interview on "How to Ace College," Richard J. Light summarizes a number of intriguing suggestions for college success. In a group, discuss which of the suggestions would be easiest for each group member to follow and why. Exchange ideas for using as many of the suggestions as you can.

CHAPTER 9

Writing and Speaking for Success

Constance Staley, University of Colorado, Colorado Springs, and R. Stephens Staley, Colorado Technical University, contributed their valuable and considerable expertise to the speech portion of this chapter.

IN THIS CHAPTER, YOU WILL LEARN

- How to get in the habit of writing down your first thoughts
- How to use reviews and revisions to strengthen your writing
- Six steps to success in preparing a speech
- How best to use your voice and body language

Think about it: Writing and speaking are direct representations of who we are. The words we write and speak communicate our innermost thoughts and feelings to others. This chapter will ask you to think of writing and speaking as *processes* (how you get there) as well as *products* (the final paper or presentation). It will help you overcome those "blocks" we all encounter from time to time.

The Power of Writing

William Zinsser, author of several books on writing, says, "The act of writing gives the teacher a window into the mind of the student."[1] In other words, your writing provides your teachers with tangible evidence of how well you think. Your writing might also reveal a good sense of humor, a compassion for the less fortunate, a respect for family, and many other things.

Put down this book for a moment and write the Zinsser quote at the top of a piece of blank paper. Look at the words for a few moments, pen in hand, and begin to write your thoughts about his statement. Don't worry about spelling, grammar, or punctuation because nobody else is going to read this. Yes, you

---

[1] William Zinsser, *On Writing Well* (New York: Harper Perennial, 1990).

147

read that correctly. Just keep writing for at least five to seven minutes. Then put your pen down and continue reading this chapter.

What happened? Were you able to write anything? Was what you wrote off track? Or did there come a point in your writing when you began to make connections from Zinsser's thought to thoughts of your own? Whatever your reaction may have been, the most important thing at this point is that you had something to say, and that you captured for later use some ideas (in writing)—even though they might have been rough.

Zinsser reminds us that writing is not merely something that writers do, but a basic skill for getting through life. He claims that far too many Americans are prevented from doing useful work because they never learned to express themselves. Because writing enables you to share your ideas, not just with a roomful of people but with thousands or millions, it can be a highly powerful tool.

Explore First, Explain Later

Very few writers, even professionally published ones, say what they want to say on their first try. And the sorry fact is that good writers are in the minority. Yet through practice, an understanding of the writing process, and dedication, people can improve their writing skills.

Writing serves two purposes. *Exploratory* writing helps you discover what you want to say; *explanatory* writing lets you transmit your ideas to others.

Explanatory writing is "published" so that others may read it (your teacher, your friends, other students, magazine subscribers, those who buy books at amazon.com), but it is important that much of your exploratory writing be private, to be read only by you as a series of steps toward your published work.

Some writers say they gather their best thoughts through exploratory writing by researching their topic, writing down ideas from their research, and adding their questions and reactions to what they have gathered. As they write, their minds begin to make connections between ideas. They don't attempt to organize, to find exactly the right words, or to think about structure. That might interrupt the thoughts that seem to magically flow onto the paper or computer screen. Of course, when they go from exploratory to explanatory, their preparation will help them form crystal-clear thoughts, spell correctly, and organize their material so it flows naturally from one point to the next.

If a teacher asks to see all of your drafts, remember that your prewriting is not a draft and keep it private.

Three Steps to Better Writing

Most writing teachers agree that the writing process consists of three steps:

- **Prewriting or rehearsing.** This step includes preparing to write by reading assigned work and doing other research. It is generally considered exploratory writing.
- **Writing or drafting.** This is when exploratory writing becomes a rough explanatory draft.
- **Rewriting or revision.** This is where you polish your work until you consider it done.

The reason many students turn in poorly written papers is that they skip the first and last steps and "make do" with the middle one. Perhaps it's a lack of time or putting off things until the night before the paper is due. Whatever the reason, the result is often a poorly written assignment.

Prewriting

Many writing experts believe that, of all the steps, prewriting is the one that should take the longest. This is when you write down all you think you need to know about a topic and then dig for the answers.

You might question things that seem illogical. You might recall what you've heard others say. This may lead you to write more, to ask yourself whether your views are more reliable than those of others, whether the topic may be too broad or too narrow, and so forth. Test your topic by writing "The purpose of this paper is to convince my instructor that . . ." Know the limits of your knowledge, the limitations on your time, and your ability to do enough research.

Writing for Organization

Once you feel you have exhausted all information sources and ideas, it's time to move to the writing, or drafting, stage. Now you will want to put things where they logically belong, build your paper around an acceptable topic, begin paying attention to the flow of ideas from one sentence to the next and from one paragraph to the next, and include subheadings where needed. When you have completed this stage, you will have the first draft of your paper in hand.

Rewriting to Polish

Are you finished? Not by a long shot. The essence of good writing is rewriting. You read. You correct. You add smoother transitions. You slash through wordy sentences or paragraphs that add nothing to your paper. You substitute stronger words for weaker ones. You double-check spelling and grammar. You continue to revise until you're satisfied. And then you "publish."

Finding a Topic

In *Zen and the Art of Motorcycle Maintenance,* Robert Pirsig tells a story about his first-year English class. Each week their assignment was to turn in a 500-word essay. One week, a student failed to submit her paper about the town where the college was located, explaining that she had "thought and thought, but couldn't think of anything to write about." Pirsig replied, "I want you to write a 500-word paper just about Main Street, not the whole town," he said.

Monday she arrived in tears, and with no paper. Pirsig's answer: "Write a paper about one building on Main Street. The opera house. And start with the first brick on the lower left side. I want it next class."

The student's eyes opened wide. She walked into class the next time with a 5,000-word paper on the opera house.

"I don't know what happened," she exclaimed. "I sat across the street and wrote about the first brick, then the second, and all of a sudden I couldn't stop."[2]

Getting started is what blocks most students from approaching writing properly. Presig had helped this student find a focus, a place to begin. She probably began to see, for the first time, the beauty of the opera house and had gone on to describe it, to find out more about it in the library, to ask others about it, and to comment on its setting among other buildings on the block.

Allocating Your Time for Writing

When Donald Murray—one of the pioneers of a "process" approach to teaching writing—was asked how long a writer should spend on each of the three stages, he offered this thought:

> Prewriting 85% (including research and rumination)
> Writing 1% (the first draft)
> Rewriting 14% (revising till it's right)

Do the figures surprise you? If they do, here's a true story about a writer who was assigned to create a brochure. He had other jobs to do and kept avoiding that one. But the other work he was doing had a direct bearing on the brochure he was asked to write. So as he was putting this assignment off, he was also "researching" material for it.

---

[2] Robert Pirsig, *Zen and the Art of Motorcycle Maintenance* (New York: Bantam Books, 1984).

After nearly three months, he could stand it no longer. So he sat at his computer and dashed the words off in just under 30 minutes. He felt a rush of ideas, he used words and phrases he'd never used before, and he was afraid to stop until he'd finished. He did some revising, sent it around the office, took some suggestions, and eventually the brochure was published.

He had spent a long time "prewriting" (working with related information without trying to write the brochure). He went through the "writing" stage quickly because his mind was primed for the task. As a result, he had time to polish his work before deciding the job was done.

Tips for Becoming a Better Writer and Thinker

To become a better writer and thinker, start writing the day you get the assignment, even if it's only for 10 or 15 minutes. That way, you won't be confronting blank-paper anxiety later in the week. Write something every day, because the more you write, the better you'll write. Dig for ideas. Reject nothing at first; then organize and narrow your thoughts. Read good writing and begin copying it; you will soon find your own writing style, and then you can stop copying the styles of others. Above all, know that becoming a better thinker and writer takes hard work, but practice—in this case—can make near-perfect.

Speaking in Public Need Not Be Scary

If the biggest writing problem for students is writer's block, then the biggest problem associated with speaking in front of others is fear.

Speaking in front of others appears to be the number-one fear of Americans. Surveys show that it's more frightening for most of us than death, sickness, deep water, financial problems, insects, or high places. Though it may be one of our most prevalent fears, it doesn't have to be. When it comes to holding forth in public, a few of us seem blessed with a wonderful sense of freedom, but most of us are more hesitant. Fortunately, your anxiety can help release the energy it takes to speak well to a group. It may help to keep the following in mind:

- Once you begin speaking, your anxiety is likely to decrease. Anxiety is highest right before or during the first seconds of a presentation.
- Your listeners will generally be unaware of your anxiety. Although your heart sounds as if it were pounding audibly or your knees feel as if they were knocking visibly, rarely is this the case.

- Some anxiety is beneficial. Anxiety indicates that your presentation is important to you. Channel your nervousness into energy, and harness it to propel you enthusiastically through your talk.
- Practice is the best preventive. The best way to reduce your fears is to prepare and rehearse thoroughly. World-famous violinist Isaac Stern is rumored to have once said, "I practice 8 hours a day for 40 years, and they call me a genius?!"

Steps to Successful Speaking

Clarify Your Objective

Begin by identifying what you want to accomplish. Do you want to persuade your listeners that your campus needs additional student parking? Inform them about student government's accomplishments? What do you want your listeners to know, believe, or do when you are finished?

Analyze Your Audience

What do they already know about your topic? If you're going to give a presentation on the health risks of fast food, you'll want to know how much your listeners already know about fast food so you don't risk boring them or wasting their time. What do they want or need to know? How much interest do your classmates have in nutrition? Would they be more interested in some other aspect of college life? What are their attitudes toward me, my ideas, and my topic? How are they likely to feel about the ideas you are presenting? What attitudes have they cultivated about fast food?

Collect and Organize Your Information

One useful analogy is to think of yourself as guiding your listeners through the maze of ideas they already have to the new knowledge, attitudes, and beliefs you would like them to have.

Imagine you've been selected as a guide for next year's prospective first-year students and their parents visiting campus. Picture yourself in front of the administration building with a group of people assembled around you. You want to get and keep their attention in order to achieve your objective: raising their interest in your school.

Get Your Audience's Attention

To help your audience understand the purpose of your talk, you must get their attention right away. You can relate the topic to your listeners:

"Let me tell you what to expect during your college years here—at the best school in the state."

You can state the significance of the topic:

"Deciding on which college to attend is one of the most important decisions you'll ever make."

Or you can arouse their curiosity:

"Do you know the three most important factors students and their families consider when choosing a college?"

Or you can begin with a compelling quotation or paraphrase:

"Alexander Pope once said, 'A little learning is a dangerous thing; Drink deep or taste not the Pierian spring.' That's what a college education is all about."

Regardless of which method you select, remember that a well-designed introduction must not only gain the attention of the audience but also develop rapport with them, motivate them to continue listening, and preview what you are going to say during the rest of your speech.

Don't Forget Yourself

Even in a formal presentation, you will be most successful if you develop a comfortable style that's easy to listen to. Don't play a role. Instead, be yourself at your best, letting your wit and personality shine through.

Ideas, Ideas, Ideas!

Create a list of all the possible points you might want to make. Then write them out as conclusions you want your listeners to accept. For the typical presentation, about five main points are the most that listeners can process. After considering your list for some time, you decide that the following five points are critical:

- Tuition is reasonable.
- The faculty is composed of good teachers.
- The school is committed to student success.
- The campus is attractive.
- The campus is safe.

As you formulate your main ideas, keep these guidelines in mind:

- Each main point should include a single idea. Don't crowd main points with multiple messages, as in the following:

1. Tuition is reasonable, and the campus is safe.

2. Faculty are good teachers and researchers.

- Main points should cover relatively equal amounts of time. If you find enough material to devote 3 minutes to point 1 but only 10 seconds to point 2, rethink your approach.

Develop an Organizational Structure

For example, you may decide to use a chronological narrative approach, discussing the history of the college from its early years to the present. Or you may wish to use a problem-solution format in which you describe a problem (such as choosing a school), present the pros and cons of several solutions (the strengths and weaknesses of several schools), and finally identify the best solution (your school!).

Begin with your most important ideas. Writing an outline may be the most useful way to begin organizing. List each main point and subpoint separately on a note card. Spread the cards out on a large surface (such as the floor), and arrange, rearrange, add, and delete cards until you find the most effective arrangement. Then simply number the cards, pick them up, and use them to prepare your final outline.

As you organize your presentation, use transitions to guide your listeners. For example:

- "Now that we've looked at the library, let's move on to the gymnasium."
- "The first half of my presentation has identified our recreational facilities. Now let's look at the academic hubs on campus."

In speaking, as in writing, transitions make the difference between keeping your audience with you and losing them at an important juncture.

Exit Gracefully and Memorably

Someone once commented that a speech is like a love affair: Any fool can start it, but to end it requires considerable skill. Plan your ending carefully, realizing that most of the suggestions for introductions also apply to conclusions.

Whatever else you do, go out with style, impact, and dignity. Don't leave your listeners asking, "So that's it?" Subtly signal that the end is in sight (without the overused "So in conclusion"), summarize your major points, and then conclude confidently.

Choose Your Visual Aids

When visual aids are added to presentations, listeners can absorb 35 percent more information, and over time they can recall 55 percent more. You may choose to prepare a chart, show a video clip, write on the board, or distribute handouts. You may also use your computer to prepare overhead transparencies or dynamic PowerPoint presentations. As you select and use your visual aids, consider these rules of thumb:

- Make visuals easy to follow. Use readable lettering, and don't crowd information.
- Explain each visual clearly.
- Allow your listeners enough time to process visuals.
- Proofread carefully. Misspelled words hurt your credibility as a speaker.
- Maintain eye contact with your listeners while you discuss visuals. Don't turn around and address the screen.

Although a fancy PowerPoint slideshow can't make up for inadequate preparation or poor delivery skills, using quality visual aids can help you organize your material and help your listeners understand what they're hearing.

Prepare Your Notes

A better strategy than reading your speech or memorizing it is to memorize only the introduction and conclusion so that you can maintain eye contact and therefore build rapport with your listeners.

The best notes are a minimal outline from which you can speak extemporaneously. You will rehearse thoroughly in advance. But because you are speaking from brief notes, your choice of words will be slightly different each time you give your presentation, causing you to sound prepared but natural. You may wish to use note cards, because they are unobtrusive. After you become more experienced, you may want to let your visuals serve as notes. Eventually, you may find you no longer need notes.

Practice Your Delivery

As you rehearse, form a mental image of success rather than failure. Practice your presentation aloud several times beforehand to harness that energy-producing anxiety we've been talking about.

Begin a few days before your target date, and continue until you're about to go on stage. Make sure you rehearse aloud; thinking through your speech and talking through your speech have very different results. Practice before an audience—your roommate, a friend, your dog, even the mirror. Talking to something or someone helps simulate the distraction listeners cause. Consider audiotaping or videotaping yourself to pinpoint your own mistakes and to reinforce your strengths. If you can ask your practice audience to critique you, you'll have some idea of what changes you might make.

Using Your Voice and Body Language

Let your hands hang comfortably at your sides, reserving them for natural, spontaneous gestures. Don't lean over or hide behind the lectern. Plan to move comfortably about the room, without pacing nervously. Some experts suggest changing positions between major points in order to punctuate your presentation. Face your audience, and don't be afraid to move toward them while you're speaking. Make eye contact with as many listeners as you can. This helps you read their reactions, demonstrate confidence, and establish command.

As you practice, pay attention to the pitch of your voice, your rate of speech, and your volume. Project confidence and enthusiasm by varying your pitch. Speak at a rate that mirrors normal conversation, not too fast and not too slow. Consider varying your volume for the same reasons you vary pitch and rate—to engage your listeners and to emphasize important points.

Pronunciation and word choice are important. A poorly articulated word (such as "gonna" for "going to"), a mispronounced word ("nucular" for "nuclear"), or a misused word ("antidote" for "anecdote") can quickly erode credibility.

Consider your appearance. Convey a look of competence, preparedness, and success. As Lawrence J. Peter, author of *The Peter Principle,* says, "Competence, like truth, beauty, and a contact lens, is in the eye of the beholder."

YOUR PERSONAL JOURNAL

Here are several things to write about. Choose one or more, or choose another topic related to this chapter.

1. If you found the writing process in this chapter helpful, explain how. If not, tell why and explain how you write best.
2. How would you rate your writing on a scale of 1 to 5, with 5 being excellent? If you rate it high, tell why. If you rate it low, explain what steps you will take to improve.
3. If you have already given a speech in college, reflect on how it went.
   a. How did you handle your anxiety?
   b. What strategies did you use to prepare?
   c. What aspect of giving the speech were you most satisfied with? Least satisfied with?

4. What behaviors are you willing to change after reading this chapter? How might you go about changing them?

5. What else is on your mind this week? If you wish to share something with your instructor, add it to this journal entry.

READINGS

Ten Tips for Better Business Writing*
By Edwin Powell

Where once Medieval monks toiled for a lifetime over handwritten manuscripts, today's electronic technology allows us to zap our words around the globe in seconds, but it hasn't made us better writers. Arguably, the opposite has occurred. In deference to speed, our writing has often become increasingly terse and sloppy as we sacrifice quality to communicate faster.

Clear, effective business writing not only reads well, it's also good for one's business and career. Managers routinely turn down job candidates whose résumés and cover letters contain mistakes in grammar, spelling, and punctuation. Likewise, supervisors can use such mistakes to weed out candidates for promotions.

The best rationale for good writing falls under the heading of common sense. People won't respond to communications they don't understand. One of the master keys to success in any line of work is the ability to convey your ideas effectively to others, be they team members, superiors, or customers. You may have the greatest idea in the history of modern thought, but unless you can bring it beyond the confines of your own mind, it isn't worth much.

In the interest of improving written communication, try the following tips next time you write a business letter, memo, proposal, or other document. You will be able to send it with confidence, knowing your message will be better understood, because good writing makes for good business.

1. Know your purpose. Before you put down the first word, you need to know what you are writing about. This is a twofold question in that you not only need to know your subject matter, you also need to understand why you are writing. Do you intend to inform the reader, persuade him or her to accept your point of view, elicit a desired action by the reader, or some combination thereof? Keeping in mind the reason you are writing helps keep you focused and concise while avoiding the temptation to wander off topic.

OfficeSolutions, November-December 2003, v20, i6, p. 36(3). Reprinted with permission.

Sherry Roberts, a Greensboro, N.C.–based writer who offers seminars on improving business writing, suggests beginning any written piece with a one-line synopsis of the main point you wish to convey, not unlike the one-line descriptions of movies found in *TV Guide.* Use the synopsis as a focus point as you write.

"Your one-line synopsis is a grain of sand; it will help you begin. Large projects can be built from it, but the grain of sand itself is neither overwhelming nor intimidating," Roberts writes in the companion booklet to her seminar. "As you write, reread your one-line reminder. It will keep you grounded, focused, and on target. Know what you want before you begin to write, and the writing will come more easily."

2. Know your audience. Understanding your readers' needs and expectations will help you craft your written work to better meet those needs and expectations. If you are writing a report to insiders with whom you share detailed knowledge of the business task at hand, you can safely skip lengthy background information and use specialized jargon without having to stop and define it.

On the other hand, if you are writing a proposal for outside investors who may not understand all the nuances of your industry, use patience in explaining potentially unfamiliar terms and processes.

3. Be a reporter. The old news reporters' style of telling the who, what, where, and why makes good sense for business writing. "The chief financial officer [who] reports sales of widgets are up 20 percent [what] in the North American market [where], thanks in part to several large orders from defense contractor General Doohickey Corp. [why]." Make sure you cover these basics to ensure you haven't left out anything important.

4. Keep it concise. Regardless of what you may have been taught in school, writing more doesn't necessarily equate to writing better—especially in a business environment, where time is precious. When you send someone a written communication—be it a memo, a proposal, or an annual report— you are asking them to invest time reading the document and mentally digesting its contents. Because the reader usually has many other pressing matters, make things easy by minimizing excess verbiage and organizing information in an accessible manner. Following the list below can help keep your writing concise.

   - Avoid long, convoluted sentences—keep it simple and direct.
   - Provide a summary for long documents.
   - Use bullet lists to express multiple ideas with minimal verbiage.
   - Avoid redundancy.

* Be direct—don't wander off topic or bury your most important points under unnecessary verbiage.

5. Keep it simple. The importance of simplicity cannot be overstated. We learn in school to make our writing sound sophisticated by using complex sentence structures and big, fancy words, but in business writing these characteristics only make writing harder to understand. For best results, use simple, direct sentence structures and plain, unambiguous words.

6. Use active voice. Passive voice, telling what happened, but not who did it, is one of the most easily overcome pitfalls to good writing. By using active voice, telling not only the action but also the actor, you provide more information for your reader and give your message a more authoritative tone. Writing "Our team closed the deal Thursday" makes a stronger statement than "The deal was closed Thursday" because it places the emphasis on who closed the deal, instead of that the deal was closed.

7. Don't offend. Political correctness may seem a nuisance, but a major part of knowing the needs and expectations of your readers is being aware of their sensibilities. Avoid language that could be interpreted as a slight against a particular gender, ethnic group, or other segment of the population.

Some of the most difficult bad habits to break involve gender, as many devices commonly used in business writing show an outdated gender bias. Many women in the workplace, for instance, take offense at receiving a business letter that opens with the salutation "Dear Gentlemen." Likewise, many of us learned in school to use masculine personal pronouns (*he, him, his*) in situations where a gender is not specified. Today, this practice receives an almost universal thumbs down. Although some writers move to the opposite extreme by using the feminine pronouns (*she, her, hers*) in an inclusive manner, the more acceptable practice is to be truly inclusive by using both (*he* or *she, him* or *her*) or circumvent the issue by using a plural. Instead of saying, "Each employee must wear his or her ID badge," it is better to say, "All employees must wear their ID badges."

8. Be consistent. There is more than one way to construct a grammatically correct sentence. Take, for instance, the issue of serial commas. *The Chicago Manual of Style* suggests using them (Crosby, Stills, Nash, and Young), while the *Associated Press Stylebook* recommends avoiding them (Crosby, Stills, Nash and Young). Likewise, whether you write a phone number as (123) 456-7890 or 123-456-7890 is largely a matter of taste.

Unless your organization uses a specific style manual for its written communications, the most important thing is to remain consistent, both within a particular document, and from document to document.

9. Don't depend on spell check alone. Sure, your word processor's spell checker is good for finding misspelled words, but we all know it's not perfect, especially if your typo happens to be a word in its own right, such as typing *fro* instead of *for.* Always supplement an electronic spell check with good old-fashioned eyeballing. Even better, find a coworker who is willing to give it a once over before you turn it in. It may even be to your mutual advantage to agree to check each other's work as a matter of course.

10. Don't just write—rewrite. Revision is a necessity in good writing. Written work seldom, if ever, reaches its complete, final, and polished form in a single draft. Revising a document—usually more than once—allows an opportunity for making major and minor fixes to improve the message. Fortunately, modern word processors make the task of revision quick and painless.

A three-draft method works well for creating well-polished documents. When working on each draft, focus on a specific set of tasks. The first (rough) draft is for setting the ideas in place, more or less as you need them to appear in the final version. The second (content review) draft is for refining those ideas, adding missing points, deleting superfluous items, and sequencing the result for a logical and comprehensible flow. The third and final (proofreading) draft is for addressing mechanical issues such as spelling, punctuation, and sentence structure. While it is fine to fix a misspelled word or misplaced punctuation mark on the first or second draft, or shift a couple of sentences around in the third draft, it is best to focus on editing tasks specific to that draft.

Delivering the Goods*

Memorable presentation starts with organizing your thoughts in writing

By Phil Venditti

Every day, for better or worse, Americans conduct approximately 33 million meetings. Many of these gatherings take place in business settings and involve oral presentations.

---

*This article appeared in the *Wenatchee Business Journal,* January 2004, v18, i1, p. C5(2). Copyright 2004 Phil Venditti. Reprinted with permission from the author.

Can you rise to the occasion when your turn comes to make such a presentation?

. . . Organizing your thoughts well in writing constitutes the first step toward successful business speaking. Information and argumentation which unfold logically can capture and retain an audience's attention the way a skilled pinball player keeps a ball in play, sounding bells and racking up points.

Once you've arrayed your central ideas logically on paper, though, another major challenge remains: actually conveying them in words, face-to-face, to a group.

Research indicates that the body language and tones of voice associated with a spoken message pack 10 times or more impact than its words do, so you should manage those nonverbal elements carefully in ways that further your purposes.

Here are some hints for smoothing out bumps on the path from ideas to action in public speaking:

1. After you're sure of your main points, bracket the body of your presentation outline with a well-defined introduction and conclusion which preview and review those points. In other words, be certain that your audience will know up front what you're going to tell them and that they will be reminded when you're done of what you've told them.

If the introduction and conclusion refer to one and the same situation or idea, like matching bookends holding together a row of volumes on a shelf, so much the better.

You might want to pose a question in your introduction, for example, and answer it in your conclusion. Memorizing a presentation or speech in full, if you had time to do it, might seem like a good way to prevent nervousness and ensure that you say exactly what you want to. Unfortunately, it's also likely to make your remarks sound canned.

You should commit your introduction and conclusion to memory, however, so you can say them with fluency and emotion.

2. Decide on a powerful "grabber" and a memorable "clincher" for your comments. These few sentences—the first and last sounds out of your mouth when you address an audience—should set your presentation apart from anything else they've ever experienced.

They should be dynamic enough to engage your listeners' awareness at a visceral as well as an intellectual level. Try using a rhetorical question, a quotation, a surprising fact, or perhaps a brief story as your first or last words. One speaker I heard at a Rotary meeting in Wenatchee began his presentation by asking each person in the audience to lightly tap the shoulder of someone nearby and then nudge that person a bit.

"Now," he said, "all of you can say after my speech that you were touched and moved."

3. Resist the urge to spout formula phrases to start and end a presentation. In my view, clichés like, "It's good to be here," and, "Thank you very much for listening," rarely amount to more than fluff. If you insist on saying such things and can do so sincerely, however, I'd suggest putting them just after your grabber and just before your clincher rather than making them your initial and final utterances.

4. Decide how you'll use movement and gestures to advantage. Many people tend naturally to freeze up when they first stand before a new audience. Their bearing looks stiff, and they hold their arms close to their bodies. If you expect to experience symptoms like these, you can take a couple of deliberate measures to loosen up.

First, consciously use the "speaker's triangle": Shift your position, even if just a foot or so, when you make the transition from one point to another in your outline.

Second, hold your hands at least waist-high throughout your entire presentation; this will increase the likelihood that you'll gesture spontaneously at least once in a while.

These strategies may feel awkward at first. As you repeat them on numerous occasions, though, they'll evolve into integral parts of your uniquely personal brand of speaking.

5. Plan to vary your tone of voice. To see whether your natural delivery style includes a large enough range of tones to be interesting, speak a few paragraphs of a manuscript to yourself with your mouth closed. Ideally, the flow of sound you hear will include melodious peaks and valleys. When you have a pretty clear idea of what you want to say, try recording yourself electronically—preferably with at least an audiotape, and ideally with videotape.

6. Assuming you don't write a word-for-word text for your presentation—and I do recommend against creating such a text—you should prepare an outline of some sort to take with you when you speak. You might want to use a "delivery outline"—a text which you mark up with a highlighter and marginal notes to show your main points and identify how you want to stress particular ideas through pacing, intonation, gestures, and audience involvement.

7. Always use some kind of audiovisual aids. My father took a class in college from a professor who once spent two hours lecturing about a complex

philosophical concept, using nothing but a small dot on the blackboard to supplement his remarks. The dot helped the professor's students follow his reasoning, if for no other reason than that it relieved them of having nothing to look at but him.

John Hilton, a respected BBC radio commentator in the 1930s and '40s, maintained a simple credo: "Truth, not tricks." Hilton was right in claiming that truth is essential to good business communication, including oral presentations.

At the same time, learning the delivery techniques we've covered here can add to the attractiveness and power of your presentations. It might even help you rise to the top of the millions of daily meetings taking place in our country.

DISCUSSION

1. Have a brainstorming session with other students and generate a list of all the potential ways you might use writing in your intended career. If you are undecided about career choice, that's fine; just try to imagine yourself in any type of work that you might enjoy. Are there any occupations in which writing will play little or no role? How will college help you build writing skills that will help you later in life?
2. What kinds of activities could you could engage in during college that will develop your speaking skills—both in the courses you take and in college-related activities outside of class?
3. Share examples of times when you have experienced a fear of public speaking. Tell what you did about it and whether it worked. Then decide which of the techniques in the chapter you might want to try.
4. Which of the ten tips for business writing can you apply to college writing? In a group, discuss which of the tips is (are) the most important and why. If the group agrees that one or more tips will be hard to accomplish, discuss ways to overcome those views.
5. In "Delivering the Goods," the author advises us to organize our thoughts in writing before preparing to speak. What's the advantage here? How can you tell when a speaker has skipped this initial step? Also, take turns in your group delivering a three-minute speech employing as many of the seven tips in the article as you can. What worked? What didn't?

Charles Curran and Rose Parkman
Marshall, both of the University
of South Carolina, Columbia,
contributed their valuable and
considerable expertise to the
writing of this chapter.

CHAPTER 10

Research and College Libraries

IN THIS CHAPTER, YOU WILL LEARN

- What the Information Age is about
- The differences between research and simply "finding stuff"
- The threats posed by GNI–galloping new ignorance
- Why information literacy is the survival skill for the 21st century
- How to focus on a topic, narrow it, and shape it
- Specific search strategies
- How plagiarism can doom a paper, a course, even a career!

Most colleges and universities describe their three major missions as teaching, research, and service. Information feeds research, and research produces discoveries that improve our quality of life. We are in the midst of an information explosion. Those who want to keep up, to participate, and to succeed in college, career, and community have to acquire the basic research and critical-thinking skills needed to make sense of the vast amount of information available at our fingertips. It means developing information literacy.

The Information Age, the Information Explosion, and the Information Society

During the agricultural age most people farmed. Now only a tiny fraction of the U.S. population work the land. During the industrial age we made things. We still do, of course, but we have automated industry so that fewer people can produce more goods. In addition, we have shipped much of our manufacturing overseas to cheaper labor markets. Now we live in the Information Age, a label that signifies the primacy of information in our everyday lives:

- Information, having overtaken *things*, is the new commodity.
- America's gross national product (GNP) is substantially information-based.

- Information doubles at ever-shortening intervals. This abundance has not made information easier to get, although the abundance creates that illusion.
- Because abundance and electronic access combine to produce prodigious amounts of retrievable information, people need highly developed sorting skills to cope.
- Most of the American workforce is employed at originating, managing, or transferring information.
- Information has intrinsic value; one can determine its benefits in dollars, and one can compute the cost of not having it.
- In the corporate world, information and knowledge combine to form *intellectual capital,* which represents the value of what people in the organization know.
- Information literacy is the survival skill for this millennium.

The Information Society

Here is an IBM-developed definition of the information society:

> *A society characterized by a high level of information intensity in the everyday life of most citizens, in most organizations and workplaces; by the use of common compatible technology for a wide range of personal, social, educational, and business activities, and by the ability to transmit, receive, and exchange digital data between places **irrespective of distance** [emphasis ours].*[1]

A student in Butte, Montana, can access the collections of the British Library in London *in seconds;* a doctor in New York can read the EKG of a patient in Brussels in *real time;* a client's computer in Hong Kong can communicate with a manufacturer in Oslo *while the company is closed for the night.* Not only is the communication instantaneous; so is the need for current, accurate, sorted, interpreted, and packaged information. Soon you, too, will need skills to compete and thrive in this fast-paced world. You also will have to make sense of a bewildering array of information.

---

[1] IBM Community Development Foundation in a 1997 report, "The Net Result—Report of the National Working Party for Social Inclusion."

Making Sense of It All

Not all examples of the mishandling and misjudging of information are as dramatic as Pearl Harbor, the Oklahoma City bombing, and September 11, 2001. Yet in each case, the right information failed to reach the right people at the right time. Lives were lost, peace was threatened, and economies were damaged.

How does one cope with the daily challenge of finding the right information to solve a given problem before it defeats us? Which airline or travel service really offers the cheapest airfare? Which variety of poisonous serpent bit the patient, and which antivenin is required to treat the victim? Which is likely to give me better service, a Subaru or a Toyota? Who steals most from a chain store, the customers who lift displayed products or the employees who help themselves to inventory?

Even though some of these questions are "academic" and others are down-to-earth questions that people ask as part of their jobs, they share a particular common characteristic. The answers are available in information agencies and/or in electronic formats.

Information Literacy

The right information in the hands of resourceful people can be an instrument of great power for them. If it just lies there, however, it is not powerful at all. Furthermore, if information is outdated, ignored, misused, or misinterpreted, it can be a source of great *unpower.* An information center with five million items has no power at all, but when you retrieve relevant sources from that center, sort them, interpret them, analyze them, and synthesize them into a well-organized project, you will knock your teacher's socks off. *That's* power! Galloping new ignorance (GNI) siphons off power. By "galloping new ignorance," we mean the assumption that the huge amounts of manageable information available at the press of a button confer knowledge. Put another way, if it is electronic, it is considered gospel. Conversely, if it is in print, it is considered obsolete. The newly ignorant rejoice at the discovery of 12,456 hits on fossil fuels. Then *abundance shock* takes hold if they realize their discovery is totally unsorted, and they frequently respond by *settling*—using the first five hits, irrespective of quality or authenticity. The reason this galloping new ignorance is so commonplace is that it infects smart people, decision makers—people who should know better but do not and whose decisions suffer as a consequence.

Confusing *information* for *understanding* is a common GNI symptom. People marvel at the information explosion and conclude that they are or can easily become informed. Many are unprepared for the blurring of lines between disciplines, the prodigious assault of publications, and the unsorted, unevaluated mass of information that pours down upon them at the press of a button.

The antidote for galloping new ignorance is learning to be information literate.

1. **Know that information matters.** It helps empower people to make good choices. The choices people make often determine their success in business, their happiness as partners, and their well being as citizens on this planet.

2. **Know how and where to find it.** If we are sick, we must know whose help to seek. If we are poor, we need to know where to get assistance. If we want to study chemistry, we need to know which schools offer degrees, how much they charge, if there are scholarships, and who will hire us when we graduate.

3. **Know how to find and retrieve information.** Once we find where to go and whom to ask, we must possess the skills to ask good questions and to make educated searches of information systems such as the Internet, libraries, and databases. We must cultivate relationships with information professionals—the librarians. We must be able to identify and define our need and to use the kinds of inquiry terminology that will give us hits instead of misses.

4. **Learn how to interpret the information you find.** While it is very important to retrieve information, it is even more important to know what to do with it. Is the information accurate? Is the author/provider a reliable source? How can you determine this?

Is it introductory? Introductory information is very basic and elementary. It does what its name implies—it introduces and provides a first impression. It often neither assumes nor requires prior knowledge about the topic. Example: *A snake is a long-bodied, legless animal.*

Is it definitional? Definitional information provides some descriptive details about a topic. Example: *Snakes are either venomous or nonvenomous. The venom may be of three types: neurotoxic, hemotoxic, or a combination of both.*

Is it analytical? Analytical information supplies data about origins, behaviors, differences, and uses. Example: *While some snakes are shy and prefer to retreat when disturbed, some are aggressive. People who mistake venomous varieties for harmless ones suffer deadly consequences.*

Is it current or dated? Is it someone's opinion, or is it a rigorously researched document? Can you lay it out in a logical sequence? Can you conclude anything? Use the *"So what?"* test: How important is this discovery?

Whom are you going to tell about your discovery, and how? Will you write a report? What guidelines for construction will you follow? Will you respect the intellectual property of others by giving appropriate credit to sources? Will you give your report orally? If you transfer this information orally, how should you prepare for your presentation? Information literacy has many facets, among them:

Computer literacy, the abilities associated with using electronic methods (search language), both for inquiry and for constructing presentations for others of what you have found and analyzed.

Media literacy, which is about facility with various formats: film, tape, CDs, and the machines that operate them.

Cultural literacy, keeping up with what has gone on and is going on around you. If someone refers to the Great Bambino or a feat of Ruthian proportion, you have to know about George Herman (Babe) Ruth, or you will not get the point. You have to know the difference between the Civil War and the Revolution, U2 and Y2K, Eminem and M&Ms, or you will not understand everyday conversation.

Researching and Presenting an Assigned Topic

Today when you tackle an information problem, you will probably consult the staff and holdings of the library at your campus as well as search the Internet. Tomorrow when you tackle an information problem, you may well consult a knowledge manager at your organization's information center and/or the Internet. In both cases you will apply the same information skills.

If you are fortunate to have an instructor who understands that information literacy skills are best practiced and learned when an inquirer has a reason for gathering information, that instructor will have given you an assignment to discover, interpret, organize, and present some findings to your classmates. What steps should you take to execute your assignment? If you are willing to practice information literacy, the survival skill you must acquire if you are to prosper in the information society, you must take these steps:

You have a topic, an inquiry task, and a product to produce:

TOPIC	INQUIRY TASK	PRODUCT
Political ethics	Definition	Paper and/or oral report
	Introduction	
	Some examples	
	Current	
	Historical	
	Problems, if any	
	Important aspects to report	
	Conclusions to draw	

Step 1. Define the topic in general terms. Any respected general dictionary can define ethics for you, but it would be a good idea to get your topic defined in context. Since your topic is *political* ethics, consult a political dictionary and an encyclopedia that would consider the political aspects of your ethics topic. For example, you will find a great article on lobbies in *The Encyclopedia of American Political History.*

Step 2. Specify and narrow your topic. After you have retrieved a definition that you determine to be complete and understandable, you are ready to search for a good introduction. What aspects of political ethics will you pursue? Even if you launch the most general of inquiries, you will very quickly discover that your topic is vast and that there are many related subtopics.

Here's where the narrowing comes in, for when you consult political ethics in the *Library of Congress Subject Headings* (LCSH) or when you check political ethics in the library's electronic catalog, you will discover some choices:

Civil service, ethics	Judicial ethics
Conflicts of interest	Justice
Corporations–Corrupt practices	Legislative ethics
Ethics, modern	Political corruption
Environmental ethics	Political ethics
Fairness	Social ethics
Gifts to politicians	

Note two things. First of all, your topic is broad. Every one of these headings leads to books and articles on political ethics. The good news is there's lots of information; the bad news is there's lots of information. For your sanity's sake, narrow your topic; get specific. In the *Library of Congress Subject Headings* you will encounter some abbreviations that may help you with your *search* and *narrow* mission. In this valuable volume, BT means *broader term* and suggests that you can get more specific. NT means *narrower term;* you *are* getting specific. RT means *related term* and identifies an additional related topic. UF means *used for* and tells you that the subject heading you have found is the standard term used by many finding tools.

Your library's catalog probably has InfoTrac® College Edition, an electronic indexing tool. *Social Science Citation Index* carries the actual words used in the titles of articles so that searchers can inquire, electronically or in print, in everyday language. Be on guard; some indexing tools, such as *The New York Times Index* and *ERIC,* have their own legal subject terms and their own thesauri or lists that you should consult before searching.

Because you may know about the efforts of lobbyists and political action committees (PACs) to influence legislation, and because this sub-topic interests you, you may decide upon *gifts to politicians* and *political corruption* as your target topics.

Encyclopedic sources will help you craft an introduction to your three-pronged topic: gifts to politicians, political corruption, and lobbyists. For instance, two editions of the previously cited and very useful specific subject encyclopedia, *The Encyclopedia of American Political History*, can supply some interesting information. If an encyclopedia has an index, use it. Your chances of finding something useful are increased manyfold if you check the index first.

Step 3. Launch your search. It is decision time. Are you going to search print or electronic sources? For best results, decide to do *both*. Where you begin is up to you. You may go after books or periodicals. Let's say you decide on periodicals, journals, and magazines first.

Your library may still subscribe to the following print indexes: *Readers' Guide, Social Science Index,* and PAIS *International Political Science Abstracts.* Even if the library has discontinued the current print subscriptions in favor of electronic ones, check out your subject headings in a three-to-five-year-old print version:

* You will see full-page displays of multiple listings.
* You will see some retrospective (historical) coverage of your topic.
* You will see titles of some articles that will further inform you.
* You may encounter some useful *see also* subject headings that may help you home in precisely on your target.

Get the serial *Editorials on File* for some real point-of-view observations. Everything you find in *Editorials on File* will be opinion. Check the indexes bound at the end of a yearly volume. You may not find *gifts to politicians, political corruption,* or *lobbying,* but under *politics* you can find gems like these: "Bradley/McCain soft money rejection," and "Campaign contributor limit," each of which leads to numerous columns of editorial reporting.

In searching articles, you should be aware that there may be a heavy dose of bias or point-of-view in some of them. Although nothing is inherently wrong with point-of-view, or with having a personal agenda, it is dangerous for an inquirer not to know that the bias is there. A great source for keeping you informed about this is *Magazines for Libraries* (LaGuardia, 2002), which will tell you about a periodical's editorial leanings. Here are some examples:

PERIODICAL TITLE	PERSPECTIVE
America	Jesuit/Catholic
Church and State	Historically Protestant
Commentary	American Jewish Committee
Commonweal	Catholic perspective
Time	Major news weekly; not opinion-free
New Republic	"Even-handed"
National Review	Conservative

Let's Go Electronic

Online periodical databases, online catalogs, and the World Wide Web allow you to quickly locate materials in the vast universe of electronic information. First, know the difference between searching online catalogs or periodical databases and the World Wide Web (WWW). Online catalogs and online periodical databases such as InfoTrac College Edition or *LexisNexis* are accessed via the Internet; the WWW only acts as a "host" to disseminate the information. Information for a database is usually stored in a single location or server owned by a company such as Gale Research. Remember, much of the information found in online periodical databases may also be found in print. Being careful to search terms relevant to your investigation will help you retrieve stuff you can use. Hence, searching InfoTrac College Edition is a lot like searching the print version of *Readers' Guide*—only much quicker.

Searching the World Wide Web, on the other hand, is a totally different story. You get different results from those you retrieve in a database. The information you seek on the WWW is not found in a single location, but is an aggregation of information from the vast universe of servers across the globe. To search the WWW, you need to use a commercial search engine such as Google, Yahoo, AltaVista, or Northern Lights. Anybody and his mama can have a Web site on the WWW, so the information you retrieve may be written by anyone—a fifth grader, a distinguished professor, a professional society, or a biased advocate! The super search engines send out little spiders, or "bots," to find key words in posted Web sites, and they may include in their files what their little electronic snoops find in the way of hits. So Joe Blow's uninformed comments on smoking and health could be right next to results from a rigorous scientific study. After a few assignments, you will quickly learn when to use a database and when information from the WWW is authoritative and sufficient.

You should know that an *index* and a *catalog* have completely different uses. A catalog—OPAC (online public access catalog)—tells you what books, magazines, newspapers, videos, and other materials your library owns. An index such as InfoTrac College Edition, *Readers' Guide,* or *America History and Life* allows you to search for articles within periodicals such as newspapers, magazines, journals, or even book chapters. To become a successful and savvy user of electronic resources, you need to establish and follow certain guidelines that work well for you:

1. Write out your topic or problem as a statement or question. "Is it *right* for *politicians* to take *gifts* from *lobbyists*?" "The influence of *lobbyists* or *PACs* has dramatically changed American *political ethics.*" (Key words are italicized.)

2. Write down several terms or synonyms for your topic so that if one search does not yield any hits, you have some back-up terms on hand.

3. Understand Boolean operators: *AND, OR,* and *NOT* are the ones most commonly used. The *OR* operator retrieves all synonyms, as in "PACs or Political Action Committees or Lobbyists." The computer always performs the OR function first. The *AND* operator retrieves only those records that have *BOTH* sets of terms, as in "PACs and Political Action Committees." Searching for "foreign films not French" will lead you to hits on all foreign films except those from France.

4. Know the difference between *subject* and *keyword* searches. "Subject" searches a controlled vocabulary list, and you need to know exact terminology in order to get good results: *political corruption—United States—history.* "Keyword" searches the entire record, including the title, notes, table of contents, or perhaps the abstract or the full text as well as the subject field: *political corruption AND United States AND history.* You may use Boolean operators in a keyword search.

5. The first time you use any electronic resource, be sure to consult the *HELP* link provided by the catalog, database, or search engine to learn specific searching techniques.

6. Understand whether you need scholarly publications, popular magazines, or both.

Scholarly (Refereed) Journals	Popular Magazines
Long articles	Shorter articles
In-depth information on topic	Broad overview of topic
Written by experts in subject/field	Written by journalists or staff reporters
Graphs, tables, or photographs to support text	Lots of color photos of people and events
Articles reviewed by peers in field	Articles evaluated by editor
Documented by works cited page	No bibliography provided, but sources credited

7. Select the correct database for your particular subject or topic. Most libraries subdivide their databases by broad general categories such as Humanities, Social Sciences, Science and Technology, Business, Health and Medicine, and Government Information. Each library loads its subscription list onto its electronic resources page. Under "Social Sciences," for example, one might find *International Political Science Abstract, America: History and Life,* and over 20 other databases. Then there are multidisciplinary databases, such as InfoTrac College Edition, that provide excellent material on most topics you encounter during your first years of college. If you are not sure which database to use, check with a librarian.

Looking Elsewhere

What if the library does not have the journal or book you really need for your research or project? The interlibrary loan department will be happy to borrow the materials for you. Most libraries allow you to submit your interlibrary loan requests online. Ask about this free service at your reference desk.

Are you a distance education student who cannot come into your college library in person? Libraries provide proxy access to their electronic materials to distance education students. To learn how, email or call the reference desk.

Be sure to use the handouts and guides available in print at the reference desk or online. You will also find online tutorials and virtual tours of the library that enable you to become familiar with the collections, service points, and policies of your library.

 ## Ask a Librarian

Librarians are information experts who are trained to assist and guide you to the resources you need. The librarians assigned to reference work or the ones who patrol the computer stations may look busy. That's because they are! But they are busy helping students with projects just like yours.

You will not interrupt them when you ask for assistance, and 99 percent of them will help you promptly and ably.

Today, you can contact a reference librarian in several ways. You can email a reference librarian and receive a quick reply. Or you may call the reference desk to ask a question such as "Do you have a copy of the report *Problems with the Presidential Gifts System*?" You can have a "live chat" online with a library staffer in real time. Or you may come to the reference desk in person.

 ## About Plagiarism

When ideas are put on paper, film, screen, or tape, they become intellectual property. Using those ideas without permission and/or without saying where you got them, and sometimes without paying for them, can cost you a grade, a course, a degree, maybe even a career. Plagiarism can mess you up big time. And it is so easy to avoid.

Just remember: If you use somebody else's exact published words, you have to give that person credit. If you use somebody else's published ideas, even if you use *your* words to express his or her ideas, you must give that person credit. Your instructor will indicate the preferred method for doing this—

with footnotes, or parenthetical references embedded in the text of your paper, and/or endnotes of some kind.

Most instructors and most college officials consider plagiarism cheating. They seldom accept "I didn't know" as a defense. They may not acknowledge that plagiarism can be inadvertent or an *oops*! thing. The Internet, which can be a tempting repository of ideas to pilfer, now offers programs that help instructors identify plagiarized assignments! Turnitin.com and Plagiarism.org are examples of Internet help available to teachers.

Buying and then submitting a term paper from one of the many thriving *term papers 'R' us* electronic mills invites one to:

1. Miss out on the genuine thrill of discovery and analysis that information literacy activities provide.
2. Give a false impression that the student knows something he does not, a fakery that will catch up with him, in school and certainly on the job.
3. Flunk out.
4. Get by, if the ruse is successful, but learn little or nothing.

As a student, your task will be to manage information for projects and presentations, oral and written. In a few years, as a technical writer for IBM, a teacher of English at a school or university, or a campaign manager for a gubernatorial candidate, your task will be the same. The information literacy skills you learn and employ as a student are the same ones that will serve you well as a successful professional.

YOUR PERSONAL JOURNAL

Here are several things to write about. Choose one or more. Or choose another topic related to libraries and research.

1. Look over the following list of common concerns and misconceptions about libraries and librarians:

   - I should automatically know how to use the library.
   - I've never had to use the library. I can get what I need from the Internet.
   - Librarians look too busy to help me.
   - The library is too big, and I never find what I need.
   - Librarians haven't helped me in the past.
   - Doing research usually requires having to talk to someone and ask for help. I don't like to do that.

Do you identify with any of these statements? Of the items listed above, are there any that you would consider misconceptions? Think about your own experiences using libraries, both the rewarding ones and the challenging or frustrating ones. What are some of your concerns or feelings?

2. Zora Neale Hurston described research as "poking and prying with a purpose." How would you describe it?

3. What behaviors are you willing to change after reading this chapter? How might you go about changing them?

4. What else is on your mind this week? If you wish to share something with your instructor, add it to this journal entry.

READINGS

Drawn to Knowledge*
By Kevin Havens

By most definitions, a library is the heart of a campus. Students gather there to research information and study quietly. The library is not just a repository of books; it symbolizes the very treasure-house of knowledge, history, and wisdom that defines the institution and the value of education.

But times have changed, and so have the perceptions of the library and its relevance. Most campus librarians report a significant decline in circulation figures, but a tremendous increase in demand for online media. Many campuses have responded by removing bookshelves and providing as many computer stations as possible. But how is this affecting meaningful learning and quality research? Is the book simply an old-fashioned "container" of information, easily replaced by the more efficient Internet?

The essence of the debate calls into question the evolving mission of the academic library. Once an institution that acquired and organized information, a library now frequently is viewed as an access point to a much greater selection of media and information that resides electronically and not physically. Most students embrace this understanding, but many faculty members are unsure of the ramifications of so radical a shift.

"College libraries can no longer be simply a repository of books and journals, nor can librarians serve only as information managers and clerks," says Michael Bell, dean of faculty at Elmhurst College in Elmhurst, Ill. "But increased information without interpretation produces more noise than

*American School & University, August 1, 2003, v75, i12. Copyright 2003 Primedia, Inc. Reprinted with permission.

knowledge, and librarians who merely manage the information flow are likely to foster more ignorance than insight."

A BALANCING ACT

School administrators and facility planners are searching for the proper balance of technology and tradition. Making library facilities more attentive to student expectations is essential. But schools also must consider the need for high-quality scholarship and guideposts to lifelong learning. These needs must be mutually supportive.

To lure students back to the library, school planners and architects are exploring creative ways to redesign, renovate or build new library structures that meet the changing academic and social needs of its student body and faculty.

Many school administrators are embracing similar design goals as they consider modern library facilities:

- **Technology and information literacy**

Providing more computers without meaningful guidance improves neither student scholarship nor teaching effectiveness. The real differentiator seems to be harnessing new media to teach critical-thinking skills.

Several schools are providing information-literacy labs as core spaces in their new facilities. These teaching spaces allow librarians to help students develop organization and information-assessment skills. This formal guidance nurtures a student's ability to discover, sort, and integrate information, and evaluate it critically. Students use the library most effectively when they understand how to navigate through the storm of information.

Some schools are enclosing these classrooms in glass so people can view the technology-enhanced instruction space and have uninterrupted views throughout the library without compromising acoustic containment.

Many students use laptop computers to research, write, and communicate with their peers and professors. A new or remodeled library facility should incorporate a robust network environment "painted" with wireless access to the campus network and Internet. A fiberoptic backbone connecting the library to the world is seen as the best "future-proofing" strategy for these evolving technologies.

- **Librarians as research collaborators**

As the mission of the academic library is re-examined, so is the role of the librarian. If information literacy training is essential to the success of a student's experience and lifelong learning habits, the library staff must assume primary responsibility to provide this training.

Librarians are moving from their traditional role as information managers to become teachers of critical-learning skills, research collaborators, and technology leaders.

Librarians no longer work behind reference counters; they try to form research partnerships with students. They teach research techniques as they help find and evaluate information.

New library interiors often incorporate workstations configured in a collaborative setting. This allows students to work individually with a librarian or in small groups.

● Reconfiguring collections

Library collections are expanding rapidly. Librarians have been integrating non-print formats—video, DVD, and sound recordings—into their collections for years while removing hard-copy materials that are available electronically. But the interest in electronic media and declining enthusiasm for print material have driven books off the main levels of many libraries. Stacks frequently are relegated to lower levels, and in some cases, are situated in a remote part of the campus, with a system in place to retrieve requested volumes.

But most librarians agree that the book will not become extinct. Despite the proliferation of electronic media, much information is available only in print. Training students to mine this source of knowledge and not only online data is part of the mission.

● Social and academic center

For a library to regain its role as the center of a college's intellectual community, it must provide venues that attract students.

Spaces that incorporate both quiet reading and discussion can become alternative hangouts for students to relax and build friendships. Many libraries create private rooms for study groups to discuss assignments or prepare class presentations.

One of the more conspicuous departures from the traditional library paradigm is having a cafe or snack area inside the library. These limited-menu coffee bars become between-class gathering spots. They frequently serve as a cyber cafe with desktop and wireless laptop capabilities.

● Looking to the future

Most academics believe that the library still is significant and should not be discarded prematurely. In fact, many campuses are attempting to restore the vitality once common in these buildings.

The core issue is not books vs. computers, but rather the nature of learning and the quality of human discourse.

Designing a modern library environment to enhance a student's experience may involve an array of initiatives that address both academic and social issues. But the question of what form this venerable institution will take in the future is still evolving.

The most enduring vestige from the past may be that comfortable armchair in the corner, perfect for curling up with a good book.

A NEW VISION

Size doesn't matter when renovating a campus library—it's how you use the space you're given. Take for example the vision of Michael Bell, dean of faculty at Elmhurst College in Elmhurst, Ill. He envisioned a library that would meet the intellectual needs of students and faculty in today's changing information environment. Yet, he saw a library that maintained its traditional responsibility to teach the critical research skills central to intellectual life.

In 2002, this liberal-arts college welcomed its 2,800 students to an expanded and reconfigured library. The $1.4 million expansion at Buehler Library added an information-literacy laboratory and a cyber cafe, complete with food and beverages and TVs for students to catch up on the day's news. The reconfiguration of the library moved books from the first level to the basement; new layouts and furniture complemented the increased role librarians would have in collaborating with students.

Elmhurst College uses the information-literacy classroom and computer lab to conduct more than 200 instructional sessions per year for students and faculty, turning the librarians into an integral part of the teaching staff.

Since the library's renovation, library traffic has increased significantly. Elmhurst College's students are embracing the concept of a library that caters to their desire for study, socialization, and information literacy.

Deserted No More*

After years of declining usage statistics, the campus library rebounds
By Andrew Richard Albanese

Few articles caused as much of a stir among academic librarians as Scott Carlson's November 2001 *Chronicle of Higher Education* piece, "The Deserted Library." But for Tjalda Nauta, Carlson's piece caused more than a stir. It helped end her 19-year tenure at the Bentley College library (Waltham, MA). "I won't blame [my departure] directly on the article," says Nauta, who was then the director of libraries at Bentley. "But the timing was bad."

Not long after the *Chronicle* piece appeared, Nauta says she had a memorable meeting with an administrator at Bentley. "His first announcement to me," she recalls, "was basically 'I don't believe we need libraries.'" Less than inspired by that level of support from her administration, Nauta ultimately

Library Journal, April 15, 2003, v128, i7, p. 34(3). Copyright 2003 Reed Business Information. Reprinted with permission.

resigned. Now director of the library at Rhode Island College (RIC) in Providence, Nauta, like many of her fellow librarians, disagreed with what she then saw as the *Chronicle's* underlying premise—that the advent of the Internet had diminished the need for the campus library. But Nauta concedes that her views on the article have softened over the past year.

"I remember how indignant I was—how indignant we all were," Nauta recalls. "I look at that article very differently now. When it came out it was as if [the *Chronicle*] was saying this is the end of the library. . . . It was [really] saying that the orientation of libraries is going to be different. And that's absolutely right. We are adapting."

REBOUND

On a Tuesday in February, the Monroe Library at Loyola University in New Orleans is almost completely deserted. Of course, that's because this particular Tuesday happens to be Mardi Gras, and the library is closed. Every other day the Monroe Library is the most popular place on campus. We've seen a tremendous increase in the number of students coming into our building and an increase in book circulation," says Mary Lee Sweat, dean of libraries at Loyola.

Indeed, after years of declining traditional usage statistics appeared to chart the nadir of the campus library, at least in the eyes of some observers, the rising numbers at Loyola now tell a different story. Despite some gloomy prognoses for the campus library during the 1990s Internet boom, the campus library appears to be experiencing a renaissance.

At RIC, for example, annual gate count at the library had declined steadily during the early years of the Internet, from 331,530 visitors in 1993–94 to a low of 240,948 in 1998–99. But since 2000, gate count at RIC has increased. Gate count for 2001–02 was back up to a healthy 282,501, its highest point since 1995–96. Figures thus far for 2002–03 put gate count on pace to rise again. Circulation figures, Nauta says, are also on the rise. And RIC is not alone.

According to a report in the March 2 edition of the *Chicago Tribune,* Illinois academic libraries, from research institutions such as Northwestern University to small private colleges like Elmhurst College, have also booked rising gate counts and usage statistics. At Illinois Wesleyan University, which opened its new Ames Library last year with more computers, more books, and a variety of instructional space, Library Director Sue Stroyan told reporters that weekly visits to the library have tripled, now up to 1,200 a week, an impressive figure for a school with an enrollment under 2,000.

At Loyola, the spacious new Monroe Library offers users five times as much space as its predecessor. Sweat says there has been no trouble filling the space with students. "Physically, the library is at the center of the campus, and it has literally changed traffic patterns on campus," she notes. "It has become a real social as well as intellectual center."

A RENAISSANCE

Brian Coutts, dean of libraries at Western Kentucky University (WKU), has also seen an increase in gate counts and circulation. "We don't think it happened just because it happened," Coutts says. "We took some proactive steps to make that happen."

Today's campus library, Courts says, is more than just a place to get resources. It's a destination that supports new, technology-driven teaching, learning, and research patterns, offering everything from books to digital databases to a social space for students to gather.

The basic idea, says Loyola's Sweat, is to offer students "one-stop shopping." At Loyola's Monroe Library, not only do students get help with finding resources and doing research, but librarians also offer a range of instructional services. "If you want students to use your library," Sweat explains, "you want to offer them everything they need. You don't want to have to send them to other places on campus."

WHAT STUDENTS WANT

"What the younger students really seem to like," RIC's Nauta observes, "is to sit with a laptop plugged into our wireless network, with their feet up." Other students, she notes, prefer a quiet place where they can spread out by themselves and not be disturbed. "Others like to sit in large groups and work together," adds Nauta. The library at RIC, Nauta says, now accommodates all those various student preferences, including the installation of a wireless network, 30 laptops for loan, and new public workstations.

Libraries have also learned from their competition, such as bookstores and Internet cafes. Many have altered their policies and practices, permitting or offering food and drink and installing comfortable furniture and an array of leisure programming, as well as multimedia instruction rooms, group study areas, and atriums where students can talk and collaborate on projects.

At WKU, Coutts says the library's resurgence is predicated on campus partnerships. For example, the library joined with the campus food service department to build a popular cafe. The library also partnered with student government to bring entertainment to the cafe and with the An Guild on campus to redecorate the lower part of the library's lounge. Another venture with the campus counseling center offers special programs in the library on everything from relationships to stress management. Through an alliance with the English Department, the WKU library has also opened a writing center to help students with their papers—offering assistance with everything from grammar and style to proper research.

Coutts also struck a deal with the campus IT department. In exchange for a small space in the library, that partnership has given library patrons what they really seem to want in the digital age: free printing. "With all the databases available now, students like to search and print articles."

What about the reference desk?

Unlike rebounding gate counts and circulation figures in campus libraries, however, reference requests, librarians say, have not gone up.

Michael Gorman, dean of libraries at California State University (CSU), Fresno, says that lower reference statistics could mean any number of things. "What's a reference question today?" Gorman asks. "A reference question years ago might have been, 'Do you have *Time* magazine?'" Today Gorman says such basic questions are easily answered on the library's Web site. "There is a great drop in the most elementary reference questions," Gorman explains, "but if you counted the more substantial reference questions—'Can you help me with my paper on Heidegger,'—I'd argue that the number is probably about the same."

Another key figure that has stayed down is the use of current periodicals. Since 1993–94, Nauta says that she has seen a 76 percent drop in the use of periodicals. "Extraordinary," she says. "We were able to track issues by bar code, and we couldn't believe how much use dropped." Those figures are mirrored at CSU, says Gorman, where current periodical use is also down roughly 80 percent.

Some of that is certainly attributable to the increasing popularity of aggregated databases and e-journals. But part of that decrease, Gorman says, points to the need for more library instruction. "There is still a tremendous need for library instruction in general and critical thinking," Gorman says. That, he says, would help students get away from the alarming practice of using the first online source that fits and help to foster better judgment when it comes to searching for, accessing, and evaluating sources.

A POST-INTERNET BOUNCE

Librarians also say that the circulation of books is likely getting a boost from what one librarian called a "post-Internet bounce." In the early days of the Internet, digital euphoria suggested that everything would soon be available at the click of a mouse, obviating the need for the traditional library. As the Internet has progressed, however, that has not happened. That realization is helping to drive traffic back to the library.

Nauta says book circulation is on the rise at RIC. And unlike the situation with e-journals, e-books have yet to take off among students. Gorman agrees. "We still circulate a lot of books," he says. Librarians also report an increase in the number of faculty who are requiring students to use traditional resources and not just Web-based resources in their work. "Because of the convenience of the Internet, students will always turn there first," says RIC's Nauta.

"Faculty now are eager to impress upon them that the whole world of information is not on the Internet."

LEGACIES

Despite the resurgence of the campus library in recent years, the notion of "the deserted library" still casts a long shadow on many campuses. The decision throughout the 1990s, by many administrators, to back off on construction or capital improvement plans has left libraries short of space. Given the economic uncertainties facing the nation, it's likely that at those schools whose administrators underestimated the future of the campus library during the Internet boom, librarians will have to make do.

On the other hand, many schools forged ahead with libraries designed to meet both the digital and traditional needs of students and faculty. The University of Arizona, which opened its Information Commons in 2002, offers a space that gives students and faculty access to traditional resources as well as computers, multimedia, and high-speed network connections. The space also hosts live "support specialists," most of whom are librarians; meeting spaces; wired classrooms; and an environment that facilitates both private and collaborative study.

Other models are also emerging. At the University of Texas at Arlington (UTA), administrators are now examining a plan that would place a network of smaller, computer-based libraries throughout the campus. Tom Wilding, director of libraries at UTA, said that the original vision for a new main library had been drawn up four to five years ago. Then one day, Wilding recalls, UTA's president took him to lunch and floated an idea. "He said, 'What if we went in a different direction?' He wasn't saying that libraries were not important, not at all," says Wilding. "He just wanted to know how I felt about doing something different."

"I thought a lot about what the library would be in the 21st century. I didn't want to have a great 20th-century library in the 21st century," says Wilding. Eventually the master plan that called a new main library the "highest priority project" was shelved at UTA, replaced by a model based on UTA's popular electronic business library. Wilding says a network of similar libraries—situated within academic units—in support of UTA's existing main library is now in the works. "It really makes you stop and think what the role of the library is in the 21st century," says Wilding.

THE MOST POPULAR RESOURCE

As technology continues to change the learning and research patterns of students and faculty, campus libraries are sure to look different in the coming decades. What they won't be, librarians say, is deserted.

The real challenge now, librarians say, is not getting students inside library walls but marketing library services outside the library. "I'm not too concerned with bringing people through the gate," says Illinois Wesleyan's Stroyan. "We don't have a problem with that." What Stroyan says she hopes to do through various marketing efforts is create better awareness of library services. "For first-year students [that means] letting them know that we can help them understand their assignments and what tools we have to help them. For seniors, letting them know that librarians are here to work with them, one on one, with their research assignments."

Such sentiments serve to remind users of the most important resource found in any campus library: librarians. "If you look at student satisfaction surveys, the library is almost always ranked the top institution on campus among students," says CSU's Gorman. That's not because of comfortable couches and lattes, he adds. "Any place you go in the library you can find someone who is looking to help you. You can't find that anywhere else on campus."

IF YOU BUILD IT, THEY WILL COME

For Mary Lee Sweat, dean of libraries at Loyola University in New Orleans, the increased use of the Edgar and Louise Monroe Library vindicates the vision of the robust academic library in a digital age. Throughout the 1990s, college and university administrators typically backed off on plans to build or renovate their libraries, convinced that with the dawn of the digital age, the need for the library as a place would likely diminish. However, for institutions such as Loyola that remained committed to library projects, both with dollars and vision, the library has proven an increasingly vital rather than vestigial entity. "On our campus," Sweat says, "students appreciate the library as a place."

Loyola's Monroe Library, which opened in 1999, is an excellent example of how the campus library remains the very heart of the academy. It offers students and faculty the perfect blend of traditional services and digital resources, as well as an inviting space to gather, whether for classes, special events, or for social interaction. At Loyola, students find not only a vast array of resources at their disposal but also innovative instructional services, media labs, and teaching rooms, and librarians eager to help with anything from finding resources and general research to web-hosting to putting together a PowerPoint presentation. In fact, the entire first floor of the Monroe Library is designated an "active learning" space, where students and instructors can congregate.

The popularity of the library is readily apparent in its usage statistics. Gate counts at Loyola rose a whopping 13.4 percent last year, with more than 792,000 visits to the library for a student population of 5,500. Circulation of books and other media rose 13.8 percent. The library also held nearly 300 instruction sessions last year, for roughly 3,500 students. So strong is the library at Loyola that it won the 2002 Excellence in Academic Library Award for universities from the Association of College and Research Libraries. The award, sponsored by Blackwells Booksellers, was presented at Loyola in a ceremony . . ., along with a $3,000 check. "It's a tremendous recognition of the library and the university and especially of the library faculty and staff," Sweat told LJ [*Library Journal*].

More programs and collections are on the way, Sweat says, including a plan to improve library services for the College of Music and to implement more information literacy initiatives on campus—activities that will surely drive even higher library use. For now, though, Sweat says she'll proudly enjoy the spotlight with her colleagues. "They are at the heart of what we do."

DISCUSSION

1. Carefully consider several topics you would be motivated to learn more about if you were required to do a research paper. Assume that you have total academic freedom for this purpose and are free to pursue anything that interests you. Share with fellow students your first and second choices. As a group, talk through how you might collect information on these topics. What sources would you use? Make sure you narrow your topic down to a manageable one. And remember: for this discussion it will not do to simply advise each other to "go to the Web"!

2. Share with fellow students some of your challenges and successes so far in using your campus library. Ideally, you should have your instructor arrange for a reference librarian to come to class as you discuss the exercise above so that she or he can react to the group reports and provide further suggestions.

3. In the reading "Drawn to Knowledge," the writer states that college libraries are in a dramatic era of transition as a result of the information age revolution. Have you noticed differences between your college library and your high school and community public libraries? In what ways has your college library changed because of the Information Age?

4. The second reading, "Deserted No More . . . ," describes a resurgence in student use of the library after a temporary decline in the first years of the Internet era. The writer calls this a "post-Internet bounce." Discuss with a group of students the various ways you make use of your library, where, when, and with whom. How are your habits similar to or different from those of your classmates? Listen carefully and see if you can glean some good tips from your classmates that might help you use this critical college success resource.

CHAPTER 11

Careers and Service Learning

Philip Gardner of Michigan State University, Linda Salane of Columbia College, and Edward Zlotkowski of Bentley College contributed their valuable and considerable expertise to the writing of this chapter.

S tudents planning for careers frequently encounter bumps along the way. Choosing a career is a process of discovery, involving a willingness to remain open to new ideas and experiences. Many of the decisions you make during your first year in college will have an impact on where you end up in the workplace.

IN THIS CHAPTER, YOU WILL LEARN

- How majors and careers are linked— but not always
- Surprising things about careers and liberal arts majors
- How to prepare a résumé and cover letter
- How your academic advisor and college catalog can be helpful references
- How service learning, internships, and co-op programs can pave the way to employment

---

Careers and the New Economy

Since the 1990s, major changes have taken place in how we work, where we work, and the ways we prepare for work while in college. In the early 21st century, organizations have become increasingly:

- **Global.** National economies have gone multinational, not only moving into overseas markets but seeking cheaper labor, capital, and resources abroad. Your career is bound to be affected by the global economy, even if you never leave the United States.
- **Boundaryless.** U.S. companies have partners throughout the world. DaimlerChrysler, the result of a merger of the U.S. Chrysler organization with the German Mercedes-Benz group, is a recent example. You may be an accountant and find yourself working with the public relations division of your company, or you may be a human resources manager who trains a number of different divisions in a number of different countries. You might even find yourself moved to a unit with a different function, as opposed to climbing up the proverbial—and often narrow—career ladder.

- **Customized.** More and more, consumers are demanding products and services tailored to their specific needs. One example is the health food supermarket. Another is the seemingly endless varieties of a single brand of shampoo or soup crowding your grocer's shelves. Such market segmentation requires constant adaptation of ideas to identify new products and services as new consumer demands emerge.
- **Fast.** When computers became popular, people rejoiced because they believed the computer would reduce their workloads. Actually, the reverse happened. Now executives are designing their own PowerPoint presentations because, as one article put it, "It's more fun to work with a slide show than to write reports." For better or worse, "We want it now" is the cry in the workplace, with product and service delivery time cut to a minimum.
- **Unstable.** Terrorist attacks, the war in Iraq, soaring gasoline prices, and the scandals within the highest echelons of major companies put the stock market into a spin and caused massive layoffs. The travel industry experienced a slump after 9/11 that is still felt today. Drops in state and federal funding have negatively affected shopping. Although, as history has taught us things will get better, it's important to know about the economy because it changes so quickly.

Surviving in a Changing Economy

As you prepare over the next few years to begin your career, remember that:

- **You are, more or less, solely responsible for your career.** Companies may assist you with assessments and information on available positions in the industry, but the ultimate task of engineering a career path is yours.
- **To advance your career, you must accept the risks that accompany employment and plan for the future.** Organizations will continually restructure, merge, and either grow or downsize in response to economic conditions. Because you can be unexpectedly unemployed, it will be wise to keep other options in mind and to invest and save what you can on a regular basis.
- **A college degree does not guarantee employment.** Of course, you'll be able to hunt through opportunities that are more rewarding, financially and otherwise, than if you did not have a degree. But just because you want to work at a certain organization doesn't mean there's a job for you there. And as the economy rises and falls, you may find yourself laid off from a job that fits you to a tee.

- **A commitment to lifelong learning helps to keep you employable.** In college you have been learning a vital skill: how to learn. *Gradus,* the Latin root of *graduation,* means moving to a higher level of responsibility. Your learning has just begun when you receive your diploma.

Now the good news. Thousands of graduates find jobs every year. Some may have to work longer to get where they want to be, but persistence pays off. If you start now, you'll have time to build a portfolio of academic and cocurricular experiences that will begin to add substance to your career profile. This Rudyard Kipling couplet from *The Just So Stories* (1902) is an easy way to remember how to navigate for career success:

I keep six honest serving men (They taught me all I knew)
Their names are what and why and when and how and where and who.

- **Why.** Why do you want to be a _____? Knowing your goals and values will help you pursue your career with passion and an understanding of what motivates you. Never say "because I'm a people person" or "because I like to work with people." Sooner or later, most people have to work with people. And your interviewer has heard this much too often.
- **Who.** Network with people who can help you find out what you want to be. Someone will always know someone else for you to talk to.
- **How.** Have the technical and communications skills required to work effectively. Become a computer whiz. Learn how to do PowerPoint presentations or improve your PowerPoint skills. Take a speech course. Work on improving your writing. More than likely, your future job will require many or all of these skills.
- **What.** Be aware of the opportunities an employer presents, as well as such unforeseen occurrences as relocation overseas. Know what training you will need to remain in your chosen profession.
- **Where.** Know the points of entry into the field. For example, you can obtain on-the-job experiences through internships, co-ops, service learning, or part-time jobs.
- **When.** Know how early you need to start looking. Find out if certain professions hire at certain times of the year.

Connecting Careers and Majors

Once you have explored your interests, you can begin to connect them to academic majors. If you're still not sure, take the advice of Patrick Combs, author of *Major in Success,* who recommends that you major in a subject that you are really passionate about. Most advisors or counselors would agree.

The reality is that most occupational fields do not require a specific major, and graduates have found a number of ways to use their majors.

Today English majors are designing Web pages, philosophy majors are developing logic codes for operating systems, and history majors are sales representatives and business managers. You do not have to major in science to gain admittance to medical school. Of course, you do have to take the required science and math courses, but medical schools seek applicants with diverse backgrounds.

Some fields do require specific degrees, such as nursing, accounting, engineering, and pharmacy, because certification in these fields is directly tied to a degree.

Exploring Your Interests

Dr. John Holland, a psychologist at Johns Hopkins University, has developed a number of tools and concepts that can help you organize your various interests, skills, and so forth, so that you can identify potential career choices.

Holland separates people into six general categories based on differences in their interests, skills, values, and personality characteristics—in short, their preferred approaches to life:[1]

Realistic These practical doers exhibit competitive/assertive behavior, prefer situations involving action solutions rather than tasks involving verbal or interpersonal skills, and like to take a concrete approach to problem solving rather than rely on abstract theory.

Investigative These people value intellectual stimulation and intellectual achievement and prefer to think rather than to act, to organize and understand rather than to persuade.

Artistic These people value self-expression and relations with others through artistic expression and are also emotionally expressive. They dislike structure, preferring tasks involving personal or physical skills.

Social These people value helping others and making a contribution to society. They satisfy their needs in one-to-one or small group interaction using strong speaking skills to teach, counsel, or advise.

---

[1] Adapted from John L. Holland, *Self-Directed Search Manual* (Psychological Assessment Resources: 1985). Copyright 1985 by PAR, Inc. Reprinted with permission.

Enterprising These people value prestige, power, and status and are more inclined than other types to pursue it. They use verbal skills to supervise, lead, direct, and persuade rather than to support or guide.

Conventional These people value order, structure, prestige, and status and possess a high degree of self-control. They are not opposed to rules and regulations. They are skilled in organizing, planning, and scheduling.

Holland's system organizes career fields into the same six categories. Here are a few examples:

Realistic Agricultural engineer, electrical contractor, industrial arts teacher, navy officer, fitness director, package engineer, electronics technician, computer graphics technician

Investigative Urban planner, chemical engineer, bacteriologist, flight engineer, genealogist, laboratory technician, marine scientist, nuclear medical technologist, obstetrician, quality control technician, computer programmer, environmentalist, physician, college professor

Artistic Architect, film editor/director, actor, cartoonist, interior decorator, fashion model, graphic communications specialist, journalist, editor, orchestra leader, public relations specialist, sculptor, media specialist, librarian, reporter

Social Nurse, teacher, social worker, genetic counselor, marriage counselor, rehabilitation counselor, school superintendent, geriatric specialist, insurance claims specialist, minister, travel agent, guidance counselor, convention planner

Enterprising Banker, city manager, FBI agent, health administrator, judge, labor arbitrator, salary and wage administrator, insurance salesperson, sales engineer, lawyer, sales representative, marketing specialist

Conventional Accountant, statistician, census enumerator, data processor, hospital administrator, insurance administrator, office manager, underwriter, auditor, personnel specialist, database manager, abstractor/indexer.

Holland's model can help you address the problem of career choice in two ways. First, you can begin to identify many career fields that are consistent with what you know about yourself. Once you've identified potential fields, you can use the career library at your college to get more information about those fields, such as daily activities for specific jobs, interests and abilities required, preparation required for entry, working conditions, salary and benefits, and employment outlook.

Second, you can begin to identify the harmony or conflicts in your career choices. Never feel you have to make a decision simply on the results of one assessment. Take time to talk your interests over with a career counselor.

Another helpful approach is to shadow an individual in the occupation that interests you. Ask your career center for help.

Starting Your Career-Planning Program

The process of making a career choice begins with:

- Understanding your values and motivations
- Identifying your interests
- Linking your personality and learning styles to those interests
- Using this information to decide on an appropriate academic major
- Researching possible occupations that match your skills, your interests, and your academic major
- Building on your strengths and developing your weaker skills
- Preparing a marketing strategy that sells you as a valued member of a professional team
- Writing a convincing résumé and cover letter.

Steps in the Job Hunt

Your search for a career should begin early in college. Here are some things you can do:

- Get a job. Even a part-time job will develop your skills and may help you make decisions about what you like—and what you don't—in a work environment.
- Register with your college's online job listing system to find listings for part- and full-time, internship, co-op, and seasonal employment.
- Find on-campus interviewing opportunities for internships in your early years and for full-time employment as a senior.
- Network with family, friends, instructors, friends of family, and acquaintances to find contacts in your field(s) of interest so that you can learn more about those areas.
- Volunteer! This can help you explore careers and get some experience in an area that interests you as you help others.
- Conduct occupational and industrial research for your field or area of geographic interest. Explore career options through informational interviews (interviewing to find out about a career), job shadowing (arranging to observe someone as he or she works), and service learning (see pages 194–195).
- Prepare a draft of your résumé and have it critiqued by your career counselor and perhaps by a professional in your chosen field.

- Get involved in clubs and organizations; work toward leadership positions.
- Explore overseas study possibilities to gain a global perspective and learn a foreign language.
- Attend career fairs to connect with employers for internships and other career-related opportunities as well as to develop a professional network.
- Attend your campus's annual job fair to see what is being offered.
- Talk to a career counselor about your skills, aptitudes, and interests. Find out what the career center offers.[2]

Some Career Do's and Don'ts

As you start examining your aspirations and interests, keep in mind these simple do's and don'ts:

Do's

1. Do explore a number of career possibilities and academic majors.
2. Do get involved through volunteer work, study abroad, and student organizations—especially those linked to your major.
3. Do follow your passion. Learn what you love to do, and go for it.

Don'ts

1. Don't just focus on a major and blindly hope to get a career out of it. That's backward.
2. Don't be motivated primarily by external stimuli, such as salary, prestige, and perks. All the money in the world won't make you happy if you hate what you're doing every day.
3. Don't select a major just because it seems "cool."
4. Don't choose courses simply because your friend said they were easy.

Getting Experience

Your campus has a variety of activities and programs in which you can participate to confirm those interests, check your values, and gain valuable skills. Here are some examples.

---

[2] Used by permission of Career Passport, Michigan State University.

- **Volunteer.** Volunteering outside of class is a valuable way to encounter different life situations and to gain work knowledge in areas such as teaching, health services, counseling, and tax preparation.
- **Study abroad.** Take a course or spend an entire term taking classes in another country and learn about a different culture at the same time. Learn to adapt to new traditions and a different pace of life.
- **Internships and co-ops.** Many employers now expect these work experiences. They want to see that you have experience in the professional workplace and have gained an understanding of the skills and competencies necessary to succeed. Check with your academic department and career center on internships available in your major.
- **On-campus employment.** On-campus jobs may not provide as much income, yet this type of employment gives you a chance to practice good work habits. Some jobs have direct connections to employment. More important, on-campus employment brings you into contact with faculty and other academic professionals whom you can later consult as mentors or ask for references.
- **Student projects/competitions.** In many fields, students engage in competitions based on what they have learned in the classroom. In the process, they learn teamwork, communication, and applied problem-solving skills.
- **Research.** Work with a faculty member on a research project. Research extends your critical thinking skills and provides insight on a subject above and beyond your books and class notes.
- **Informational interviewing.** One way to learn more about a career is to talk directly with the people in it. By arranging to meet with people who could be your peers, as well as those who are doing the hiring, you'll learn more about job requirements.

Service Learning[3]

One of the most effective ways to explore careers is through a program called "service learning." Service learning is a teaching method that combines meaningful service to the community with related classroom learning, all for academic credit.[3]

> **Serving.** The service itself should address a genuine community need, as determined by existing or student-led community assessments.

---

[3] For more information on service learning, go to the Web site of the W. K. Kellogg Foundation: http://learningindeed.org/about/index.html. Courtesy of the W. K. Kellogg Foundation. Reprinted with permission.

Linking. The service project is designed to meet not only a real community need, but also classroom goals. Through service learning, students demonstrate to teachers what they are learning and how they are meeting specific academic standards.

Reflection and analysis. The teacher structures time and methods for students to reflect on and analyze their service experience. Through this process, students learn and understand the complexity of community issues. In addition, students understand how to view such issues in their broader social, political, and economic contexts.

Although a student may learn a lot through traditional community service, service learning does not leave such learning to chance. Instead, it surrounds the service experience with carefully designed reflection activities to help students prepare for, process, and pull together different aspects of their experience.

For many students, service learning means knowing not just about things but how to do them. It juxtaposes theories and ideas with concrete personal experience and, in doing so, helps students learn how to act on their knowledge and put theory to the test.

When you step outside the traditional role of knowledge "consumer" and become a knowledge "producer" in your own right, you will be taking a huge step toward becoming a "lifelong" learner—one who knows how to learn outside the bounds of a formal classroom.

YOUR PERSONAL JOURNAL

Here are a number of topics to write about. Choose one or more, or choose another topic related to this chapter.

1. What internal (feelings, emotions) and external (parents, peers) influences have affected your thoughts about majors and careers? How do you feel about those choices?
2. What other majors and/or careers have you been thinking about? Why do these appeal to you? If you're not considering other careers and majors, why are you dead set on the one you've chosen?
3. What factors are important to you in deciding on a major and a career?
4. What sort of service learning course would appeal to you? Why?
5. What behaviors are you willing to change after reading this chapter? How might you go about changing them?
6. What else is on your mind this week? If you wish to share it with your instructor, add it to this journal entry.

READINGS

The University of Social Justice*

Beyond community service, colleges educate for social change.

By Melissa Snarr

To borrow a term from social movement theory, universities can be "movement halfway houses" that educate leaders for social justice. Higher education institutions have trained and nurtured numerous social movements and activists that have changed our world. The Student Nonviolent Coordinating Committee, which played a key role in the civil rights movement, came from a coalition of college students. Northern college students infused Freedom Summer's voter registration drives. More recently, student networks have rapidly expanded protests of corporate globalization and the U.S. Army's School of the Americas. Anti-sweatshop and living wage movements also are building momentum because of students.

These movements emerge, in part, because university faculty and staff are part of the conscientizing process of young people. Universities emphasize systemic analysis of social problems. They prize critical thinking skills. They encourage creative use of language and symbols. Combine these skills with higher education's focus on developing leaders, and we can see the potential of the universities to produce multiple generations of justice seekers.

We find the summons in our institutions' mission statements, the statements that no student, faculty, or staff ever really reads. But it's there, the call to moral learning and social justice. At some schools, the commitment is explicit: "Loyola Marymount understands and declares its purpose to be: the encouragement of learning, the education of the whole person, the service of faith, and the promotion of justice." At others, the call is embedded in an understanding of the proper use of knowledge: "Emory's mission lies in two essential, interwoven purposes: through teaching, to help men and women fully develop their intellectual, aesthetic, and moral capacities; and, through the quest for new knowledge and public service, to improve human well-being."

Universities experience enormous pressure to deliver a marketable product. But higher education is called to be more than a conduit for career-making. Our students are more than clients. Classically, education was meant for the

---

Sojourners, May-June 2003, v32, i3, p. 28(6). Reprinted with permission from Sojourners. 1-800-714-7474. www.sojo.net.

whole person—for "full human flourishing." As University of Chicago professor Martha Nussbaum notes, U.S. higher education has been devoted particularly to the "cultivation of the whole human being for the functions of citizenship and life generally." At the core, universities are more than service providers with privileged clients. We are moral actors shaping the character and justice of society.

But educating change agents for social justice is not the same as encouraging increased volunteerism on campus, which is embraced much more easily by institutions and a broad political spectrum. As community service hours are required by many high schools for graduation, students arrive at college open to giving time to "those less fortunate." In fact, the Higher Education Research Center's most recent freshmen survey reported that 84 percent of students had volunteered in the last year.

At the same time, only 4 percent of college students have ever given time or money to a political organization. Less than 15 percent of voters under the age of 25 voted in the last election. The civic engagement of many young adults today is decidedly local, short-term, and apolitical (although the recent burst of antiwar organizing seems an important exception).

These statistics introduce a contrast between the approaches to "service" and "moral learning" that are embedded in our universities. As Keith Morton, director of the Feinstein Institute for Public Service at Providence College has noted, most of the service programs in our universities focus on "understanding the 'other' and, in so doing, reshaping one's self-identity." In order to sensitize students to difference and the need for social cooperation, short-term service programs often focus on what service means for the student and his or her character formation. Volunteer activities thus center on charitable activities and/or temporary relationships that ameliorate immediate needs. The goal for student development is to realize the necessity and richness of a character based on giving and caring for the other.

While this "personal development" approach to service is worthwhile, the model also misses things. Big things. Absent are historical, economic, and political analyses that help students understand how social issues are structured in a specific community, in a specific place, at a specific time. Absent are social justice lenses that challenge students to understand social arrangements and how social change occurs. Absent is an emphasis on political engagement as a key activity for those who care about people and communities.

Making the connection between personal development and social justice models is not easy for many universities and students. College students are in a developmental stage that focuses on interpersonal relationships and learning. Thus tracking how bank loans affect economic development in southwest Atlanta is not always seen as meaningful service. Students flock in droves to reading and tutoring programs in local elementary schools. But few of those students can articulate how property taxes impact school resources—and even fewer will ever vote in a local school board election.

Negotiating the threshold from interpersonal learning to structural analysis is one of the core challenges for moral learning in the university. The "service learning" movement within higher education has offered several avenues for making these connections.

First, the teaching process of many courses is shifting in higher education. Service learning models encourage many professors to pair in-class time with hands-on fieldwork. A student might work in a local addiction clinic while she studies, in class, the social and economic influences on drug use. Deep reflection on the practice in the clinic helps both student and professor change the way classes are taught and texts are read.

Second, service learning approaches to education also change the content of academic courses. Several universities are now creating programs focused on community building and social change. Here the focus is on reading across multiple disciplines to understand the strengths and needs of communities. Community development literature is read next to economic and social theory, ethics, and environmental studies. The collaborative nature of intellectual development in the classroom, matched with the hands-on nature of group projects, forces students beyond individualized models of social change.

Universities that nurture change agents are those that bring together the personal and the political. They break through cycles of remedial charity and systematically address preventative justice. Or as my college mentor often bellowed, they call us to be "poverty warriors," not just poverty companions.

RELATED ARTICLE: THE COMMON GOOD

Exploring Social Change on the Stage, Street, and Classroom

The University of San Francisco, whose motto is "Educating Minds and Hearts to Change the World," challenges students to put both intellect and motivations to work for the common good. For example, in USF's year-long, residential Erasmus Project, sophomores devote five hours a week to community action. Projects range from the library (researching fair trade coffee for Global Exchange) to the street (serving breakfast to day laborers and collecting their stories). The day laborers' stories will be passed on, as the basis of a possible play, to students in USF's Performing Arts and Social Justice major.

Guadalupe Chavez, an Erasmus alumna earning a master's degree at USF's Center for Teaching Excellence and Social Justice, finds in her alma mater the kind of education she wants to give her future students: "I think politics and education go well together—I don't think it can be any other way." Nor is she waiting for graduation to start educating others. Her Peace and Justice Studies minor requires fieldwork; hers was to help eighth graders in San

Francisco's Mission District form a social justice club, in which students talk about everything from local gangs and sweatshops to the prospect of war in Iraq.

Combating College-Grad Stress Syndrome*

Despite the dismal job outlook . . . these tips could make the search
less daunting.

By Susannah Chen

For college seniors, the next two semesters should be the best part of college—a well-deserved chance for some R&R before going out into the real world. But it's that foray into the real world that has prospective graduates viewing the next nine months as a countdown to doomsday, as many of them could graduate without a job.

Unemployment has been on the rise since 2001, and experts can't agree when the picture will brighten. [In spring 2003] U.S. companies said they wouldn't be hiring any more grads than they did in 2002, according to data from the National Association of Colleges & Employers.

The shrinking job market has affected parents, too, who may be hard pressed to support their unemployed college grads. "Before, students had a safety net called mom and dad," says Patricia Rose, director of Career Services at the University of Pennsylvania. "Now, that net isn't as broad and deep."

BEYOND PEP TALKS

More than ever, soon-to-be graduates are relying on their universities to help them find jobs. While many schools are sticking to tried-and-true job-search techniques like résumé workshops and on-campus recruiting, others are supplementing these methods.

Like most schools, Claremont McKenna College has long counted on alumni and trustees to help new grads, but lately it has also been exploring an underused network of parents with students still in school. "Parents of other current students have an affinity for the college and might find interest in [those] who are graduating from the college," says Jefferson Huang, dean of students at Claremont McKenna.

Another way schools are helping students is by offering counseling that goes beyond the standard pep talk. Jerry Houser of Caltech's Career Development Center says students who are anxious about the job search might

---

procrastinate, which can then make their anxiety worse. He tells them to start looking early and stick with it, likening his role to being more like a parent than a counselor. "You'd think students would get more active because of the fear and the uncertainty," he says. "They actually hide or get less active."

Here are several specific tips to help get students started.

Talk to companies, whether or not they're hiring:

Says Claremont McKenna's Huang: "Even if they're not recruiting today, we want to keep the relationship there so when they do pick up—which they will—they'll come back to us shortly. We're cultivating relationships." It's just as important for individuals to nurture relationships. It will give you a leg up when there are job openings.

Professional associations—like the National Society of Accountants or the National Social Science Assn.—provide newcomers with a wealth of resources to explore uncharted territory. These groups also offer discounted memberships to students and hold special events dedicated to industry newbies. "It gives students an automatic network," says Micael Kemp at the University of California at Santa Barbara.

And students looking to develop a relationship beyond the superficial will find help in a number of organizations that offer mentoring programs pairing neophytes with seasoned pros. "Mentors can help guide [students] into entry-level positions," Kemp points out.

Add Mom and Dad to your networking list:

Yes, you thought you would be savoring your imminent independence, not looking to your parents for more help. But even if they aren't in a position to float you though a prolonged bout of unemployment, they can help you in other ways. Fred Pollack, author of *The College Senior's Survival Guide to Corporate America,* advises parents to assist their kids in building networks by asking around at work or having graduating seniors come into their workplace and observe, even if no jobs are available.

Your folks could also pitch in by taking over some of the administrative duties that come with the job search. "You only have a window of time [during the day] when you can call companies," Pollack says. "You can utilize time by talking to people while someone else is helping with email or running to the post office [for you]."

Keep an open mind:

University of Pennsylvania's Rose encourages her students to "look a little more broadly in the field or find similar opportunities in other fields." Students looking into Wall Street–type jobs should consider investment management in addition to investment banking.

Be willing to work for free:

With entry-level positions scarce and companies working with reduced staff, many organizations need help. They just can't pay much for it. "Develop an internship proposal," says Shonool Malik, the assistant director at the MIT Careers Office. By studying up on the company's needs and industry trends, you'll be well prepared to sell yourself, and they'll be pleasantly surprised by your initiative.

Be honest about what you're looking for:

If you talk to someone about doing an internship, don't confuse the issue by asking for a job. Same with an informational interview. Advises Caltech's Houser: "Ask them who they know. Tell them you're interested in their career." That interest often leads to secondary referrals and invites to get-togethers.

Don't use grad school as a fallback:

An internship, a temp job, or even a position in retail will help pay off student loans while buying you time to plan your next move. Don't incur more debt for a degree you're not sure you want—or need for your professional pursuits. "Use that period to start making decisions about what field attracts you and what you want to stay away from," says Kemp. "You're better off getting someone to pay you to work it out."

If you start at the bottom, there's no place else to go but up:

If you do get an offer, don't automatically reject it if it isn't quite as high-paying or glamorous as you would have hoped. After all, even famed Hewlett-Packard (HPQ) CEO Carly Fiorina started her career as a secretary one summer at the company she now runs. [Update: Fiorina stepped down as HP's CEO in early February 2005.]

DISCUSSION

1. When students are asked what they most want out of a college education, the most commonly reported answer is "to get a good job." Engage a group of fellow students in a discussion about what this statement means to each of you. How is your decision to attend college related to your career goals? What thoughts has this chapter stimulated in you about college and careers?

2. Share with fellow students what kinds of knowledge and skills you want to bring to the new knowledge-based economy. As you listen to your fellow students do the same, reflect upon the knowledge and skills you possess

now versus those you want to acquire during college. Contrast yours with those reported by your fellow students and let them inspire you!

3. The article "The University of Social Justice" contrasts the idea of the college experience as vocational preparation versus one that prepares students to go forth and invest their energies, at least in part, in creating some greater order of social justice. Do you see any connections between your personal development and the more idealistic notion of achieving social justice? How might some college activities help develop your career skills as well as your obligation to society? Compare your thoughts with those of other students.

4. Much can and will change by the time you finish college and begin looking for employment. Nevertheless, consider whether you might adopt any of the suggestions offered in the article "Combating College-Grad Stress Syndrome" now, even though you are still in your first year. Given the importance of "getting a good job" to most college students, it's never too early to start thinking about how to apply what you are learning and doing now to that eventual goal.

CHAPTER 12

Relationships

Tom Carskadon of Mississippi
State University contributed his
valuable and considerable
expertise to the writing of this
chapter.

Now that you're in college, are classes and studies the first thing on your mind? Student journals suggest that what often takes center stage are relationships—with dates, lovers, or lifelong partners; with friends and enemies; with parents and family; with roommates, classmates, and coworkers; and with new people and new groups.

Relationships strongly influence your survival and success in college. If you are distracted by bad relationships, you will find it difficult to concentrate on your studies. If you are supported by good relationships, you will be better able to get through the rough times, reach your full potential, stay in college, and enjoy it.

Dating and Mating

Loving an Idealized Image

Swiss psychiatrist Carl Gustav Jung identified a key aspect of love: We each have an idealized image of the perfect partner, which we unconsciously project onto potential partners we meet. The first task in any romantic relationship, then, is to look beyond the initial attraction and see that the person you are in love with really exists! Anyone who can make your knees go weak and your mouth go dry at a single glance can affect your perceptions as well as your body. Are you in love, or are you in lust? People in lust often sincerely believe they are in love, and more than a few will say almost anything to get what they want. But would you still want that person if sex were out of the question? Would that person still want you?

Folklore says love is blind. Believe it. Check out your perceptions with trusted friends. If they see a lot of problems that you do not, at least listen to them. Another good reality check is to observe the other person's friends. Exceptional people rarely surround themselves with jerks and losers. If the person of your dreams tends to collect friends from your nightmares, wake up!

Off Limits!

Some "fishing grounds" are strictly off limits. Never become romantically involved with your teacher or someone who works over or under you. If you date a subordinate, when the relationship ends you may find yourself accused of sexual harassment, fired, or sued. Even dating coworkers carries major risks; it will be much harder to heal from a breakup if you must continue to work together.

Gay and Lesbian Relationships

Although most people build intimate relationships with someone of the opposite sex, some people are attracted to, fall in love with, and make long-term commitments to a person of the same sex. Gay or straight, your sexuality and whom you choose to form intimate relationships with are an important part of who you are.

You need to know that professionals do not consider homosexuality a disease or a mental disorder. Most experts—and most gays and lesbians—believe that sexual orientation is inborn, and that no amount of "treatment," prayer, or anything else is going to change it.

If you are heterosexual, these facts may be puzzling, even troubling, to you. But try putting the shoe on the other foot, as psychologist Robert Feldman suggests. If questions like the following seem stupid to you, they seem just as stupid when heard by gays and lesbians about their sexuality:

> *What caused your heterosexuality? When and how did you choose it? Why do you flaunt your heterosexuality and try to involve others in this lifestyle? Why do you heterosexuals think about sex so much? Wouldn't a good relationship with a skilled homosexual lover make your heterosexuality go away?*

Your sexuality is your own; it isn't dictated by your family, by society, or by what the media present as normal. Although listening to your feelings is important, it may also help to talk about those feelings with someone you trust.

Consult a professional counselor, who helps people with these issues every day. (Most campuses have professional counseling available.) Read about sexuality and sexual orientation. It is important to remember that relationships that involve communication, trust, respect, and love are crucial to all people.

Developing a Relationship

Early in a relationship, you may be wildly "in love." You may find yourself pre-occupied—if not obsessed—with the other person, with feelings of intense longing when you are apart. When you are together, you may feel thrilled and blissful, yet also insecure and demanding. You are likely to idealize the other person, yet you may overreact to faults or disappointments. If the relationship goes awry, your misery is likely to be intense, and the only apparent relief from your pain lies in the hands of the very person who rejected you. Social psychologist Elaine Walster calls this the stage of *passionate* love.

Most psychologists see the first stage as being unsustainable—and that may be a blessing! A successful relationship will move on to a calmer, more stable stage. At this next stage, your picture of your partner is much more realistic. You feel comfortable and secure with each other. Your mutual love and respect stem from predictably satisfying companionship. Walster calls this more comfortable, long-lasting stage *companionate* love.

If a relationship is to last, it is vital to talk about it as you go along. What are you enjoying, and why? What is disappointing you, and what would make it better? Is there anything you need to know? If you set aside a regular time and place to talk, communication will be more comfortable.

Long-Distance Relationships

Many students arrive at college while still romantically involved with someone they left behind. If you restrict yourself to a single, absent partner, you may miss out on a lot, and this often leads to cheating or resentment. Our advice for long-distance relationships: Keep seeing each other as long as you want to, but with the freedom to pursue other relationships, too.

Becoming Intimate

Sexual intimacy inevitably adds a new and powerful dimension to a relationship. We suggest the following:

- Don't hurry into it.
- If sexual activity would violate your morals or values, don't do it. And don't expect others to violate theirs. You do not owe anyone justifications, nor should you put up with attempts to argue you into submission.

- If you have to ply your partner with alcohol or other drugs to get the ball rolling, you aren't engaging in sex—you are committing rape.
- Consult a professional about pregnancy prevention. A pregnancy will drastically curtail your freedom and social life, and finding time for your studies will be much harder. Conception can occur even when couples take precautions. Data based on real-life (as opposed to theoretical) use indicate that students who are sexually active for five years of college and use condoms for birth control all five years have, on average, about a 50–50 chance of having to deal with a pregnancy during college.

When passions run high, physical intimacy can feel like emotional intimacy but sex is an unsatisfying substitute for love or friendship.

Genuine emotional intimacy is knowing, trusting, loving, and respecting each other at the deepest levels, day in and day out, independent of sex. Establishing emotional intimacy takes time—and, in many ways, takes more courage. If you build the emotional intimacy first, not only the relationship but even the sex will be better.

An interesting question is whether sex actually adds to your overall happiness. Believe it or not, a thorough review of the literature on happiness finds no evidence that becoming sexually active increases your general happiness. Sex relieves horniness, but it doesn't ensure happiness. Loving relationships, on the other hand, are powerfully related to happiness.

If you want sexual activity but don't want all the medical risks of sex, consider the practice of "outercourse," mutual and loving stimulation between partners that allows sexual release but involves no exchange of bodily fluids.

Getting Serious

Although dating more than one person can help you clarify what you want, multiple sexual relationships can be dangerous. Besides the health risks involved, it's rare to find a good working relationship where the partners have sex with others. Sexual jealousy is very powerful and can arouse insecurities, anger, and hurt in a heartbeat.

Being exclusive provides the chance to explore a relationship in depth and get a taste of what marriage might be like. But if you are seriously considering marriage, consider this: Studies show that the younger you are, the lower your odds of a successful marriage. It may also surprise you to learn that trial marriage or living together does not decrease your risk of later divorce.

Above all, beware of what might be called "the fundamental marriage error": marrying before both you and your partner are certain about who you are and what you want to do in life. If you want to marry, the person to marry is someone you could call your best friend—the one who knows you inside and out, the one you don't have to play games with, the one who prizes your company without physical rewards, the one who over a period of years has come to know, love, and respect who you are and what you want to be.

Breaking Up

In a national study of 5,000 college students, 29 percent reported they had ended a romantic relationship during their first year in college.

Change can be scary to think about and painful to create, but sometimes it's the only thing to do. When you break up, you lose not only what you had, but also everything you thought you had, plus many cherished hopes and dreams. No wonder it hurts. But remember that you are also opening up a world of new possibilities.

If it is time to break up, do it cleanly and calmly. Don't be impulsive or angry. Explain your feelings and talk them out. If you don't get a mature reaction, take the high road; don't join someone else in the mud.

What about being "just friends"? You may want to remain friends with your partner, especially if you have shared and invested a lot. You can't really be friends, however, until both of you have healed from the hurt and neither of you wants the old relationship back. That usually takes a year or two.

If you are having trouble getting out of a relationship or dealing with its end, get help. Expect some pain, anger, and depression. Your college counselors have assisted many students through similar difficulties. In fact, relationship problems are the most common student concern that college counselors hear about. It is also a good time to get moral support from friends and family. Read a good book on the subject, such as *How to Survive the Loss of a Love*.

You and Your Parents

If you are on your own for the first time, your relationship with your parents is going to change. A first step in establishing a good relationship with your parents is to be aware of their perceptions. Here are their most common ones:

- Parents fear you'll harm yourself. You may take risks that make older people shudder. You may shudder, too, when you look back on some of your stunts.
- Parents think their daughter is still a young innocent. Yes, the old double standard (differing expectations for men than women, particularly regarding sex) is alive and well.
- Parents know you're older but picture you as much younger. Maybe it's because they loved you so much as a child they can't erase that image.

- Parents mean well. Most love their children, even if it doesn't always come out right; very few are really indifferent or hateful.
- The old have been young, but the young haven't been old. Parental memories of youth may be hazy, but at least they've been there.

Some families are truly dysfunctional. If love, respect, enthusiasm, and encouragement are just not in the cards, look around you. Other people will give you these things, and you can create the family you need. With your emotional needs satisfied, your reactions to your real family will be much less painful.

Try setting aside regular times to update your parents on how college and your life in general are going. Ask for and consider their advice. You don't have to take it. Finally, realize that your parents are not here forever. Mend fences while you can.

Married Life in College

Both marriage and college are challenges. With so many demands, it is critically important that you and your partner share the burdens equally; you cannot expect a harried partner to spoil or pamper you.

If you are in college but your spouse is not, it's important to bring your partner into your college life. Share what you're learning in your courses. See if your partner can take a course, too—maybe just to audit for the fun of it. Take your partner to cultural events—lectures, plays, concerts—on your campus. If your campus has social organizations for students' spouses, try them out.

Electronic Relationships

Nowadays, through electronic mail, message boards, interest groups, dating sites, and chat groups, it is possible to form relationships with people you have never met.

For instance, there is a student who has regular email correspondence with the following group, who all met online: an aspiring screenwriter in New Jersey, an undercover narcotics agent in Michigan, a professional animator in Georgia, a college teacher in Connecticut, a high school student in Arizona, a librarian in California, a strip-club bartender in Tennessee, a mother in Pennsylvania, a police officer in Australia, a flight attendant in Illinois, an entrepreneur in Louisiana, a psychologist in Colorado, a physician in training in Texas, a schoolteacher in Canada, and college students in five states and three countries.

The downside? Electronic relationships may be more transient and unpredictable than "real world" ones. People may not be what they seem. Meeting them in real life may be delightful—or disastrous. You could literally be corresponding with a state prisoner! Be very cautious about letting strangers know your name, address, telephone number, or other personal information, and about considering face-to-face meetings.

If you find yourself spending hours every day with people on the computer, you are probably overdoing it. Don't let electronic relationships substitute for "real" ones in your life. By the way, your college counselors have experience dealing with students suffering from "computer addiction."

Roommates

Roommates range from the ridiculous to the sublime. You may find a lifetime friend or an exasperating acquaintance.

With any roommate, establish your mutual rights and responsibilities in writing. Many colleges provide contract forms that you and your roommate can use. If things go wrong later, you will have something to point to.

If you have problems, talk them out promptly. Talk directly—politely but plainly. If problems persist, or if you don't know how to talk them out, see your residence counselor if you live on campus, or seek assistance at the counseling center if you live off campus.

On-Campus Involvement

Organizations help you find friends with similar interests. And remember, new students who become involved with at least one organization are more likely to survive their first year and remain in college.

To go Greek or not to go Greek? Greek-letter social organizations (fraternities and sororities) are not all alike, nor are their members. Some students love them. But other students may find them philosophically distasteful, too demanding of time and finances, and/or too constricting. Take a good look at the upperclass students in the organization. If what you see is what you want to be, consider joining. If not, steer clear.

Many campuses have residence halls or special floors for students with common interests or situations, such as first-year students; honors students; students in particular majors; students desiring quiet space; students who shun tobacco, alcohol, and drugs; students interested in protecting the environment; and so on. These often provide very satisfying experiences.

Off-Campus Involvement

Co-op Programs

Many schools have co-op programs in which you spend some terms in regular classes and other terms in temporary job settings in your field. They offer an excellent preview of what work in your chosen field is actually like, thus helping you find out if you have made the right choice. They give you valuable experience and contacts that help you get a job when you finish school; in fact, many firms offer successful co-op students permanent jobs when they graduate.

Alternating work and school terms may be a more agreeable schedule for you than eight or ten straight terms of classes would be, and it may help you keep your ultimate goal in mind. Co-op programs can help you pay for school, too. And don't forget service learning, as discussed in Chapter 11.

Relationships are an integral part of your education and can consume a majority of your waking hours. Whether you're a traditional-age new student living on or off campus, or a returning student with family responsibilities, be sure to approach your relationships with the same effort and planning as you would approach your course work. Long after you have forgotten whole courses you took, you will remember relationships that began or grew in college.

YOUR PERSONAL JOURNAL

Here are a number of topics to write about. Choose one or more. Or choose another topic related to this chapter.

1. This chapter advises you to date others before making a commitment to one individual, but not to have more than one sexual relationship at a time. What is your reaction to that?
2. If you are a married student, what do you see as your biggest problems in balancing your family and your education? What is your plan for dealing with those problems?
3. Describe your relationship with your parents. Has it changed now that you are in college? What is your plan for maintaining and improving it?
4. If you have made friends with some people who are very different from you, write about those relationships and what you have learned from them.
5. If you have a roommate, describe the best and worst things about living with that person. What is your plan for dealing with the things that bother you?

6. What behaviors are you willing to change after reading this chapter? How might you go about changing them?
7. What else is on your mind this week? If you wish to share it with your instructor, add it to this journal entry.

READINGS

College Women Say College Men Don't Ask for Dates*

Most college women plan to get married and many expect to meet their future husbands at school; however, the college dating scene does not offer realistic opportunities to get to know potential partners, according to a study of heterosexual women at U.S. colleges and universities commissioned by the Independent Women's Forum. Although more than eight in 10 women (88%) say they are generally happy with the social scene at their colleges, they describe the campus climate as offering limited romantic options.

The most common forms of sexual interaction between college women and men offer either far more or far less commitment than most college women prefer. Women at all universities studied refer to the practice of "hooking up" as widespread, defining it as a casual sexual encounter (which may or may not include intercourse) often fueled by alcohol, with no emotional attachment involved or implied.

Although less than half (40%) of women surveyed indicate they have participated in such an encounter, over nine in 10 students (91%) say hook-ups occur fairly or very frequently (50% say very frequently) at their colleges. Women who have participated in a hook-up report feeling ambivalent afterward; most express feelings of confusion and awkwardness, even if they also felt "sexy" as a result of the encounter.

Women also say that most women who have hooked up end up waiting to find out whether the man is interested in pursuing a further relationship. Although some women believe participating in casual encounters is a sign of assertiveness, they also acknowledge that most often it is the woman who then allows the man to determine the nature of any further relationship. And many women who describe feeling hurt or rejected by such experiences blame themselves for having gotten involved in the first place—or for reacting emotionally to a sexual encounter.

Marketing to Women, September 2001, v14, i9, p. 7. © 2001 EPM Communications, Inc., www.epmcom.com. Reprinted with permission.

Women say that while men who engage in a lot of casual hook-ups tend to be described as "studs" or "players" by other students, women who behave in the same fashion acquire epithets such as "slut," "ho," "skanky," "couch," and "trash." Some women say they engage in casual sexual activities to avoid the bother of a committed relationship, which they see as being too time-consuming. Given the model for the most common type of romantic relationship observed among college students, this is not surprising.

College students describe the typical committed relationship at school as a very intense, fast-moving relationship, in which the members of the couple spend virtually all of their waking and sleeping hours together.

Relationships that progress more slowly are rarer on campus, say women, even though most would prefer such relationships—or even the opportunity to go on "old-fashioned" dates with a variety of people before getting involved with just one. Less than half of college women (37%) report having been on more than six "real dates" since they've been at college. Even junior and senior women have experienced few dates at college: 47% of juniors and 50% of seniors have been on more than six dates. Further, many say the few dates they have had were tied to a structured social occasion, such as a school dance or Valentine's Day.

Six in 10 women (60%) report having had at least one boyfriend while at college, even though some of them have never been on "real dates" with their boyfriends. Much of social and romantic interaction centers around simply "hanging out" in the dorms.

Women in the study are critical of the lack of structured social interaction and clarity about relationships on campus, and more than half (51%) say there are not clearly understood informal rules about relationships on their campuses. Women also complain about the men on campus being too passive about asking out women in whom they have an interest, and being more likely to prefer hook-ups than dates or relationships. Six in 10 women (61%) agree with the statement "There aren't many guys here (on campus) who want a committed relationship." Women are also invariably the ones who initiate a discussion about the nature of a relationship.

Many women note that they are trying to establish friendships with possible partners before getting romantically involved, but that there is often confusion in this case as to whether social activities are dates or merely friendly.

While the vast majority of college women (83%) consider marriage a very important personal goal, and 53% say they would like to meet their future mate while at college, the collegiate social scene does not appear to be conducive to getting to know potential mates. For the most part, women describe hooking up as being a purely physical encounter (some even cite the lack of conversation involved as a point in favor of hooking up). And "joined at the hip" relationships are so intense and exclusionary that women involved in them feel cut off from socializing with others even in a non-sexual way.

Nevertheless, 83% of college women agree with the statement "The things I do in my relationship today will affect my future marriage," and 86% believe that if they do get married, their marriage will last their whole lives.

A College Student's First Lesson Often Is How to Live with a Stranger*
By Patrice Relerford

Meridith McLane is excited. High school is over, and college is just weeks away.

McLane, 18, who graduated in May from Crossroads School, will start Xavier University in Cincinnati this fall. Although she soon will move hundreds of miles away from her family and friends, she won't be alone. She'll live in a residence hall and have a roommate. Everyone she meets will be someone new—a big change for a teenager who pretty much went to school with the same kids for years.

"I'm always willing to try new things," McLane said of the friendships she will strike up.

Relationships between roommates can be among the most lasting memories of college. A roommate is often the first friend you make, and some remain close for the rest of their lives. Of course not all roommate situations are idyllic. Still, say those in the know, there are ways to enhance this relationship or at least help it get it off to a good start.

Jill Stratton is associate director of residential life at Washington University. Stratton said sharing a room with anyone, let alone a stranger, can greatly influence a college student's overall experience.

"College students (who live on campus) spend about 70 percent of their time in residence halls," Stratton said. If they get along with their roommates and others in the dorm, they are likely to have a good freshman year, she said. "But if it's not a good place for them to be—if there's tension—it can negatively impact them," she added.

McLane is too pumped to think about what can go wrong. To get the relationship going, she and her roommate called each other and sent emails throughout the summer.

What McLane knows about her roommate makes her feel optimistic. When they talked about their families, interests and boyfriends, McLane discovered

*St. Louis Post-Dispatch, August 12, 2003. Reprinted with permission of the St. Louis Post-Dispatch, copyright 2003.

they are both die-hard soccer fans. They immediately planned a road trip and bought tickets for a World Cup soccer game in Columbus in September.

Beth Lauchstaedt likes that McLane already has a feel for her roommate. Lauchstaedt serves as a residence hall coordinator at the University of Missouri at Columbia, managing student staff members and programs in three residence halls.

Lauchstaedt recommends contacting roommates over the summer to help break the ice. Nowadays, schools often send housing assignment letters to students before they arrive on campus that provide roommate contact information. That way everyone gets to know a little about each other before they meet.

During the getting-to-know-you conversation, Lauchstaedt advises roommates to discuss their background, interests, and the items they will bring for the room. "That way you're not meeting them cold, it allows you to put the facts with the face," she said.

During his freshman year, Kent Adams, 19, shared a suite with three guys at Southwest Missouri State University in Springfield, Mo. Although he and his roommates attended Kirkwood High School together, they had never lived with each other. Luckily, the four had no major brawls, but small incidents bothered Adams.

"You get to see what people are really like when you live with them," Adams said.

It took some time for Adams to adjust to his roommates' living habits, particularly how neat or messy they were. They sometimes argued over taking out the trash and what to watch on TV. He also stopped studying in his room. Too many other students would hang out at his suite because it was the largest on their floor. This fall, Adams will try living in a fraternity house.

Dee Kauffman is the assistant director of residential life at St. Louis University and has worked in education for 10 years. Over the years, Kauffman said, the worst conflicts have arisen between roommates who came to campus already friends.

Kauffman said friends often are afraid to talk about conflicts because they worry they will destroy their friendship. But Kauffman said even friends should discuss how to handle late-night phone calls, keeping the room clean, and other living habits because everyone eventually reaches a breaking point.

To reduce conflicts, SLU has a lower student-to-staff ratio in the residence halls for first-year students. In addition, residence advisors receive extensive training on how to handle freshmen issues.

At Mizzou [University of Missouri], Brittany Paris, 19, of St. Louis, reached a point where she didn't know what to say to her roommate. She grew tired of trying to make her roommate help clean their room. It wasn't that she disliked the girl or that Paris was a neat freak. But she could no longer look at the growing piles of clothes, books, and moldy food her roommate left around.

"She had no cleaning ethic whatsoever," Paris said. "Everything was always junky." The experience was a culture shock for Paris. This school year she will live on campus, but she decided against letting the school randomly assign her a roommate.

Schools typically offer assistance in navigating these new relationships, but differ in how they handle roommate issues. During freshmen orientation at Washington University, students fill out an agreement stating how they will live. Bedtimes, cleanliness, and other issues are discussed by roommates and student staff members. The agreement is a reference point whenever conflicts arise, Stratton said.

At Mizzou, intervention is typically a last resort. Getting too involved in students' lives conflicts with the idea that college helps them become adults, Lauchstaedt said. Students are expected to work out their differences themselves. If they decide they need assistance, a staff member will help draw up a "roommate contract." In it, students outline things that are bothering them, such as bringing guests to the room all the time. Then they decide how to address the problems.

Despite all the horror stories, many first-year roommate experiences turn out well. Kenyatta Thacker, 24, is still friendly with her former freshman-year roommate. Thacker, now a junior at the University of Missouri at St. Louis, spent a year living in the residence halls. Now she has her own apartment, but she still deals with roommate issues.

Thacker, who mentors freshmen students, said many arrive at college not used to sharing anything. She advises making trade-offs and compromising. For instance, if one roommate brings a computer the other can provide a VCR or DVD player. The two can share the expense of a small refrigerator. However, some roommates want certain possessions to be off limits. No problem, but they should probably agree to that ahead of time, says Thacker.

Although there are pitfalls, living with a stranger can be a good experience. Thacker said it simply requires bluntness and not avoiding issues that need to be discussed.

"The most important question is what are your pet peeves," Thacker said. "They are going to get on your nerves. Ask so you don't take things personally."

DISCUSSION

1. Your text claims that the greatest influence on college students is that of other college students. Discuss your reactions to this assertion. So far in

college, which relationships are the most influential in the key decisions you make?

2. College students often set both academic and career goals—and the authors of this text have encouraged you to do this, too. Try setting *relationship goals* for yourself for your time in college. Kick around this idea, and its possible merits, in a group discussion.

3. The first reading discusses the social/dating—or lack of "dating" scene on residential campuses for traditional-aged college students, with special focus on the phenomenon of "hooking up." Discuss with fellow students how this compares to what really happens on your campus. What are the implications for your academic success and social satisfaction?

4. The second reading considers the challenges facing residential college students moving away from home for the first time and living with a roommate who essentially is "a stranger." Regardless of where you live and with whom, your living arrangements have a big influence on your chances for success as you start college. With your group, create a list of strategies that might help any college student make the most out of his or her residential situation.

CHAPTER 13

Appreciating Our Differences

J. Herman Blake, Iowa State University, and Joan Rasool, Westfield State College, contributed their valuable and considerable expertise to the writing of this chapter.

IN THIS CHAPTER, YOU WILL LEARN

- How diversity in America has changed and is changing
- Why it isn't easy to label an individual as a member of a certain cultural group
- The value of sharing your uniqueness with others
- What colleges are doing to promote healthy diversity
- How to fight discrimination and prejudice on campus
- How the "old minority" is becoming the "new majority"

For years, the United States prided itself on being one nation united by a common culture. Subcultures (Hispanic, African-American, Asian-American, and others) were encouraged to shed much of their cultural identities and become part of the whole.

Then, in the wake of the civil rights movement of the sixties, this concept of a "melting pot" vanished, replaced by an ideal called "diversity," where different ethnic groups, instead of melding into one another to produce an "American ethnicity," would celebrate their own cultures as well as the general culture.

Many view diversity as a more tolerant ideal than the melting pot, claiming it allows people to preserve their identities instead of forcing them into assimilation. Others argue that "diversity" encourages the belief that culture is genetically transmitted and racially specific. All of this is perhaps an oversimplification of what diversity actually stands for. As a new college student, you should understand that individuals belonging to various cultural, ethnic, and racial groups share common traits not only with others of their particular group, but also with others beyond their group.

What did you learn about people who were different from you when you were growing up? How might college help change your attitudes toward people of other races, ethnicities, and cultures?

Race, Ethnic Groups, and Culture

The word *race* generally refers to a group of people who are distinct from other people in terms of certain inherited characteristics: skin color, hair color, hair texture, body build, and facial features. *Ethnic group* can refer to people of different races or to people of the same race who can be distinguished by language, national origin, religious tradition, and so on.

Culture refers to the material and nonmaterial products that people in a society create or acquire from other societies and pass on to future generations. Culture includes a society's beliefs, values, norms, and language. For example, many European societies believe children should learn to be independent and self-sufficient at an early age, whereas Hispanic cultures tend to place a high value on strong family ties. As people from different ethnic groups marry one another and have children, the word *race* is slowly becoming insufficient as a descriptor of individuals with mixed heritages, and many such people are refusing to fill in the line asking for "race" on numerous government and business forms, especially when their only choices are white, black, Asian, Hispanic, and the ubiquitous "other."

The Changing U.S. Population

When the Census Bureau completed its count of the American population in April 2000, we learned that the United States had 281 million people within its 50 states and territories. During the 20th century, the number of Americans had increased by more than 200 million people, a phenomenal and unprecedented rate of change.

When the latest figures were revealed, the director of the Census Bureau, Kenneth Prewitt, stated that not only was the United States a dynamic nation in terms of population growth, it was the only nation in the world where virtually every group represented had its origins in another country. Seldom before had we thought about the diverse origins of the American population as we did in the last portion of the 20th century.

You undoubtedly will encounter this diversity during college, and most definitely in your postcollegiate life. Social change over the past 100 years has changed the face of America, and the results of these changes will become increasingly apparent in the early part of the new century.

In a 10-year study of college student success, Harvard University Professor Richard J. Light found that an overwhelming majority of his students reported that the impact of racial and ethnic diversity on learning was both strong and positive.[1] Such experiences are occurring among college students from all types of institutions. In a letter to his teacher at a university in Iowa, where racial minorities are a very small percentage of the population, a recent white college graduate who is now a corporate executive wrote, "A day doesn't go by that I don't use something I learned from African-American Studies."

A Century of Change

Figures from the 2000 Census show that the United States has greater racial diversity, greater ethnic diversity, and more foreign-born residents than ever before. Women play a much greater role in every aspect of American life. And emerging lifestyles make it imperative that students become more sensitive to and knowledgeable about others as well as themselves.

Race and ethnicity are much more complex ideas than commonly assumed. In counting the American population in 2000, the Census Bureau used five categories of race, plus two additional categories for people of "some other race" or "two or more races" (see Table 13.1).

People from Hispanic or Latino backgrounds are not considered a race, but an ethnic group. The Census Bureau reports that more than 35 million Americans (12.5% of the total) identify themselves as Hispanic. If we add these numbers to those of other minorities, we can see that racial and ethnic minorities together represent more than one-third of the U.S. population at the beginning of the 21st century.

While little changed in the first half of the 20th century, the second half was a different matter. Not only racial distribution changed but the definitions

Table 13.1   Total U.S. Population, 2000, by Race

White	75.1%
Black or African-American	12.3
American Indian/Alaska Native	0.9
Asian	3.6
Hawaiian/Pacific Islander	0.1
Some other race	5.5
Two or more races	2.4

Source: U.S. Bureau of the Census, "Overview of Race and Hispanic Origin: 2000," *Census 2000 Brief*, C2KBR/01-1, March 2001, by Elizabeth M. Grieco and Rachel C. Cassidy.

---

[1] Richard J. Light, *Making the Most of College: Students Speak Their Minds* (Cambridge, MA: Harvard University Press, 2001), pp. 9–10, and chapters 7, 8.

of race also changed. The American Anthropological Association reports that since 1900, more than 30 different racial terms have been used to identify populations in the U.S. Census. Regardless of definitions, however, it is clear that the United States is more racially diverse than ever before, and this diversity is apparent at many colleges and universities.

Another aspect of present-day American diversity is the changing distribution of country of origin. In 1900, 13 percent of all Americans were foreign born. This percentage declined to 7 percent by 1950, and grew to 8 percent by 1990. What is significant, however, is the dramatic change in the places from which these new Americans came. By the end of the 20th century, more than 26 million persons of foreign birth were living in the United States, many of them as naturalized citizens. In 1999, 50.7 percent of all foreign-born residents were from Latin America, most of them from Mexico or Central America. Another 27.1 percent were born in Asia, and 15.1 percent were born in Europe. The remaining 6.2 percent were born in other areas of the world.[2]

In the past, racial differentiation was often viewed in terms of whites and blacks (see Table 13.2). Blacks are still a major racial group in America, but they have been increasingly joined by Asians, American Indians, and Alaska Natives. What's more, definitions of race are expanding so that Native Hawaiian and Other Pacific Islanders are now counted as a separate race.[3]

Recently, the Census Bureau acknowledged that a growing number of Americans are of more than one race. In the 2000 census, more than 6 million people described themselves as multiracial. Although most indicated they were of two races, some indicated as many as five races. It's harder now than ever before to categorize any individual.

Besides race and country of origin, a third dimension of American diversity is ethnicity. As we said earlier, an ethnic group is defined by cultural characteristics that are voluntary, such as language, lifestyle, cuisine, or other

Table 13.2   Trends in U.S. Population by Race

TIME	POPULATION	WHITE	BLACK	OTHER
1900	76 million	87.9%	11.6%	0.5%
1950	151 million	89.5%	10.0%	0.5%
2000	291 million	75.1%	12.3%	*see below

* American Indian/Alaska Native, 0.9; Asian, 3.6; Hawaiian/Pacific Islander, 0.1, some other race, 5.5; two or more races, 2.4.
SOURCE: Census Bureau.

[2] U.S. Bureau of the Census, "PPL-123, Profile of the Foreign-Born Population in the United States: March 1999," issued August 2000.

[3] U.S. Bureau of the Census, "Overview of Race and Hispanic Origin," *Census 2000 Brief,* issued March 2001.

patterns of social organization. Race and ethnicity intersect in various ways. In the 2000 census, for example, nearly half (48%) of all Latinos indicated their race as white. Others described themselves as black or American Indian, and many indicated that they represented two or more races.

Can you understand why the concept of "race" is becoming less and less distinct today?

The Many Dimensions of Diversity

Even though we may think race and ethnicity are clearly distinct concepts, such is not the case. In fact, race and ethnicity are basically social concepts we use to categorize and define people according to their physical appearance or the way they act or sound. *No reputable social scientist would ever assert there is any biological or scientific foundation for the idea of race.*

In a discussion of their decision to expand the racial categories in the 2000 enumeration, the Census Bureau cited "changing lifestyles and emerging sensitivities" among the people of the United States as reasons for the revised categories.

In one class in a large university, the instructor assumed that students who looked Asian would consent to being considered Asian, yet three students objected very strongly to being so categorized. One student wrote that he was *not* Asian, he was Vietnamese. Another wrote that she was Filipino. Still a third wrote, "I am of the Hawaiian race." Students who were referred to as Hispanic or Latino had similar reactions. Some asserted that they not only were Puerto Rican, they were not a minority. In their homes, they were the majority group. Enrollment in a large mainland university led to their being categorized in a number of ways that they rejected.

Another example of the intersection and interaction of race, ethnicity, and national origin can be seen in a *New York Times* series on race in America.[4] Two young men, born in Cuba and growing up as good friends, emigrated separately to the United States and settled in Miami. As Latinos of Cuban birth, they shared a common origin and ethnicity. They shared a common language. But once in the United States, they found they were considered two different races. As a result, it became difficult to maintain their childhood friendship, and they ultimately grew apart. One man was white, the other black.

This last example shows that the *concept* of race is still powerful in the United States. The consequence is that physical appearance—including skin complexion, hair texture, and eye shape—is an important part of our categorization of others and ourselves.

---

[4] Correspondents of *The New York Times, How Race Is Lived in America: Pulling Together, Pulling Apart* (New York: Henry Holt and Company, 2001).

The Concept of Race on Campus

As you observe your campus environment, you will see clear evidence of the significance of race in the way students interact with one another and how they view others as well as themselves. This is a particularly intense experience for black or African-American students. Such groups as the Black Student Alliance (Union) as well as black fraternities and sororities are crucial to the participation and success of black students in predominantly white institutions. Although black students rarely seek to isolate themselves from the larger campus community, they are seldom welcomed into the campus community based on their individual merits and special qualities. Instead, they are often seen and perceived as black, with little understanding of who they really are. Whenever someone asks, "Why do all the black students sit together in the cafeteria?" you might do well to ask if they have ever noticed that all the white students also sit together. Transcending the boundaries of race in college will require that all students become extremely sensitive to one another and aware of how race affects perceptions, understandings, and experiences.

To a profound degree, ideas of race affect how students perceive themselves and how they perceive others, and may well affect the opportunities for shared activities. What's more, as we have seen, ideas of race are changing even though fundamental notions of race persist. College is the one place where many of these concepts and their related structures can be bridged if students can find common ground for interaction and cooperation.

What Does the Future Hold for You, for Me, for Us?

In considering diversity and the American future, the past provides some indication of what may happen. At the start of the 20th century, European Americans represented 88 percent of the total population. By the beginning of the 21st century, that number had dropped to 75 percent. Regardless of where, diversity is becoming more and more an everyday experience in society.

The dynamic and rapid nature of this change is apparent when we realize that in 1996 the Census Bureau projected that the minority population would not reach one-third of the total until the year 2020. This proportion has been reached more than 20 years ahead of the predictions.[5]

If the present rates of change continue, we can expect minorities to make up 50 percent of the U.S. population by the year 2030. This will mean that

---

[5] U.S. Bureau of the Census, "Population by Race and Hispanic Origin 1990–2050," *Current Population Reports,* February 1996, Series P25-1130, Tables I and J.

when you reach the height of your personal and professional future, half of all Americans will belong to racial or ethnic minorities. What will diversity mean then? Will the term "minority" still be appropriate? Some see an amalgam of peoples that will lead to a new race, a "monochrome society."[6] Though we cannot predict in specific terms what the future will be, it is safe to say that it could be considerably different from the present.

It matters little what metaphors are used or what predictions are made. The future will be dynamic and different, just as our recent past has been. As Amitai Etzioni points out, "We came in many ships, but now we ride in the same boat."[7]

Gays and Lesbians

You can't tell someone's sexual orientation just by appearance. The fact that a person is gay or lesbian doesn't mean he or she is attracted to all people of the same sex (Are you attracted to all people of the opposite sex?). Also, being gay or lesbian is rarely a choice. Each year, scientists find further evidence indicating that sexual orientation may be influenced by genetic as well as environmental factors. Last, most child molesters are white male heterosexuals—not homosexuals.

Returning Students

Adult students (those 25 and older) are enrolling in college courses in record numbers. Women may make this choice after raising children, to learn skills for a new career. Other adults, men and women, may decide it's time to broaden their horizons or prepare themselves for a better job with a higher starting salary. Many returning students work full-time and attend school part-time. Given the potential stressors of family and work, their persistence is remarkable.

Students with Disabilities

Students with learning disabilities cannot easily learn some academic skills, such as listening, thinking, speaking, writing, spelling, or doing math calculations. Even though they lack certain abilities, these students are of normal or above-average intelligence and are motivated to learn coping strategies that

---

[6] James W. Russell, *After the Fifth Sun: Class and Race in North America* (Englewood Cliffs, NJ: Prentice-Hall, 1994).

[7] Amitai Etzioni, *The Monochrome Society* (Princeton, NJ: Princeton University Press, 2001).

aid them in facing different types of academic situations. Most learning disabilities are not readily apparent. If a friend confides to you that he or she is having problems with basic skills, you might urge that person to contact the academic skills center.

When you see a student with a physical disability, the most respectful thing to do is to greet him or her just as you would any other person. If the student is in your class, you probably should not go out of your way to offer help unless the person asks for it. A quadriplegic student once asked his teacher how he could explain to another student that he did not want her to always help him write his papers.

Discrimination and Prejudice on College Campuses

Unfortunately, acts of discrimination and incidents of prejudice are rising on college campuses. Although some schools may not be experiencing overt racial conflict, tension still exists; many students report having little contact with students from different racial or ethnic groups. A national survey, "Taking America's Pulse," conducted for the National Conference of Christians and Jews, indicated that blacks, whites, Hispanics, and Asians hold many negative stereotypes about one another. The good news is that "nine out of 10 Americans nationwide claim they are willing to work with people of all races—even those they felt they had the least in common with—to advance race relations."[8]

You should be aware that in addition to being morally and personally repugnant, discrimination is illegal. Most colleges and universities have established policies against all forms of racism, anti-Semitism, and ethnic and cultural intolerance. These policies prohibit racist actions or omissions, including verbal harassment or abuse that might deny anyone his or her rights to equity, dignity, culture, or religion. Anyone found in violation of such policies faces corrective action, including appropriate disciplinary action.

If college is where you seek an education and develop values for life, appreciating people who are different from you is one of its major lessons. Regardless of the "group" you belong to, all college graduates have one thing in common: a degree that is the mark of an educated person. If you avoid the chance to know people from other groups, you'll be missing out on many of the benefits of your education.

---

[8] "Survey Finds Minorities Resent Whites and Each Other," *Jet* 28 (March 1994).

YOUR PERSONAL JOURNAL

Here are a number of topics to write about. Choose one or more. Or choose another topic related to this chapter.

1. Many people today are enthusiastic about diversity. Others say, "Whatever will be will be. I don't think it's right to go out of my way to make friends with someone from another culture." What do you think?
2. Write down five adjectives that you would use to describe yourself to someone you have never met or spoken with. Do any of the adjectives describe your race, gender, sexual preference, ethnicity, or culture? Or is your self-description based on other characteristics? Write the adjectives on a card and don't put your name on it. Then pass it around the group and see if one or more students can identify you.
3. An older student arrives at class 10 minutes late each day and explains that she has to feed her child breakfast and drop him off at day care. How do you think the instructor should handle this?
4. How can you benefit from having a diverse set of friends? How can they benefit?
5. What behaviors are you willing to change after reading this chapter? How might you go about changing them?
6. What else is on your mind this week? If you wish to share it with your instructor, add it to your journal entry.

READINGS

Don't Forget the Women*
African-American female college students.
By M. Rick Turner

With so much media attention focused on the plight of young African-American males, I fear that the experiences and challenges African-American females face often go unnoticed. This seems to be especially true for those attending predominantly white institutions. As a follow-up to my article "Where the Boys Are," appearing in the Spring 2000 issue of *Black Issues in*

Black Issues in Higher Education, May 10, 2001, v18, i6, p. 34. Copyright 2001 Black Issues In Higher Education. Reprinted with permission.

Higher Education, I felt compelled to make sure that I, too, did not commit the unpardonable sin of ignoring our young women.

Our young women carry the burden of simultaneously being ambassadors for the race and cheerleaders for our young men. They encourage our males to get involved in university life so they can somehow ease the feelings of alienation.

Although African-American females don't talk too much (at least not with me) about the dearth of African-American males at our institution, I cannot help but believe that there are several serious social consequences to this issue. In the words of one African-American female, "Finding a man is a challenge because your choices are limited. First, because not many black males are admitted to the university and the numbers are getting smaller and smaller. So the number of black women and men is disproportionate. Many African-American women feel that African-American men are doing a good job surviving and that they should be given credit for being here because they could be involved in so many things that have nothing to do with going to school."

Over the past several years, I have asked African-American females in my sociology class to write papers and to conduct mini research projects and interviews with other African-American students about their experiences at the University of Virginia. Through their findings and my own conversations with female students in the Office of African-American Affairs, I am getting a better understanding of what it means to be a black female here.

Two third-year students, Miya Hunter and Chantale Fiebig, voluntarily emailed their thoughts to me. They seem to fully understand that the socialization of African-American females into womanhood is a complex process, and that the mother–daughter relationship, in particular, is central to understanding their experiences at a predominantly white selective institution. They both agree, as do many others with whom I have talked, that in order for African-American women to feel comfortable with who they are at UVA (or any campus), they need to feel strongly supported at home.

Black women often face many challenges in having their voices heard in classrooms. In many cases, students find themselves the only African-American in a class. They feel a certain degree of anxiety because they are expected to represent the black race as a whole. In the face of these issues, it becomes even more important that home is a constant source of encouragement, affirmation, and reassurance. It is critical that young women who question themselves at college feel as though they have a source of unconditional acceptance from home.

During the spring 2000 semester, LaTasha Levy, a fourth-year student in my class, conducted interviews and heard that there is often a "coldness" and tension among black females, too often over males.

African-American women often feel compelled to compete in fashion, in appearance, and for men. Although this type of competition is often healthy and somewhat natural in male–female relationships, it is also important to take note of what Hunter and Fiebig stated in their email to me: "In order to be here [at the university], they [African-American females] are active women who have proven that they possess initiative, an appreciation of education, and a willingness to work hard. None of these strengths should be compromised in efforts to cultivate a newfound social life, to enhance one's appearance, or to attract male attention. Many women are able to enjoy healthy social lives while nurturing the positive traits that helped them arrive here in the first place. . . ."

Many African-American women recognize that they must address issues of respect for themselves and for each other. They must begin to have ongoing, open, and honest discussions about self-esteem, assertiveness, and internalized racism.

They must reflect upon how society, their upbringing, and/or early experiences with African-American women cause them to perceive each other with some level of mistrust and envy. Of course, as Levy noted in her work, "not all African-American women have to be best friends, nor should they consider themselves natural enemies. Sisterhood may in some respects seem Utopian, yet it is definitely something worth striving for."

Students Reveal the Reality of College Diversity*
By James M. O'Neill

America's most selective colleges have long defended affirmative action in admissions as vital to the kind of diverse campus that improves the academic experience for all students.

But many at those colleges express frustration at how diversity plays out once classes begin. They say:

Schools view diversity through too narrow a prism and students tend not to mix socially, short-circuiting the benefits of diversity.

Colleges might be diverse ethnically but fail the test for socioeconomics or political thought. They are largely composed of middle- and upper-middle-income students, and conservative political views are given short shrift.

Diversity should go well beyond race—though it is race that is the focus of the recent national debate about affirmative action.

Knight Ridder/Tribune News Service, June 11, 2003, p. K1259. Copyright 2003 Knight Ridder/Tribune. Reprinted with permission.

[When] the U.S. Supreme Court [was deciding in 2003 that narrow use of] affirmative action in admissions is legal, many selective colleges [were] on edge, worried that the student diversity they carefully craft [would] be at risk.

With that as a backdrop, *The Philadelphia Inquirer* conducted interviews with 45 students, chosen randomly, at seven selective colleges in the region . . . finding a jumble of opinions on affirmative action and diversity and how they affect the college experience.

From the University of Pennsylvania to Haverford College, from Bryn Mawr to Swarthmore, students offer up stories about how much more diverse the student body is compared with their mostly white, middle-class, suburban high schools.

"My freshman dorm was like the United Nations," said Jacquelene Kahn, a Swarthmore junior. "My roommate was from Singapore. Down the hall was someone from Ireland. Upstairs was someone from Nigeria."

That diversity generates a better classroom discussion, students say. Jillian Smith, a Dickinson College sophomore, said her courses on urban issues were better served by the presence of students who grew up in the inner city. "You can read about something, but that doesn't mean you necessarily comprehend fully. Any time a [city] student shared a story, everyone in class understood more."

Penn junior Brooke Dairman said one of her best friends on campus was someone she met by chance, an African-American who grew up in North Philadelphia. "It was eye-opening," she said. "It showed me that friendships can transcend race. I was afraid that race would constantly be a centerpiece of our interaction, but it turns out we're just people who are friends."

Students say they actively sought out schools with diverse student bodies because they knew that would add value to their education. Bryn Mawr senior Rachel Brodsky put it this way: "If the idea of liberal arts education is to prepare you to think critically, it means you have to challenge your biases."

But students say their schools fail to build campuses with political diversity.

"There's definitely a liberal bias. Conservative opinions are shut down and dismissed offhand," said John Anderson, a Swarthmore senior. "When a conservative point of view is brought up, there's a knee-jerk reaction that it can't be valid."

Students suggest that the overwhelming liberalism fosters a self-censorship among conservatives who are unwilling to speak up in class or in social settings to provide the conservative view on issues.

"Haverford might look diverse, but everyone thinks the same," said Jennie Gibson, a sophomore who doesn't like to mention her conservative positions on campus. "I like debate, but there's a difference between that and having people call you stupid when you say you support President Bush."

Students also generally have the impression that their selective campuses are not diverse economically. Yet Swarthmore, for instance, points out that half its students are on financial aid, with the average aid package of loans and grants now $25,146.

That aid ensures that less affluent students get to have the same experience as their wealthier peers, Swarthmore president Alfred Bloom said. As a result, he said, "It is not surprising that students themselves are not fully aware of the broad range of economic diversity within our student bodies."

Although they give high marks for campus ethnic diversity, students cite many forms of self-segregation: Athletes sitting together in the dining halls; frat houses exuding an aura of exclusivity; African-Americans living together in designated dorm space; the plethora of clubs dedicated to Latino, African-American, and other minority issues almost exclusively populated by students from those backgrounds.

"I do see self-separation, but people with similar ideas will tend to stick together," said Melissa Yarborough, a Bryn Mawr sophomore. "Minorities need a support group when they're in a sea of people different from them."

Minority students say white students often do not show interest in attending events sponsored by the minority organizations. "It's the old saying, 'You can draw a horse to water but you can't make him drink,'" said Kwesi Jefferson, an Ursinus freshman. "Students are not always interested in absorbing a diverse environment."

College presidents have heard this before. "We do recognize that these programs sometimes create a dilemma," Penn president Judith Rodin said. "Our students tell us although the programs are appreciated and helpful, they sometimes result in self-segregation among minority groups." But, she said, "We feel strongly that these programs are valuable."

Students have their own ideas about how to ensure that diverse views are encouraged. They point to their professors.

"Diversity has to be reflected in the faculty," Keya Anjaria, a Penn junior, said. "If you don't have a critical mass of faculty of color, students of color will never have a voice. So much of the dynamic of a university for students is seeking the evaluation, respect, and validity from the people you study under."

Ursinus president John Strassburger agrees. A "way to intrude on students' natural clannishness is through diversifying the faculty," he said. "They can and do play major roles in getting diverse students to engage in conversation out of class as well as in."

Some say that, because they often develop important long-term friendships with those they meet early on as first-year students, freshman housing is a key tool to ensure social mixing. Most schools assign freshmen randomly.

But some white students say another program targeted to freshmen works against mixing. Many schools hold a week or more of events for minority first-year students before the rest of the freshman class arrives, designed to help them build leadership skills and deal with being a minority on a mostly white campus.

White students argue that, during that time, minority students tend to bond and form cliques that are difficult for white students to join.

"That's a fair criticism," Bryn Mawr president Nancy Vickers said. "But minorities say the program is among the single most important experiences of college. We need to strike a balance between the comfort zone for students of different backgrounds wanting to find people like themselves and what we can achieve socially by bringing minority groups on campus."

Minority students generally said they do not experience overt racism on selective campuses. "But there's overt ignorance," said Ursinus's Jefferson. "Like white students using urban vernacular to me, saying, 'What up, homie?' I have no problem with that in itself, but I do have a problem with the assumption that because I'm black, I would automatically talk that way."

Every student interviewed saw campus diversity as a worthwhile goal. But the mechanics of affirmative action are not so uniformly praised. Some, like Penn freshman Andrew Dulberg, were uncomfortable with the idea that students with lower grades and test scores would be chosen over others with more stellar credentials partly because of race.

Swarthmore freshman Lauren Fety said affirmative action is "very, very, very not perfect." She thinks about her friends back home in Oregon who come from lower-income backgrounds, who have no role models to inform them about selective colleges as an option, who had no access to advanced placement courses to improve their credentials, but who would not benefit from affirmative action—or even aggressive college recruiting—because they are white.

Other students were quick to defend affirmative action as a vital mechanism in the admissions process. They argue that, even beyond the goal of diversity, affirmative action is needed until larger societal problems, including lingering racism, are overcome.

Penn's Dairman put it this way: "If all educational opportunity in America was fair and equal, admissions without affirmative action would work. But there are still socioeconomic problems that impact the quality of education . . . and we need to make up for that."

DISCUSSION

1. Experts who study the nature of "diversity" on college campuses believe that every campus has a unique "climate" for diversity. Discuss with your classmates what this climate is on your campus.

2. First ask yourself this question and then discuss your initial reactions to it with fellow students: Have you experienced any changes in your thinking/understanding of the role of diversity in American society since you began college?

3. The article "Don't Forget the Women" refers to African-American college females. If you are a member of that group, share with other students whether or not this portrait of African-American women at a highly selective public university struck you as being valid for your campus. If you are not an African-American female, what insights did you gain from reading this piece that might give you more empathy and understanding for the challenges faced by this group?

4. In the second reading, "Students Reveal the Reality of College Diversity," students at four elite, private, residential colleges and universities in the Philadelphia area described their views on diversity. Would your opinion of diversity on your campus be similar or dissimilar to what is described by the students cited in this article? Where did this writer get it right, or wrong, based on your own experiences? What are the implications for your success in college?

CHAPTER 14

Alcohol, Other Drugs, and Sex

Sara J. Corwin, Bradley H. Smith, Rick L. Gant, and Georgeann Stamper, all of the University of South Carolina, Columbia, contributed their valuable and considerable expertise to the writing of this chapter.

IN THIS CHAPTER, YOU WILL LEARN

- Factors in sexual decision making
- Advantages and disadvantages of contraceptive methods
- Ways to prevent sexually transmitted infections
- What to do if your relationship is abusive
- Three reasons college students drink
- The realities of abusing prescription drugs and tobacco
- The agony of Ecstasy and other illegal drugs

Wwe know from numerous studies that about 75 percent of traditional-age college students have engaged in sexual intercourse at least once. Drinking, smoking, and drug abuse are also a concern on college campuses. You will probably want to think about these things and decide what's comfortable for you. Furthermore, we hope you'll conclude (1) that choosing to have sex also means choosing to protect yourself against unwanted pregnancy, unwanted sex, and sexually transmitted infections (STIs), and (2) that choosing whether to drink, smoke, or take illegal drugs also means making your own decisions instead of following the crowd.

Not all first-year students are sexually active. However, college seems to be a time when recent high school graduates begin to think even more seriously about sex. Regardless of the reasons, it can be helpful to explore your sexual values and to consider whether sex is right for you at this time.

Sexual Decision Making

Although the sexual revolutions of the 1960s and 1970s may have made premarital sex more socially acceptable, people have not necessarily become better equipped to deal with sexual freedom. The rate of STIs among college students has increased, and unwanted pregnancies are not uncommon.

If you are in your late teens or early 20s, you may feel you are invincible or immune from danger. There are so many pressures to become sexually active; at the same time, many factors may discourage sexual activity:

ENCOURAGERS	DISCOURAGERS
Hormones	Family values/expectations
Peer pressure	Religious values
Alcohol/other drugs	Sexually transmitted infections
Curiosity	Fear of pregnancy
The media	Concern for reputation

With such powerful pressures on each side, some people get confused and overwhelmed and fail to make any decisions. Often, sex "just happens" and is not planned.

Birth Control

What is the best method of contraception? It is any method that you use correctly and consistently each time you have intercourse. We hope you will choose a birth control method and adopt some strategies for avoiding sexually transmitted infections (STIs). That's the bottom line.

Table 14.1 compares the major features of some common methods, presented in descending order of effectiveness. The "typical use effectiveness" numbers represent the percentage of women experiencing an unwanted pregnancy in 1 year per 100 uses of the method, with the normal number of human errors, memory lapses, and incomplete or incorrect use. A low number indicates the method is more effective, while a high number signals less effectiveness.

Sexually Transmitted Infections (STIs)

In general, STIs continue to increase faster than other illnesses on campuses today, and approximately 5 to 10 percent of visits by U.S. college students to college health services are for the diagnosis and treatment of STIs. If you choose to be sexually active, particularly with more than one partner, exposure to an STI is a real possibility.

STIs are usually spread through the following types of sexual contact: vaginal–penile, oral–genital, hand–genital, and anal–genital. Sometimes, however, STIs can be transmitted through mouth-to-mouth contact. There are more than twenty known types of STIs; in Table 14.2, we discuss the most common ones on campuses.

Table 14.1   Methods of Contraception

STERILIZATION

Failure Rate[a]
Female: 0.05% Male: 0.15%
Advantages Provides nearly permanent protection from future pregnancies.
Disadvantages Not considered reversible; not a good option for anyone wanting children at a later date.

NORPLANT

Failure Rate[a] 0.05%
Advantages Highly effective. Works up to 5 years. Allows sexual spontaneity. Low hormone dose makes this medically safer than other hormonal methods.
Disadvantages Removal may be difficult. Very expensive to obtain initially. Insurance may not cover cost. Does not protect against STIs.

DEPO-PROVERA

Failure Rate[a] 0.3%
Advantages Highly effective. Allows for sexual spontaneity. Relatively low yearly cost.
Disadvantages A variety of side effects typical of progestin-type contraceptives may persist up to 6-8 months after termination. Does not protect against STIs.

ORAL CONTRACEPTIVES

Failure Rate[a] 0.5%
Advantages Highly effective. Allows for sexual spontaneity. Most women have lighter or shorter periods.
Disadvantages Many minor side effects (nausea, weight gain), which cause a significant percentage of users to discontinue. Provides no protection against STIs.

INTRAUTERINE DEVICE (IUD)

Failure Rate[a] 1-2%[b]
Advantages May be left in for up to 10 years, depending on type. Less expensive than other long-term methods.
Disadvantages Increased risk of complications such as pelvic inflammatory disease and menstrual problems. Possible increased risk of contracting HIV, if exposed.

CONTRACEPTIVE PATCH

Failure Rate[a] N/A. Appears to be less effective in women weighing more than 198 pounds.
Advantages Convenient. New patch applied once a week for three weeks. Patch not worn fourth week and woman has a menstrual period.
Disadvantages Similar to oral contraceptives. No protection from STIs.

CONDOM

Failure Rate[a] 14%
Advantages Only birth control method that also provides good protection against STIs, including HIV. Actively involves male partner.
Disadvantages Less spontaneous than some other methods because must be put on right before intercourse. Some men believe it cuts down on pleasurable sensations.

FEMALE CONDOM

Failure Rate[a] 21%
Advantages Highly safe medically; does not require spermicide. Theoretically provides excellent protection against STIs—almost perfectly leakproof and better than male condom in this regard.
Disadvantages Has not gained wide acceptance. Visible outer ring has been displeasing to some potential users.

DIAPHRAGM

Failure Rate[a] 20%
Advantages Safe method of birth control, virtually no side effects. May be inserted up to 2 hours prior to intercourse. May provide small measure of protection against STIs.
Disadvantages Wide variation in effectiveness depending on consistent use, the fit of the diaphragm, and frequency of intercourse. Multiple acts of intercourse require use of additional spermicide.

CERVICAL CAP

Failure Rate[a] 20-40%[c]
Advantages Similar to diaphragm, but may be worn longer—up to 48 hours. May provide small measure of protection against STIs.
Disadvantages Not widely available due to lack of practitioners trained in fitting them.

Continued

Table 14.1   Methods of Contraception (continued)

SPERMICIDAL FOAMS, CREAMS, JELLIES, FILM, AND SUPPOSITORIES	**PERIODIC ABSTINENCE**
Failure Rate[a] 26%	**Failure Rate**[a] 25%
Advantages Easy to purchase and use. Provide some protection against STIs, including HIV.	**Advantages** Requires no devices or chemicals.
Disadvantages Lower effectiveness than many methods. Can be messy. May increase likelihood of birth defects should pregnancy occur.	**Disadvantages** Requires period of abstinence each month, when ovulation is expected. Requires diligent record keeping. Provides no protection against STIs.
COITUS INTERRUPTUS	**CHANCE OR NO METHOD**
Failure Rate[a] 19%	**Failure Rate**[a] 85%
Advantages Requires no devices or chemicals and can be used at any time, at no cost.	**Advantages** No monetary costs or side effects.
Disadvantages Relies heavily on man having enough control to remove himself from the vagina well in advance of ejaculation. May diminish pleasure for the couple.	**Disadvantages** High risk for pregnancy and STIs.

[a] Failure Rate: the percentage of women experiencing an unintended pregnancy within 1 year per 100 uses of the method with the normal number of human errors, memory lapses, and incorrect or incomplete uses.
[b] Range depends on type of IUD: Progesterone T, Copper T 380A, or LNg 20.
[c] Range depends on the number of children a woman has had; women who have not given birth may have a lower percentage.

Source: Adapted from Rebecca J. Donatelle and Lorraine G. Davis, *Access to Health*, 6th ed., p. 175. Copyright © 2000 Allyn & Bacon.

Options for Safer Sex

Celibacy One choice you always have is not to have sex with others. Even if 75 percent of college students are having sex, that still leaves 25 percent who are not.

Abstinence Abstinence (with a partner) encompasses a wide variety of behaviors, from holding hands to more sexually intimate behaviors short of intercourse.

Masturbation Although many people are uncomfortable talking (or even reading!) about masturbation, it is a common sexual practice for people of all ages. Self-stimulation (or with a partner) can provide a safe sexual outlet and is one way to learn about our bodies and our feelings.

Monogamy A safe behavior, in terms of disease prevention, is having sex exclusively with one partner who is uninfected. However, having a long-term monogamous relationship is not always practical, because many college students want to date and may not be interested in becoming serious. Your chances of remaining healthy are better if you limit the number of sexual partners and maintain a relationship disease-free over a reasonably long period.

Table 14.2 Sexually Transmitted Infections

SEXUALLY TRANSMITTED INFECTION	WHAT IT IS	SYMPTOMS	TREATMENT	DANGERS	HOW TO AVOID IT
Chlamydia	Bacterial infection	Include mild abdominal pain, discharge, and pain and burning with urination. In some people, no symptoms appear.	Antibiotics	In women, can progress to pelvic inflammatory disease (PID) and lead to infertility.	Abstinence or monogamy with an uninfected partner Condoms reduce but do not eliminate the risk of infection.
Human Papilloma Virus	Virus	None. Warts can be detected by a physician during physical exam.	No cure. Treatment includes burning, freezing, chemical destruction, or laser surgery.	Causes venereal warts. HPV has been associated with cervical cancer in women.	HPV can spread even when condoms are used. Routine screening for HIV by a physician is advised.
Gonorrhea	Bacterial infection	In men, burning sensation during urination, discharge from penis, swollen testicles. In women, discharge from vagina, vaginal bleeding between periods. Can also infect anus and throat, in cases of transmission via oral/anal intercourse.	Antibiotics	If untreated, gonorrhea can cause pelvic inflammatory disease, male infertility, difficult urination, and life-threatening spread to blood or joints.	Abstinence or monogamy with an uninfected partner. Condoms reduce but do not eliminate the risk of infection.
Herpes	Virus	Blisters or lesions on the genital area. In some cases, no symptoms appear.	No cure. Medications can reduce length and severity of outbreaks.	Most likely to be transmitted just before or after lesions appear.	Condoms, abstaining from sex before, during, and after outbreak.
Hepatitis B	Virus	Stomach virus, yellowing of the skin and eyes	No cure. Rest and healthy diet are prescribed. A vaccine is available to prevent it.	100 times more contagious than HIV. May lead to permanent liver disease.	Avoid unprotected sex and contact with infected blood.
Human Immunodeficiency Virus (HIV)	Virus that causes AIDS	Often there are no symptoms. There are many possible symptoms. Only an HIV test can diagnose HIV	No cure. Various medications are available to lessen symptoms and prolong life	Although medications can prolong life and prevent the onset of AIDS, the disease eventually kills.	Use condoms, make sure partner is uninfected.

Condoms In addition to being a contraceptive, the condom can help prevent the spread of STIs, including HIV. The condom's effectiveness against disease holds true for anal, vaginal, and oral intercourse. The most current research indicates that the rate of protection provided by condoms against STIs is similar to its rate of protection against pregnancy (90–99%). Note that only latex rubber condoms—not lambskin or other types of "natural membrane" condoms—provide this protection. Use a water-based lubricant (such as KY Jelly) to keep the condom from breaking.

Unhealthy Relationships

Intimate Partner Violence

Some individuals express their love in strange and improper ways. It's called intimate partner violence: emotional, abusive, and violent acts occurring between two people who presumably care very much for each other. First-year students may be easy targets.

Approximately one-third of all college-age students will experience a violent intimate relationship. Almost every 15 seconds, a woman in the United States is battered by her boyfriend, husband, or live-in partner. And nearly half a million women report being stalked by a partner in the previous year.

Though statistics indicate that the majority of abusers involved in intimate partner violence are male, females can also be physically, emotionally, and verbally abusive to their partners.

It's important to recognize the warning signs and know what to do if you find yourself (or know a friend) in an abusive relationship.

- An abuser typically has low self-esteem, blames the victim and others for what is actually his or her own behavior, can be pathologically jealous of others who approach the partner, may use alcohol or drugs to manage stress, and views the partner as a possession.
- A battered person typically has low self-esteem, accepts responsibility for the abuser's actions, is passive but has tremendous strength, believes no one can help, and thinks no one else is experiencing such violence.

What to Do If Your Relationship Is Abusive

Tell your abuser the violence must stop. If you don't want sex, say no firmly. Call the police, consult campus resources (women's student services, the sexual assault office, and so forth), call a community domestic violence center or rape crisis center, or call someone else on campus you can trust. Find a counselor or support group on campus or in the community. You can even obtain a restraining order through your local magistrate or county court. If the abuser is a student at the same institution, schedule an appointment with your campus judicial officer to explore campus disciplinary action. Once you decide to make a break, it's wise to remove yourself from the other person's physical presence. This may include changing your daily patterns. For further advice, contact your counselor to find out about restraining orders, listing the abuser's name at the front desk, changing your locks, securing windows, and taking other precautions.

To support a friend whose relationship is abusive, be there. Listen. Help your friend recognize the abuse. Be nonjudgmental. Help your friend contact campus and community resources for help. If you become frustrated or frightened, seek help for yourself as well.

Sexual Assault

Anyone is at risk for being raped, but the majority of victims are women. By the time they graduate, an estimated one out of four college women will be the victim of attempted rape, and one out of six will be raped.

Tricia Phaup of the University of South Carolina, Columbia, offers this advice on avoiding sexual assault:

- Know what you want and do not want sexually.
- Go to parties or social gatherings with friends, and leave with them.
- Avoid being alone with people you don't know very well.
- Trust your gut.
- Be alert to unconscious messages you may be sending.
- Be conscious of how much alcohol you drink, if any.

If you are ever tempted to force another person to have sex:

- Realize that it is *never* okay to force yourself sexually on someone.
- Don't assume you know what your date wants.
- If you're getting mixed messages, ask.
- Be aware of the effects of alcohol.
- Remember that rape is legally and morally wrong.

The following people or offices may be available on or near your campus to deal with a sexual assault: campus sexual assault coordinator, local rape crisis center, campus police department, counseling center, student health services, student affairs professionals, women's student services office, residence life staff, local hospital emergency rooms, and campus chaplains.

Making Decisions about Alcohol and Other Drugs

Even if you don't drink, you should read this information because 50 percent of college students reported helping a drunken peer (friend, classmate, study partner) in the past year.

A number of surveys have confirmed that your peers aren't drinking as much as you think they are, so there's no need for you to try and "catch up." Most students are off by almost half—and that's the truth.

In the final analysis, it's your decision to drink or not to drink alcoholic beverages; to drink moderately or to drink heavily; to know when to stop or to be labeled as a drunk who isn't fun to be around. Alcohol can turn people into victims even though they don't drink: people killed by drunk drivers or people who suffer from the behavior of an alcoholic family member.

According to most college presidents, alcohol abuse is the greatest single threat to students' health, safety, and academic performance. Over the course of one year, about 20 to 30 percent of students report serious problems related to excessive alcohol use.

Why College Students Drink

Social Learning

Students drink alcoholic beverages for many reasons, but those reasons can be divided into two major categories: (1) social learning and (2) a desire to feel good or not to feel bad. Social learning simply means learning by watching others. The major sources of social learning for drinking are parents, mass media, and peers.

Parents A parent who comes home from a hard day at work and says, "I need a drink" may be conditioning his or her children to use alcohol as a stress-relief drug.

Mass Media Commercial marketers have learned that associating sex appeal, the outdoors, and healthy-looking young people with their products catches your attention and encourages you to think favorably about their product.

Peers The best social predictor of your drinking behavior is the behavior of the people you hang out with, especially friends and close associates. A drinking game may drive a group of friends to drink more than usual. Also, the overall campus culture or the behaviors of members of clubs or Greek societies can influence your decisions about drinking. You may feel you need to change your drinking habits to be accepted by certain groups.

Drinking to Feel Good or Not to Feel Bad

At low to moderate doses, alcohol is a drug that can produce feelings of relaxation or pleasure. When people do something that is pleasurable, they are likely to do it again. This process is called positive reinforcement. So if one drink makes you feel good, it may encourage you to drink more frequently.

Related to the concept of drinking to feel good is the phenomenon of drinking not to feel bad. Some people may experience temporary relief of unpleasant feelings when drinking, such as feeling less tense or less sad. In extreme cases, a person may drink to forget. When people do something that stops them from feeling bad, they are likely to do it again.

Alcohol and Behavior

At low doses, alcohol has a stimulating effect on the human brain, making you feel animated and energized. More drinks may make you feel rowdy or boisterous. This is where most people report feeling a buzz from alcohol. After that, alcohol starts to act as a depressant. When the brain starts to slow down, your coordination, thinking, and judgment may be impaired. So as soon as you feel that buzz from alcohol, remember that you are on the brink of losing coordination, clear thinking, and judgment.

As you consume more alcohol, you will become progressively less coordinated and less able to make good decisions. Ultimately, most people who have had too much to drink become severely uncoordinated and may begin falling asleep, falling down, or slurring their speech. Eventually, heavy drinkers tend to suffer memory loss or blackouts. This may lead to nausea and vomiting. Commonly associated with nausea is a feeling of dizziness or a sensation that the room is spinning, a result of the disruption of the brain's balancing system.

Unfortunately, even after you pass out and stop drinking, your alcohol level can continue to rise as alcohol in your stomach is released to the intestine and absorbed into the bloodstream. Your body may try to get rid of alcohol by vomiting, but you can choke if you are unconscious, semiconscious, or severely uncoordinated. A person who is extremely drunk will show signs of severe alcohol poisoning such as an inability to wake up, slowed breathing, fast but weak pulse, cool or damp skin, and pale or bluish skin. People exhibiting these symptoms need medical assistance *immediately*. If you ever find someone in such a state, remember to keep the person on his or her side with the head lower than the rest of the body. Check to see that the airway is clear, especially if the person is vomiting. Even if the person is not vomiting, a severely drunk person lying on his or her back can be so relaxed that the airway can close if the tongue is blocking the back of the throat.

If a drinker passes out but does not have these severe symptoms, someone should watch him or her carefully and check back frequently until the person is awake. Even then, you may need to protect him or her from doing something dangerous, such as falling down a flight of stairs or starting a fire.

Alcohol can be fatal if you drink enough of it. You may also be more susceptible to accidents in an intoxicated condition. To be on the safe side, avoid strong drinks made with high-alcohol-content distilled spirits (such as 151-proof rum) or multiple shots of distilled spirits.

Consequences for All

Surveys conducted since the early 1990s have consistently shown a negative correlation between grades and the number of drinks per week—and not just for heavy drinkers. Findings are similar for both two-year and four-year institutions (see Table 14.3 below).

Alcohol Addiction

According to the medical definition, someone is alcohol-dependent or alcoholic if he or she exhibits three of the following symptoms:

1. A significant tolerance for alcohol
2. Withdrawal symptoms such as the shakes
3. Overuse of alcohol
4. Attempts to control or cut down on use

Table 14.3   Comparison of Percentage of Students Reporting Alcohol-Related Problems
Experienced by Light to Moderate Drinkers, Heavy Drinkers, and Frequent Heavy Drinkers

PROBLEM	LIGHT TO MODERATE DRINKERS	HEAVY DRINKERS	FREQUENT HEAVY DRINKERS
Got behind on schoolwork	9	25	48
Missed a class due to drinking	10	33	65
Argued with friends while drinking	10	24	47
Got hurt or injured	3	11	27
Damaged property	3	10	25
Got in trouble with campus police	2	5	15
Had 5 or more alcohol-related problems since the beginning of the school year	4	17	52

SOURCE: Data from Henry Weschler et al., "Changes in Binge Drinking and Related Problems among American College Students between 1993 and 1997: Results of the Harvard School of Public Health College Alcohol Study," *Journal of American College Health* 47 (1998): 57-68.

5. Preoccupation with drinking or becoming anxious when you do not have a "stash"
6. Making new friends who drink and staying away from friends who do not drink or who do not drink to get drunk
7. Continued heavy drinking despite experiencing alcohol-related social, academic, legal, or health problems

Fortunately, most college students do not become alcoholics. However, if you or someone you know is progressing toward alcoholism, you should contact a source on campus that can help. Student health centers are almost always a good place to start, but many other sources are available. Your course instructor, residence hall advisor, or academic advisor should be able to help you decide where to seek help for yourself or someone you care about.

Tobacco—The Other Legal Drug

Tobacco use is clearly the cause of many serious medical conditions, including heart disease, cancer, and lung ailments. Over the years, tobacco has led to the deaths of hundreds of thousands of individuals.

Unfortunately, cigarette smoking is on the rise among college students. "The rise in this group is really an alarming sign," says Henry Wechsler of Harvard University. A 1998 survey indicated that smoking among college students had risen 28 percent in four years, with nearly 30 percent of college students smoking. Because more women than men now smoke, the rate of lung cancer in women is rapidly approaching or surpassing rates in men. Chemicals in tobacco are highly addictive, making it hard to quit. Although young people may not worry about long-term side effects, increased numbers of respiratory infections, worsening of asthma, bad breath, and stained teeth should be motivations to not start smoking at all.

Prescription Drug Abuse and Addiction

An estimated 9 million people ages 12 and older used prescription drugs for nonmedical reasons in 1999, nearly triple the number for the previous year. Three classes of prescription drugs are the most commonly abused: opioids, central nervous system (CNS) depressants, and stimulants. We will discuss them briefly.

Opioids These pain relievers include morphine, codeine, and such branded drugs as OxyContin, Darvon, Vicodin, Demerol, and Dilaudid. Opioids work by blocking the transmission of pain messages to the brain. Chronic use can result in tolerance, which means that users must take higher doses to achieve the same initial effects, and can ultimately lead to addiction. Taking a large single dose of an opioid could cause a severe reduction in your breathing rate that can lead to death. It appears that college students' nonmedical use of pain relievers is on the rise and that many individuals may engage in "doctor shopping" to get multiple prescriptions for the drugs they abuse.

CNS Depressants These substances can slow normal brain function and, taken properly, can be useful in the treatment of anxiety and sleep disorders. If one develops a tolerance for CNS depressants, however, larger doses will be needed to achieve the same initial effects. If one stops taking them, the brain's activity can rebound and race out of control, possibly leading to seizures and other harmful consequences.

Stimulants Stimulants are a class of drugs that enhance brain activity, causing an increase in alertness, attention, and energy that is accompanied by elevated blood pressure and increased heart rate. Taking high doses of some stimulants repeatedly over a short time can lead to feelings of hostility or paranoia, as well as dangerously high body temperatures and irregular heartbeat.[1]

Ecstasy

A troubling trend on college campuses is the increased use of a synthetic drug called MDMA, or Ecstasy. While many young people believe that MDMA is safe and offers nothing but a pleasant high for the $25 cost of a single tablet (How bad can it be if it's that cheap?), the reality is far different.

MDMA exerts its primary effects in the brain on neurons that use the chemical serotonin to communicate with other neurons. The serotonin system plays an important role in regulating mood, aggression, sexual activity, sleep, and sensitivity to pain. As MDMA significantly depletes serotonin, it takes the brain a significant amount of time to rebuild the amount needed to perform important physiological and psychological functions.

Controlled studies in humans have shown that MDMA has potent effects on the cardiovascular system and on the body's ability to regulate its internal temperature. Of great concern is MDMA's adverse effects on the pumping effi-

---

[1] Adapted from "Prescription Drugs: Abuse and Addiction." National Institute on Drug Abuse, part of the National Institutes of Health, a division of the U.S. Department of Health and Human Services.

ciency of the heart. And since MDMA radically alters serotonin levels, heavy users experience obsessive traits, anxiety, paranoia, and sleep disturbance. Another study indicates that MDMA can have long-lasting effects on short-term, visual, and verbal memory and other mental functions.[2]

Other Illegal Drugs

Illegal recreational drugs, such as marijuana, cocaine, Ecstasy, LSD, and heroin, are used by a much smaller number of college students and far less frequently than alcohol. These drugs are significant public health issues for college students, however, and we hope that the comparative statistics shown in Table 14.4 and the brief additional information that follows will provoke further reading and discussion.

All the drugs listed in Table 14.4, with the exception of alcohol, are illegal. The penalties associated with their possession or use tend to be much more severe than those associated with underage alcohol use. In contrast to earlier recommendations regarding the potential for moderate and lower-risk consumption of alcohol, we cannot offer such advice for illicit drugs (except to never share drug needles). Side effects include the potential for long-term abuse, addiction, and severe health problems.

In addition, athletic departments, potential employers, and government agencies do routine screenings for many of these drugs. Future employability, athletic scholarships, and insurability may be compromised if you test positive for any of these substances.

Table 14.4 Usage of Alcohol and Other Drugs on College Campuses

Drug	% Using at Least Once in Preceding Year	% Using during Previous 30 Days
Alcohol	83%	70%
Marijuana	31%	19%
Cocaine	3.9%	1.6%
Amphetamines	6.9%	3.1%
Designer drugs (Ecstasy, etc.)	3.6%	1.3%

Source: C. A. Presley and J. S. Leichliter, *Recent Statistics on Alcohol and Other Drug Use on American College Campuses: 1995-96.* Carbondale: The Core Institute, Southern Illinois University.

---

[2] Excerpted from "Ecstasy: What We Know and Don't Know About MDMA: A Scientific Review." National Institute on Drug Abuse, part of the National Institutes of Health (NIH), a division of the U.S. Department of Health and Human Services.

YOUR PERSONAL JOURNAL

Here are a number of things to write about. Choose one or more, or choose another topic related to this chapter.

1. Is it okay for people to use alcohol or other drugs to put themselves in a sexy mood? Or, after drinking or using drugs, might people indulge in sexual behaviors that they really didn't intend to? If so, how might they feel about it afterward?
2. What are the qualities of healthy intimate relationships? Think of your own intimate (not necessarily sexual) relationships, past or present. How would you characterize them? Healthy, unhealthy, or a combination?
3. If you know someone who drinks heavily on a regular basis, write how you feel about that person. If you don't know anyone like that, write how you feel about heavy drinking.
4. How does your campus culture encourage drinking behavior? Use of illegal drugs? How does your campus culture discourage drinking behavior? Use of illegal drugs?
5. What behaviors are you willing to change after reading this chapter? How might you go about changing them?
6. What else is on your mind this week? If you wish to share something with your instructor, add it to this journal entry.

READINGS

Diversity of Students Lowers College Binge Drinking Rates*

Drinking rates among the highest-risk drinkers on American college campuses—those who are white, male, and underage—are significantly lower on college campuses with larger proportions of minority, female, and older students, according to a study published in . . . *American Journal of Public Health.*

The study, "Watering Down the Drinks: The Moderating Effect of College Demographics on Alcohol Use of High-Risk Groups," is the first to examine the

---

Alcoholism & Drug Abuse Weekly, November 10, 2003, v15, i43, p. 3(2). Copyright 2003 Manisses Communications Group, Inc. Reprinted with permission.

role of college student demographics and diversity in moderating binge drinking among high-risk students.

The study found that greater diversity on campuses may serve as a risk-protective factor, even for those who were binge drinkers in high school.

Researchers with the Harvard School of Public Health College Alcohol Study (CAS) examined whether colleges with larger enrollments of students from demographic groups with lower rates of binge drinking exert a moderating effect on students from groups with higher binge drinking rates. They analyzed data from 52,312 college students at 114 colleges from the 1993, 1997, 1999, and 2001 CAS surveys.

According to the study, binge-drinking rates vary among student subgroups. African-American and Asian, female, and older students have lower rates of binge drinking than do white, male, and younger students.

"Our major finding is that white students, underage students, and men were less likely to be binge drinkers if they attend college with more minority, older, and women students," Henry Wechsler, Ph.D., principal investigator of the study and director of CAS, told *Alcoholism & Drug Abuse Weekly*.

College student binge drinking is defined by Wechsler and other public health researchers as the consumption of five or more drinks in a row at least once in the past two weeks for men, and four or more drinks in a row for women. According to the study, research indicates that this style of binge drinking is associated with lower grades, vandalism, and physical and sexual violence.

"The number one public health problem of college students is binge drinking, which is responsible for a number of problems to the drinker, such as missing classes, becoming injured, and getting into trouble with the police," said Wechsler. The secondhand effects from the binge-drinking behavior affects other students through such behaviors as physical assault, vandalism, and noise, said Wechsler.

According to the study, white, male, underage students who did not binge drink in high school would be less likely to take up binge drinking at schools with more minority, female, and older students. The study also found that white, male, underage students who were binge drinking in high school would be less likely to continue binge drinking at schools with more minority, female, and older students.

The higher the percentage of minority, female, and older students in a school, the lower the binge drinking rates for total students and high-risk subgroups, researchers found.

According to the study, the percentage of female students was significantly associated with lower binge drinking rates for total students and high-risk subgroups among small/medium schools. The percentage of female students had no significant effect on binge rates in large schools. Researchers said this may have been because the gender ratio did not vary very much significantly at larger campuses.

The study found that although various interventions have been attempted to help lower the level of binge drinking on college campuses, colleges have not yet examined housing and admission policies and student demographics. Although most colleges are trying to do something to lower the level of binge drinking on its campuses, one area not being examined has been the role of demographics, said Wechsler.

Researchers indicated that student-body composition and demographic diversity should be examined by colleges wishing to reduce their binge drinking problems, researchers said. Having more minority students, older students, and women should provide more models of abstention and responsible drinking and should lower the overall binge-drinking rate.

According to researchers, the findings help explain why fraternities and sororities and segregated freshmen dormitories that provide the highest concentrations of binge drinkers account for the bulk of alcohol problems on campus.

The study indicated that encouraging more older students to live on campus and in fraternity houses may be one practical application of the findings. Another may be decreasing the heavy concentration of young, male, white students in residential arrangements.

Colleges should encourage older students to live on campus and make it more financially desirable by altering financial arrangements in some way, Wechsler said. "The policy of grouping all freshmen together and separating freshmen from older students may make for a concentration of heavy drinkers," Wechsler said.

According to researchers, the findings suggest practical solutions for predominantly white colleges, including:

- Creating a campus environment that would attract a diverse student body;
- Increasing the number of minorities on campus;
- Encouraging more women and older students to live on campus, and in fraternity and sorority houses;
- Decreasing the heavy concentration on campus of likely high-risk drinkers who are overwhelmingly young, male, and white.

Survey Finds High Number of College Students Using Tobacco Products*

Significant proportions of college students use tobacco, typically in the form of cigarettes and cigars, according to a survey reported in the *Journal of the American Medical Association.*

---

*The Brown University Digest of Addiction Theory and Application, December 2000, v19, i12, p. 3. Copyright 2000 Manisses Communications Group, Inc. Reprinted with permission.

Nancy A. Rigotti, M.D., and colleagues from Massachusetts General Hospital surveyed the use of tobacco products in a sample of students from 119 U.S. four-year colleges as part of the Harvard College Alcohol Survey. That study surveyed randomly selected, cross-sectional samples of students in 1993, 1997, and 1999. The data reported in the current paper were gathered in 1999.

The colleges surveyed were located in 39 states and represented all regions of the U.S.

The questionnaire assessed demographic factors, substance use, satisfaction with education, and students' interests and lifestyle choices. Subjects were asked if they had ever smoked a cigarette, cigar, or pipe, or used smokeless tobacco.[3]

The investigators found that 60 percent of college students surveyed had ever tried a tobacco product, one-third within the past month. Cigarettes were the most commonly used tobacco product, with 53.4 percent of students reporting having smoked one in their lifetime, 38.1 percent in the past year, and 28.5 percent in the past month. The plurality of most current smokers (43.6%) smoked between 1 and 10 cigarettes per day, although a significant minority (12.8%) smoked one or more packs per day.

Men were more likely to use any tobacco product than women (53% vs. 41.3%) and to have used tobacco in the past year (37.9% vs. 29.7%). However, most of the difference was due to non-cigarette tobacco use among men, since, the investigators report, men and women had nearly identical cigarette current smoking rates (28.4% vs. 28.5%).

Among non-cigarette tobacco products, cigars were the most commonly used, with more than one-third of students reporting having ever smoked a cigar. Nearly 25 percent had smoked a cigar in the past year, and 8.5 percent had smoked a cigar in the past month. However, less than 1 percent of current users reported smoking cigars daily.

Students who used tobacco typically use more than one tobacco product, investigators found. More than half of tobacco users (51.3%) reported using more than one tobacco product. The most frequent combinations were cigarettes and cigars (19.7%), cigarettes and pipes (12%), and cigarettes, cigars, and smokeless tobacco (6%). Men were more likely to use multiple tobacco products than women.

In terms of demographic factors, investigators found that the median age of first cigarette use was 14 for both men and women. Median age for first cigar use was 17 for men and 18 for women.

Tobacco use was linked with being male and white. Students who used tobacco were more likely to smoke marijuana, binge drink, have more sexual

---

[3] Rigotti N.A., Lee J.E., Wechsler H.: U.S. college students' use of tobacco products: Results of a national survey. *JAMA* 2000; 284: 699–705.

partners, have lower grades, and spend more time socializing with friends. Tobacco users were less likely to rate athletics or religion as important or to be satisfied with their education.

Study Limits

The authors note that this study may have a nonresponse bias, since only 60 percent of students surveyed returned the questionnaire. They also note that measures of tobacco use depended upon students' self-reports.

Authors' Conclusions

Based on this data, the authors conclude that tobacco use among college students is more prevalent than previously realized, mainly because tobacco use is not limited to cigarettes. Cigars, smokeless tobacco, and, more rarely, pipes are also used. College students who use tobacco are likely to be white, single, and experimenting with other risky behaviors. They are also often part of a lifestyle that values social life over education, athletics, or religion.

Authors' Recommendations

Colleges offer a potential site for interventions to discourage tobacco use. Colleges' alcohol and substance use prevention and treatment programs should also target tobacco. In addition, environmental changes—such as making all college buildings, including dorms, smoke-free—can help to protect nonsmokers and discourage occasional users from becoming regular users.

DISCUSSION

1. Your authors recognize that students do *not* want pious and moralistic "thou shalt nots" jammed down their throats; and that many students believe "I've heard it all before." With that as a context on which to base a discussion, talk with fellow students about what you have read in this chapter that might still be worthy of consideration and possible action.
2. It should be apparent to you that the topics of college student sexuality, alcohol consumption, and drug use are pervasive in the media portrayal of college life and are big issues with some of the people in authority on college campuses. Are they correct in seeing these as major issues for college students? Why?
3. One of your readings reports that the extent of "binge drinking" in the highest cohort of students engaging in this behavior (white, male, underage students) occurs at lower rates on campuses where there are higher rates of African-American, Asian, female, and older students. The reading

offers some possible hypotheses for this finding. Discuss with fellow students what you think may explain why the more characteristically heaviest drinkers may consume at lower levels on some campuses than others.

4. In the reading on tobacco use, note again the researchers' conclusions that use is more prevalent in the very same group in which binge drinking is also more likely to be found: white males who are experimenting with other risky behaviors. Discuss with other students just what is going on with young, white males in our society. Why are they behaving differently from other groups on college campuses? What are the implications of this for your success in college?

CHAPTER 15

Staying Healthy

JoAnne Herman and Danny Baker, both of the University of South Carolina, Columbia, contributed their valuable and considerable expertise to the writing of this chapter.

IN THIS CHAPTER, YOU WILL LEARN

- How to achieve and maintain good physical and mental health
- The importance of maintaining balance in your life
- The most common health problems college students face
- How to deal with depression and anxiety
- How to stay safe on campus

Most students can handle the transition to college just fine using various coping mechanisms. Others drink too much or smoke too much. Some overeat or develop an eating disorder like bulimia or anorexia. Some become so stressed that their anxiety overwhelms them.

This chapter explores the topic of *wellness*, which is a catchall term for taking care of your mind and body. Wellness means making healthy choices and achieving balance. Wellness includes reducing stress, keeping fit, keeping safe, and avoiding unnecessary risks.

Stress

When you are stressed, your body undergoes rapid physiological, behavioral, and emotional changes. Your breathing may become more rapid and shallow. Your heart rate quickens, and your muscles begin to tighten. Your hands may become cold and/or sweaty. You may get a "butterfly" stomach, diarrhea, or constipation. Your mouth and lips may feel dry and hot, and you may notice that your hands and knees begin to shake or tremble. Your voice may quiver or even go up an octave.

You may also experience confusion, trouble concentrating, inability to remember things, and poor problem solving. You may feel fear, anxiety, depression, irritability, anger, or frustration, have insomnia, or wake up too early and not be able to go back to sleep.

Stress has many sources, but two seem to be prominent: life events and daily hassles. Life events are those that represent major adversity, such as the death of a parent or close friend. Researchers believe that an accumulation of stress from life events, especially if they occur over a short period of time, can cause physical and mental health problems.

The other major source of stress is daily hassles. These are the minor irritants that we experience every day, such as losing your keys, having three tests on the same day, problems with your roommate, having to pay for an unexpected emergency repair, or caring for a sick child.

Managing Stress and Depression

The best starting point for handling stress is to be in good shape physically and mentally. When your body and mind are healthy, it's like inoculating yourself against stress. This means you need to pay attention to diet, exercise, sleep, and mental health. But what if you do all these things and still feel "down" or panicky? You may have a chronic case of depression or anxiety. A specialist can tell you if your symptoms are caused by chemical imbalances in your body—something that you may not be able to correct on your own. It's important to seek help, which may include psychotherapy, medication, or a combination of the two. If you don't have a local doctor, head for the campus health center.

Modifying Your Lifestyle

You have the power to change your life so that it is less stressful. You may think that others, such as teachers, supervisors, parents, friends, or even your children, are controlling you. Of course, they do influence you, but ultimately you are in control of how you run your life. Lifestyle modification requires that you spend some time reflecting on your life, identifying the parts of your life that do not serve you well, and making plans for change.

For instance, if you are always late for class and get stressed about this, get up 10 minutes earlier. If you get nervous before a test when you talk to a certain classmate, avoid that person before a test. Learn test-taking skills so you can manage test anxiety better.

Your caffeine consumption can also have a big impact on your stress level. Consumed in large quantities, caffeine may cause nervousness, headaches, irritability, an increase in heart rate, stomach irritation, and insomnia—all symptoms of stress.

Relaxation Techniques

You can use a number of relaxation techniques to reduce stress. Learning them is just like learning any new skill. It takes knowledge and practice. Check with your college counseling center, health clinic, or fitness center about classes that teach relaxation. These classes are often advertised in the student newspaper. Some colleges and universities have credit courses that teach relaxation techniques. You can also learn more about relaxation at any bookstore or library, where you'll find a large number of books on relaxation techniques. In addition, you can buy relaxation tapes and let an expert guide you through the process. The technique you choose will be based on your personal preference.

Exercise and Rest

Exercise is an excellent stress management technique, the best way to stay fit, and a critical part of weight loss. The beta endorphins released during exercise can counteract stress and depression. While any kind of recreation benefits your body and soul, the best exercise is aerobic. In aerobic exercise, you work until your pulse is in a "target zone" and keep it there for 20 to 30 minutes. You can reach your target heart rate through a variety of exercises: walking, jogging, running, swimming, biking, walking a treadmill, or using a stair climber. Choose activities you enjoy so you will look forward to your exercise time.

Getting adequate sleep is another way to protect you from stress and help alleviate the symptoms of depression. Although college studies require hours of homework, it's unwise to stay up till the wee hours of the morning. Most people need a minimum of six hours of sleep a night. Getting enough rest makes you more efficient when you are awake. It also helps make a lot of other activities more enjoyable. If you regularly have trouble sleeping, get medical advice. Sleep deprivation takes a terrible toll on the body.

Nutrition and Body Weight

"You are what you eat" is more than a catchphrase; it's an important reminder of the vital role diet plays in our lives. You've probably read news stories telling how more and more young people are obese than ever before in our history. Many attribute this to the proliferation of fast food restaurants, which place "flavor" and "filling" before "healthy." One chain even made its burgers larger in response to consumer research.

So what to do? It's not easy at first, but if you commit to a new eating regime, you will not only feel better, but you'll be healthier—and probably happier. Ask your student health center for more advice, including the newest food pyramid (Figure 15.1) that shows you how to follow a healthy diet. If your college has a nursing program, it might be another source of information on diet. Meanwhile, here are some suggestions:

1. Restrict your intake of red meat, real butter, white rice, white bread, potatoes, and sweets. "White foods" are made with refined flour, which has few nutrients—so you're only getting empty carbs (translation: calories). Instead, go for fish, poultry, and soy products, and use whole wheat

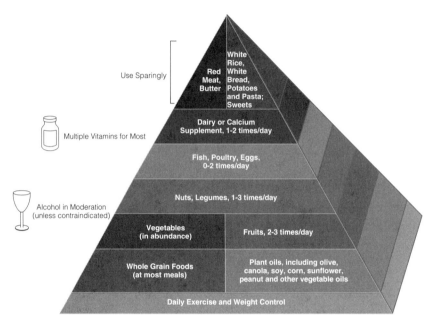

Walter Willett's Healthy Eating Pyramid

Figure 15.1

Source: Reprinted with permission of Simon & Schuster Adult Publishing Group from *Eat, Drink, & Be Healthy: The Harvard Medical School Guide to Healthy Eating* by Walter C. Willett, M.D. Copyright © 2001 by President and Fellows of Harvard College.

breads. (Speaking of carbs, you're probably aware of the Atkins and South Beach low-carb diets. They work on some people and not on others. It's wise to ask your doctor before following one of them.)

2. Eat vegetables and fruits daily. These are important building blocks for a balanced diet. Instead of fruit juices, which contain concentrated amounts of sugar (more empty calories), go for the fruit instead.

3. Avoid fried foods—fries, fried chicken, and so forth. Choose grilled meats instead. Avoid foods containing large amounts of sugar, such as donuts.

4. Keep your room stocked with healthy snacks, such as fruit, vegetables, yogurt, and graham crackers.

5. Eat a sensible amount of nuts and all the legumes (beans) you want to round out your fiber intake.

6. Make sure the oils you buy are either polyunsaturated or monounsaturated. While oils are 100 percent fat, they don't mess with your cardiovascular system unless you use too much of them and start gaining weight. Avoid trans-fatty acids and saturated fats when shopping for oils. These are substances that clog arteries.

7. Always read the government-required nutrition label on all packaged foods. Check sodium content (sodium will make you retain fluids and increase your weight) and the number of fat grams. A goal to strive for is a diet

with only 20 percent fat. So if you read that a product has 160 calories per serving and only 3 grams of fat, it's a good choice. For a quick way to check, double the number of calories per serving, move the decimal point twice to the left, and compare the number to the fat grams per serving.

Obesity

People have been joking about the "freshman 15" forever, the 15 pounds that new college students traditionally put on. But it's no joke that new college students tend to gain an excessive amount of weight during their first term. There are a lot of reasons, among them increased stress, lifestyle changes, new food choices, changes in physical activity, and alcohol consumption. In addition to following the nutrition guidelines above, other ways to avoid obesity are eating smaller meals more often, getting regular exercise, keeping a food journal (to keep track of what you are actually consuming), and being realistic about dieting.

Eating Disorders

Some students suffer from anorexia nervosa (anorexia is the common term) or bulimia. Anorexia is self-starvation. Bulimia is the "binge and purge" disease, in which a person gorges on food and then vomits it up. Both eating disorders are psychological conditions that need treatment.

There are no drugs specifically designed for these eating disorders, but a doctor may recommend an antidepressant, since depression is one of the root causes of these disorders and may worsen the longer the individual engages in anorexic-bulimic behavior. Often, the best help is counseling. Your counseling or health center should have professionals on staff to help anorexics and bulimics cope with, and eventually learn to modify, their eating habits.

If you or a friend exhibits symptoms of one of these conditions, it is important to seek assistance. Watch for these warning signs:

- Extreme participation in dance, gymnastics, or wrestling to take off more weight.
- Loose-fitting clothing that masks body shape and provides warmth.
- Incessant diet soda intake.
- Frequent colds.
- Carbohydrate cravings, such as for potato chips or cookies.
- Shopping at several stores to conceal purchases of food or laxatives.[1]

---

[1]List excerpted from Robert Finn, "Detective Work May Be Needed to Spot Eating Disorders: Clinical Pearls," (Psychosomatic Medicine), *Clinical Psychiatry News*, September 2003, v31, i9, p. 62(1). Copyright 2003 International Medical News Group. Reprinted with permission.

While there is no cure for anorexia or bulimia, a wise counselor can help victims of this disease work their way toward a healthy lifestyle.

Suicide

Suicide is the second leading cause of death, after drinking, among college students. About 1,100 college students kill themselves each year. The reasons include general depression, loneliness, the breakup of a relationship, poor grades, a lack of close friends, or a combination of factors. Often someone who decides to take his or her own life dies without leaving a reason.

Most suicidal people send out signals to us (see Table 15.1 for warning signs); often, sadly, we simply don't believe or hear them. A potential suicide needs help as soon as possible. It may be difficult to convince someone—or yourself—that help is needed.

If someone you know is considering suicide, the most important things you can do are listen and stay with the person to make sure he or she is safe. Avoid arguments and advice giving. And when the time is right, escort the person to the campus health or counseling center or a local hospital.

Finally, remember there is no shame attached to having a mental health problem. Most depression and anxiety occur when chemical imbalances in your system clash with stressful times in your life. Proper counseling, medical attention, and legal prescription drugs carefully chosen by a doctor can turn your world toward the bright side.

Table 15.1   Some Warning Signs of Suicide

• depression	• change in eating habits
• feeling hopeless or helpless	• diminished sexual interest
• anger or hostility	• low self-esteem
• inability to feel pleasure	• no hope for the future—believing things will
• feeling guilt	never get better, that
• isolation or withdrawal	nothing will ever change
• impulsive behavior	• giving things away that are valued
• thinking a lot about death	• ending important relationships or commitments
• talking about dying	• promiscuity
• recent loss including loss of religious faith, loss	• severe outbursts of temper
of interest in friends, sex, hobbies, or other	• drug use
activities previously enjoyed	• not going to work or school
• change in personality	• being unable to carry out normal tasks
• change in sleep patterns	of daily life

Stress and Campus Crime

With all the stress you may be experiencing from relationships and your studies, one thing you certainly want to avoid is becoming a victim of crime. College and university campuses are not sanctuaries—criminal activity occurs on campuses regularly. It is important to take proactive measures to reduce criminal activity on your campus. The first step is to become familiar with how you can protect yourself as well as your personal property.

Most institutions of higher learning are engaged in active crime prevention programs. If you live on campus, your resident advisor will be aware of crime prevention information and may sponsor crime prevention speakers as part of your residence hall programming.

Personal Property Safety

Most campus crime involves theft: books stolen and sold back to bookstores, computers and other expensive items stolen and traded for cash. To reduce the chances of such occurrences, follow these basic rules:

- Record the serial numbers of your electronic equipment, and keep the numbers in a safe place.
- Mark your books on a preselected page with your name and an additional identifier such as your driver's license number. Remember on which page you entered this information.
- Never leave books or book bags unattended.
- Lock your residence even if you are only going out for a minute.
- Do not leave your key above the door for a friend or roommate.
- Report lost or stolen property to the proper authority, such as the campus police.
- Don't tell people you don't know well about your valuable possessions.
- Keep your credit or bank debit card as safe as you would your cash.

Automobile Safety

- Keep your vehicle locked at all times.
- Do not leave valuables in your vehicle where they can be easily seen.
- Park in well-lighted areas.
- Maintain your vehicle properly so it isn't likely to die on you.
- Register your vehicle with the proper authorities if you park on campus. This identifies your vehicle as one that belongs on campus and assists police when they patrol the campus for unregistered vehicles belonging to potentially dangerous intruders.

Personal Safety

- Find out if your campus has an escort service that provides transportation or an escort during the evening hours. Are you familiar with the hours and days of service? Use this important service if you must travel alone during evening hours.
- Write down and memorize the telephone number for your campus police. Are your police commissioned officers with the power to arrest? Do they receive special training in preventing crime in an academic community?
- If your campus has emergency call boxes, find out where they are and how to operate them.
- Be aware of dark areas on campus and avoid them, particularly when walking alone.
- During evening hours, travel with at least one other person when going to the library or other locations on or near campus.
- Let someone know where you will be and a phone number where you can be reached, particularly if you go away for the weekend. Sometimes parents call and become concerned when they can't reach you. An informed roommate can minimize the potential for parental concern.
- While jogging during the early evening and early morning, wear reflective clothing. And find a jogging partner so that you are not alone in situations where help is not readily available.

The majority of violent crimes on or near college and university campuses involve alcohol or drug use. Friends watch out for friends. Look out for one another. Be aware that some "friends" may not have your best interests at heart.

Your behavior both on and off campus should be proactive in terms of reducing opportunity. Remember the difference between fear and concern. Fear is an emotion that generally appears after a critical incident. However, responses to fear are short-lived, and we soon return to old habits. Concern, on the other hand, allows us to make safety measures a part of our everyday routine. Be concerned.

YOUR PERSONAL JOURNAL

Here are a number of topics to write about. Choose one or more, or choose another topic related to stress management or campus crime.

1. If you have been feeling stressed lately, write about it. Name the stressor, describe how you are feeling both mentally and physically, list possible rea-

sons for your stress, and describe the possible options you have for dealing with it.

2. It's been said that anticipating a potentially stressful event can be worse than the actual event. What were your biggest concerns before you came to college? Was your stress justified or not? Write about the lessons you have learned from this transition.

3. After reading the information on eating healthy, what steps do you plan to take to change your diet?

4. What reason can you offer for the number of suicides among college students? What can anyone do to reduce this number?

5. What behaviors are you willing to change after reading this chapter? How might you go about changing them?

6. What else is on your mind this week? If you wish to share it with your instructor, add it to this journal entry.

READINGS

Surviving the Everyday Stuff*

The coauthor of The Ultimate College Survival Guide *tells you how to cope with weight gain, illness, and dirty laundry when you're living on your own.*
By Janet Farrar Worthington

Drop the chalupa. No, really, put it down. Now look in the mirror, and consider the dreaded "Freshman 15." Imagine yourself stuffed like a sausage into those retro–Lenny Kravitz hip-huggers that looked so good when you bought them. Look out—the zipper is feeling the strain, and if that waistband button pops off, some poor bystander could lose an eye. The "Freshman 15," an almost universal college phenomenon, happens when people who have been used to fairly sensible, balanced diets suddenly have too much freedom—to snarf late-night pizza, fries with every meal, and daily ice cream from the "build-your-own-sundae bar" in the dining hall. The result: Until they figure out how to eat right, they blimp up into chunky little Pillsbury dough people.

Actually, if your worst problem as a freshman is a hefty tummy, your problems are pretty small. But sometimes it's the "small" everyday things that can get you down. Here's a troubleshooting guide to help you survive some of the everyday stuff—eating right, keeping clean clothes, and maintaining your health.

Careers & Colleges, March-April 2003, v23, i4, p. 22(4). Reprinted with permission.

THE "FRESHMAN 15"

Let's face it: Ordering a Diet Coke with the Meat-Lover's Pizza special from the place that delivers until 2 a.m. isn't going to "cancel out" the extra sausage. When your mom told you to eat your vegetables, she probably didn't mean french fries and onion rings. And fried mozzarella sticks aren't the ideal source of daily calcium or vitamin D.

But how do you stay trim when temptation is everywhere—especially in the dining hall with its "Wednesday Burrito Night"? Is it hard for freshmen to eat a balanced diet?

"Oh, my God, yes," says Charisse Lyons, a recent graduate of the University of South Carolina in Columbia. "I don't know if I gained the Freshman 15, but I definitely gained. I always ate on campus. I think I ate a hamburger every day my freshman year." Although healthy food was available, it's not as good as the junk," she adds, and having a comprehensive meal plan—with Pizza Hut and Taco Bell outposts in campus eateries—actually made things worse.

"Eating junk food does catch up with you," says Lyons, who shed the extra pounds when she moved into a campus apartment where she could cook her own meals. "You'll go home for the holidays, and everybody's like, 'What happened to you? You've been eating!' I think the best thing to do is get a small meal plan, buy your own fruits and vegetables, drink water, and take advantage of the gym."

Eating "healthy" just requires some common sense. If you're buying food in a grocery store, shop for a balanced meal—including proteins, fruits, and vegetables, etc. Take a few seconds to check out the labels. You can do a lot just by consistently selecting low-fat, or better yet, fat-free versions of fatty favorites, such as mayonnaise, cookies, salad dressing, tortilla chips, and cheese. (Note: Beware of sneaky wording. The phrase, "light yogurt," for example, may just mean it's made with Nutrasweet instead of sugar; even though it has fewer calories, it may have just as much fat as regular yogurt.)

Controlling Your Intake

Here are some more tips on conquering the "battle of the bulge."

- **Don't reward yourself with junk food.** You've studied four solid hours for your economics test. It's nearly midnight, and somebody's sending out for pizza. "You deserve it," says your well-meaning roommate—who has the metabolism of a racehorse and couldn't gain weight if she chugged Crisco. Cover your ears. If you must order something, go light. Get a grilled chicken sandwich or a Greek salad. Listen instead to the bathroom scales: They're screaming. "No, no! Get off me, Tubby!"

- **Stock your own food.** If you can, rent a small refrigerator; if you can't afford it, stockpile some snacks that don't have to be kept cold: a few little containers of low-calorie pudding or applesauce, low-fat granola bars or pretzels (most pretzels have no fat), or boxes of fruit juice or V-8. Get a hot pot and fix yourself some soup.

- **Check out the whole menu.** In the breakfast line, look beyond that custard-filled doughnut and see what else is out there. Check for grapefruit, a hard-boiled egg, and toast (plus jelly has no fat). Look for whole-grain cereal (fiber is always nice) and skim milk. At lunch and dinner, choose the salad and fruit plates.
- **Exercise.** Every little bit helps—even if it's just taking the stairs instead of the elevator, or jogging up and down the halls of your dorm, or around your room for 10 minutes a night.
- **Drink lots of water.** You're supposed to drink eight glasses a day, anyway. It's good for the skin, and it works wonders on the appetite—you don't get nearly so hungry if you're already sloshing around full of water.
- **Find a food buddy.** It's easier to go through anything if you're not alone. Seek out friends who are also trying to stay trim.

Advice for Vegetarians

College dining can be especially tricky for vegetarians. Shelley Habbersett ran into trouble during her sophomore year at Westchester University in Pennsylvania. "Because I wasn't eating meat, I didn't know exactly where to get my protein," she says, "so I ate a lot of carbs." And she gained weight. "I actually went to a nutritionist to see what was going on. I was worried because I was getting tired; I didn't know what was wrong with me." The nutritionist's good advice was to eat more fruits and veggies, plus protein-rich foods like peanut butter and beans. This diet put her back on track.

LESSONS IN LAUNDRY

When Malik Husser started out at the University of South Carolina, he had relatively few problems adjusting—even though he came to the 26,000-student campus from the tiny town of Goose Creek, South Carolina. But one thing really ticked him off his freshman year—rudeness in the laundry room.

"When I first got to college, I hated the laundry room," he says. "People would leave their clothes in there forever when I really needed the dryer or washer, so I'd be sitting around waiting."

Because he wanted to be nice, Husser says he didn't feel right raking other people's clothes out of the washer or dryer. On the other hand, when it was his clothes in there, his fellow launderers weren't always so tactful.

"I had to get used to people taking my stuff out of the washing machine and putting it on the side," he says. "I had to really adjust to that."

Eventually, Husser developed a strategy of precision timing—knowing exactly how long he could stay away for the washer and dryer cycles, and returning the instant his clothes were done.

Unless you babysit your clothes in the laundry room, or watch the clock like a hawk, ready to swoop down on your loads and whisk them on the next phase of the process, you may find yourself in the same boat. Rude launderers also strike loads of clothes that are still in the dryer. Sometimes they take out still-damp laundry just to make use of the dryer time somebody else—you—just paid for. Sometimes, if they like a particular garment, they have even been known to help themselves to it.

Laundry List

- **Avoid marathon laundry sessions.** Yes, it takes only one night to wash and dry six loads at once—but that's one long, tedious night. If you do quick loads throughout the week, you'll save time in the long run.
- **Invest in a folding clothes rack.** Some students save lots of money and time by never paying to dry their clothes. They just wash them and bring them back wet to hang up in their rooms.
- **Wash clothes on weekdays.** Avoid the Sunday-night crowd.
- **Wash like colors together.** It is the sadder but wiser student who washes a red shirt with white socks in hot water.
- **Temperature matters.** Institutional hot water is really hot. The general rule is use hot or warm water for whites or lights, and use cold for colors. If you're washing everything in one load and you know nothing is going to "bleed," it's probably safe to use warm. If you're not sure, go for cold.
- **Check out local laundromats.** Some places offer "laundry by the pound" service. If you're totally stressed by exams and schoolwork, you might want to splurge and have someone else do your laundry for you.

Washin' Wares

- **A sturdy plastic laundry basket.** You'll probably keep it forever. You can use it to stow loose clothes or loose gear, particularly when you're moving in or out.
- **A laundry bag.** If your room is too cramped, this may be the way to go. It probably holds just as much as a basket, and it can be stored much more easily. (However, because air flow in laundry bags tends to be poor, your clothes may be prone to mildew.)
- **Powder or liquid detergent.** Go to a low-priced store like Wal-Mart and buy a big box or bottle. Don't waste your money buying micro-Tide in the laundry room.
- **Stain remover, odor remover, and bleach.** These "three horsemen" of the laundry apocalypse can make a huge difference in your appearance. Remove any stains before you wash clothes. Don't count on the detergent alone to do the job. Spray odor remover, such as Febreze, on anything that stinks—including piles of clothes just sitting around your room. And finally,

when it comes to bleach: Don't fear it, embrace it. Use it whenever you wash whites, and they'll come out looking crisper and more like new. Hint: Add the bleach to your regular detergent when the water is first running, BEFORE you put in the clothes. Undiluted bleach can "spot" and ruin clothes.

- **Optional:** A mesh bag for delicate items such as hosiery and lingerie that you probably should, but don't want to, wash by hand.

IF YOU GET SICK

Eating right and exercising will hopefully prevent illness. But sickness may still come knocking, and some problems you can treat yourself with a well-stocked medicine chest (see checklist). But you should see a doctor if:

- You have a fever of greater than 101 degrees that doesn't get better with aspirin, ibuprofen, or acetaminophen. Be especially cautious of a fever associated with a shaking chill.
- You have severe pain that's unexplained—not caused by a muscle injury, tension headache, menstrual cramps, or mid-cycle pain, which some women experience about two weeks after their last menstrual period.
- You're unable to keep down food or water for more than 24 hours.
- You're unable to urinate, or you haven't had a bowel movement in several days.
- You notice any unusual discharge, blood in your urine or bowel movements, or blood when you cough.
- You experience burning when you urinate, which could be a sign of irritation or infection.
- You're having upper respiratory problems. If you've been coughing for several days, cough syrups don't help and your chest is getting sore, or if you're short of breath and can't take a deep breath.
- You have a sore throat that lasts longer than a couple of days.
- You're feeling excessively fatigued for several days and can't "perk up."
- You become severely depressed or begin to have suicidal thoughts.

Medicine Chest Checklist

Stock up now, because it's inevitable: Sooner or later, you will get sick, and chances are, it won't be during normal business hours—and worse, you'll have a paper due or a big test the next day. You'll probably need:

- **Something for a headache.** You can get brand names, or buy generic medications, which are generally just as good and a lot cheaper. The basic ones are aspirin, acetaminophen (the key ingredient in Tylenol), ibuprofen (found in Advil or Motrin), and naprosyn (found in Aleve). Before you buy, read the labels. Some pain relievers do not mix well with alcohol and can damage your liver. Others can irritate your stomach.

- **Antihistamines or decongestants for colds.** Again, read the label: Some of these can make you sleepy. Others can make you wired. Also, it's better to buy drugs that need to be taken every four to six hours, instead of the 12-hour kind. This way, no matter how they affect you, they'll wear off a lot sooner.
- **Cough drops or cough syrup.** The basic choices are a cough suppressant to soothe your throat or an expectorant to loosen up congestion in your chest.
- **Bandages.** Get a multipurpose box, with a variety of sizes.
- **Antacids.** Indigestion happens, particularly after late-night pizza. Some people prefer the kind you drink; others would rather chew pills like Tums, or take acid-blocking tablets that work for hours.
- **Medicine for diarrhea or an upset stomach.** You definitely don't want to go shopping for this when you need fast relief for a digestive tract out of whack.
- **Cotton balls, tissues, swabs, and tweezers.** These are essential for all types of minor body repairs.

The Dark Side of College Life: Academic Pressure, Depression, Suicide*
By Daniela Lamas

Caitlin Stork tried to kill herself the first time when she was 15. She was hospitalized, discharged, and attempted suicide again.

The doctors diagnosed depression and put her on Paxil. It wasn't until the drug drove her into a manic state that she was diagnosed with bipolar disorder, and prescribed lithium. Stork is now a senior at Harvard University, still taking the mood-stabilizing lithium and the anti-psychotic Seroquel.

"You would never believe how much I can hide from you," Stork wrote for a campus display on mental health. "I'm a Harvard student like any other; I take notes during lecture, goof off . . . but I never let on how much I hurt."

Stork is one of a growing number of college students coping with mental illness. More students, with more serious problems, are using campus mental health centers than ever before. The number of depressed students seeking help doubled from 1989 to 2001, according to one study, and those with suicidal tendencies tripled during the same period.

Suicide is the second-leading killer of college students—with an estimated 7.5 deaths per 100,000 students per year, according to a study of Big 10 campuses from 1980 to 1990. Three New York University undergrads died in three separate apparent suicides this fall (2003).

It's a complicated landscape, where it's easier to find blame than answers. Doctors and students point to increased academic pressure, starting at a much earlier age. In addition, there's easy access to drugs and alcohol in a culture where stress is the norm and sleepless nights a badge of honor.

Students with serious mental illness also are getting diagnosed and medicated earlier. As such, some young adults—like Stork—can make it to college, while they might not have years earlier. Colleges acknowledge this is a hot issue. With limited funds, they've hired more psychiatrists, stepped up hours at counseling centers, instituted outreach programs throughout the campus, and instructed teachers to watch students during exam times.

"Around this time, it's very, very hard, but we don't turn people away," said Florida State University's counseling center director, Dr. Anika Fields, who called the weeks before first-semester exams "crunch period."

But critics say colleges need to do more. There's little evidence of which interventions work best, stigma still surrounds mental illness, and students describe a disconnect between counseling centers and the campus population.

Many schools simply aren't ready, says Stork: "The science is advancing faster than the universities."

At the University of Miami, the number of students with psychiatric appointments at the counseling center has more than tripled in the past 10 years—from 61 in the 1991–1992 school year to 264 last year. "That's a big, big jump," said Dr. Malcolm Kahn, the center's director. "The good part is that there's less stigma about having this kind of problem, and getting treatment for it."

It's no different at FSU, where there were 1,235 sessions with psychiatrists in the 2001–2002 school year, up from 306 psychiatric sessions five years ago.

"They keep coming. Sometimes they come on their own, sometimes they come because they may have heard us speak at orientation, sometimes their parents urge them, or the staff, or their friends," said Fields, who noted that students requesting non-emergency appointments have to wait at least one month.

Florida International University's counseling center added a campus psychiatrist last year—a service just over half the colleges nationwide offer, according to a national survey of counseling center directors. This is particularly useful as exams approach.

"Even if they won't come in when they're depressed, or anxious, they will come in when it starts to affect their grades," said Dr. Cheryl Nowell, who directs FIU's counseling and psychological services center.

A bill before Congress acknowledges this swell, seeking to add funds for campus counseling centers. The bill cites evidence that depression nearly doubles in the freshman year.

Indeed, students' problems are more severe than they were five or 10 years ago, said Dr. Jaquie Resnick, who directs the University of Florida's counseling center and heads the Association of University and College Counseling Center Directors—an observation backed up by 85 percent of her colleagues in the national survey.

"And this is just the beginning. We're starting to smell it, starting to see smoke on the horizon," said Peter Lake, a professor of law at Stetson University who co-authored "The Rights and Responsibilities of the Modern University: Who Assumes the Risks of College Life?" He believes mental illness—particularly self-inflicted injury—will soon eclipse alcohol as the No. 1 issue on campuses.

Already, Kahn sees students with depression, anxiety, academic problems, family and relationship problems, and eating disorders. Many come to college having previously sought treatment. For those whose parents were supportive during high school—keeping them on their medication—the freshman year can be challenging.

"Once you go off to college, you're the one responsible," Stork said. "But one of the problems with mental illness is that when you get sick, you stop being responsible."

For students without diagnosed mental illness, it's still hard to recognize whether problems exist, and to ask for help. Having more counselors helps, they say, but it's not enough.

"A lot of students aren't that comfortable going up to a psychiatrist, and saying, 'Hey, I need some help,'" said Peter Maki, a University of Miami student and member of the group Counseling, Outreach, Peer Education (COPE). Maki, a psychobiology major, is one of a group of students trying to turn COPE from a group that does "secretarial work" to a link between counseling center and student body.

"There's definitely a gap," said Ashley Tift, a University of Miami senior who chairs COPE. She referred a friend to the counseling center who was depressed and drinking too much. It helped, but she wouldn't have known where to turn if she weren't involved with COPE.

At Harvard, Stork heads a student group, the Mental Health Awareness and Advocacy Group. At a conference last year, members learned that personal contact has been proven the best way to reduce stigma—better than education. They created an annual mental health awareness week, with panels, relaxation techniques, and prominently displayed student narratives on bulletin boards in a heavily trafficked campus area. An undergrad with obsessive-compulsive disorder wrote about her need to wash her hands 50 times per day. A depressed freshman considered taking too many pills, lying in bed while everyone else seemed to welcome the new opportunities and activities.

With these and her own experiences in mind, Stork urges Harvard's resident advisors to "err on the side of nosiness" rather than risk missing a student in trouble.

When all safety nets fail, there's the threat of suicide. In a nationwide study, 9 percent of college students admitted to "seriously considering attempting suicide" between one and 10 times in the 2002–2003 school year and just over 1 percent actually tried to kill themselves.

Jed Satow was a sophomore at the University of Arizona when he committed suicide in 1998. He was impulsive, acted without thinking of consequences, but neither his friends, professors, or parents recognized his actions as signs of depression, said his father, Phil Satow.

"People don't know when their roommate or friend has crossed the line. This sort of thing is not generally talked about," said Satow, president and founder of the Jed Foundation, a nonprofit that aims to decrease the youth suicide rate. "The reality is that there needs to be cultural changes on college campuses to deal with stress and depression."

The Jed Foundation has a free Web site, Ulifeline.org, which links students to mental health centers, information and anonymous screening for issues including depression, eating disorders, and suicide. Colleges can subscribe, enabling students to avail themselves of all the services.

"This allows students on their own, without stigma, to be screened 24 hours a day," Satow said. "If you take a public health approach, alerting the whole campus in what to look for, in all probability more kids like my son will come in. It's a real communal problem."

CAMPUS MENTAL HEALTH SURVEY

In a survey of nearly 20,000 students on 33 campuses, college students reported experiencing the following within the 2002–2003 school year:

Feeling overwhelmed by all they had to do:

	Male %	Female %	Total %
Never:	10.8	2.6	5.4
1–10 times:	68.8	64.5	65.8
11+ times:	20.4	32.9	28.8

Feeling so depressed it was difficult to function:

	Male %	Female %	Total %
Never:	60.6	52.6	55.2
1–10 times:	33.3	39.8	37.7
11+ times:	6.1	7.6	7.1

Seriously considering attempting suicide:

	Male %	Female %	Total %
Never:	90.8	89.1	89.7
1–10 times:	8.2	10.0	9.4
11+ times:	1.0	0.8	0.9

Attempting suicide:

	Male %	Female %	Total %
Never:	98.6	98.7	98.6
1–10 times:	1.2	1.2	1.3
11+ times:	0.3	0.1	0.1

Source: American College Health Association, National College Health Assessment: Reference Group Executive Summary, Spring 2003.

SOME SYMPTOMS OF DEPRESSION

Think your friend or child might have a problem? The following are some symptoms of depression, from the National Institute of Mental Health. Not everyone who is depressed experiences every symptom.

- Persistent sad, anxious, or "empty" mood
- Feelings of hopelessness, pessimism
- Feelings of guilt, worthlessness, helplessness
- Loss of interest or pleasure in hobbies and activities, including sex
- Decreased energy, fatigue, being "slowed down"
- Difficulty concentrating, remembering, making decisions
- Insomnia, early-morning awakening, or oversleeping
- Appetite and/or weight loss or overeating and weight gain
- Thoughts of death or suicide; suicide attempts
- Restlessness, irritability
- Persistent physical symptoms that do not respond to treatment, such as headaches, digestive disorders, and chronic pain

DISCUSSION

1. Discuss whether "maintaining balance" is a realistic goal for college students. Do you actually know other college students who have achieved balance in their lives? If so, how did they do that? Discuss how you might learn from them.
2. This chapter offers a number of strategies for reducing stress in college. Discuss whether or not we "covered all bases." Can you identify any strategies that fellow students employ to reduce stress but actually have the opposite effect?
3. Often, stress results in positive outcomes. Share those with your group.
4. Does the reading "Surviving the Everyday Stuff" stimulate your own thinking about how college is influencing your eating patterns? Have your eating habits changed since you came to college? Compare your habits with those of your discussion group. What specific stressors are influencing your eating patterns, and what can you do to modify them?
5. One of the chapter readings reports on mental health challenges affecting college students, with special attention to depression and suicide. One trigger for depression may be the sense of "loss" of their pre-college lives, and hence a type of grieving for that lost life before something better replaces it. Reflect on your own college experience to date and think about what you have "lost" and "gained." Compare some of these outcomes with those of others in your group. Is your experience typical? Better? Worse?

Conclusion

In developing this text, we have attempted to expose readers to three concepts:

1. Making it through your first term successfully takes both academic and personal efforts.
2. Reading from other sources enriches your knowledge of the critical points for that success.
3. You will feel more comfortable working in study groups, and that, in turn, will make college more inviting and help you make new friends.

We know how stressful and frustrating beginning college can be. Both of us had a discouraging and somewhat scary first year, in the sense that we earned mediocre grades, made little effort to meet new friends, and perhaps had our priorities out of order. So in choosing the chapter topics for this book, we singled out the 15 areas we felt were most important for new college students of any age or background.

Only you can tell us if we made the right choices. Therefore, we urge you to email us with your comments on the text: John Gardner, **gardner@ FyFoundations.org** and Jerry Jewler, **jjewler@sc.rr.com**

All that's left to say is to wish you a wonderful college experience that will carry your success over to your future career. By following the suggestions between the covers of this book, you'll have the skills and the confidence to let prospective employers know how special you are.

Glossary/Index